MW00613580

FIGURES OF
BUDDHIST
MODERNITY
IN ASIA

FIGURES OF BUDDHIST MODERNITY IN ASIA

Edited by
Jeffrey Samuels,
Justin Thomas McDaniel,
and Mark Michael Rowe

UNIVERSITY OF HAWAI'I PRESS
Honolulu

© 2016 University of Hawai'i Press
All rights reserved
Paperback edition 2018

Printed in the United States of America

23 22 21 20 19 18   6 5 4 3 2 1

Library of Congress Cataloging-in-Publication Data

Names: Samuels, Jeffrey, editor. | McDaniel, Justin, editor. | Rowe, Mark (Mark Michael), editor.
Title: Figures of Buddhist modernity in Asia / edited by Jeffrey Samuels, Justin Thomas McDaniel, and Mark Michael Rowe.
Description: Honolulu : University of Hawai'i Press, [2016] | Includes bibliographical references and index.
Identifiers: LCCN 2015048892 | ISBN 9780824858544 (cloth : alk. paper)
Subjects: LCSH: Buddhists—Asia—Biography. | Buddhism—Asia. | Buddhism and culture—Asia.
Classification: LCC BQ840 .F54 2016 | DDC 294.3092/25—dc23
LC record available at http://lccn.loc.gov/2015048892

ISBN 978-0-8248-5855-1 (pbk.)

University of Hawai'i Press books are printed on
acid-free paper and meet the guidelines for permanence
and durability of the Council on Library Resources.

Designed by Milenda Lee

Contents

Contents by Buddhist Tradition

Contents by
Region and Country

East Asia

China

Hong Kong

Japan

Korea

Taiwan

Southeast Asia

Cambodia

Laos

Myanmar/Burma

Singapore

Introduction

Beyond Traits, Sects, and
Regions: New Approaches to
the Study of Buddhists in the
Modern World

JUSTIN THOMAS MCDANIEL, MARK
MICHAEL ROWE, AND JEFFREY SAMUELS

Three Buddhist Figures

Nakazawa's haunted eyes gaze out the window at the mountains in the distance as he says: "I never thought I'd see the sun set over Mount Zao again. I haven't been able to see it from here since I was a kid." His view of the mountains has come at a terrible cost. He is sitting in a small, prefabricated trailer in the middle of a postapocalyptic wasteland of housing foundations and debris—all that is left of the neighborhood after the tsunami of March 11, 2011, swept everything out to sea. A few days later and across town, Nakazawa's son looks at post-disaster satellite images of the area. He finds the enormous temple roof, intact, three neighborhoods over. "They found a body under it," he says.

The sect has donated this trailer as a temporary refuge. Although no one is allowed to live in the disaster area, Nakazawa comes down most afternoons and raises a small flag so people passing by know he is there and available for visitors. Many of his parishioners come to ask about the future of the temple and the graveyard outside. They are all staying here, but no one yet knows where that "here" will actually be.

The last of eleven children born into Jōdoji, a Pure Land temple on the coast of Sendai, Nakazawa took over after his siblings went into teaching and business: "I was the only one left in the barn." He explains that, despite the poor response to his "terrible" high school Hawaiian band ("they used to shout all kinds of stuff at us during the dance parties"), he loved to pull out his ukulele for the summer *obon* festivals held on temple grounds every year. He speaks of his childhood, when he would help fishermen by rubbing stinky fish fat on their nets to make them slide through the water more efficiently. The men would then give him a parcel of small fish that he would cook on a hibachi grill before snapping off the heads, dipping them in soy, and eating them whole. His eyes light up for the first time as he recalls the taste.

Mostly, though, Nakazawa talks about the neighborhood, which still acts as a kind of phantom limb for him. As he describes the background and family of each member of the community, he points—as if they were still there, as if he could still step out of the temple gates, walk a few paces, and knock on their doors. There is the man with the local tofu business, who lost all his machinery and has decided to call it quits; the young family who had a machinery store "just out back"; and the fathers, mothers, and grandparents who still go down to the water and scream at the sea to return their loved ones. All in all, Nakazawa lost 140 parishioners to the disaster; two are still missing, including a two-year-old child. He spent his sixty-third birthday, ironically also on March 11, conducting memorial rites for them, reading each name aloud as he generated merit on their behalf.

Ven. Dhammananda was a Sri Lankan monk sent to Malaysia in 1952 to cater to the religious, linguistic, and social needs of the Sri Lankan diaspora communities living there. He arrived in Malaysia during the ongoing communist insurgency. Learning of his presence, the British High Commissioner at the time—Sir Gerald Templer—asked the monk to preach to the residents living in the New Villages about Buddhism and its relationship to nonviolence in the hope of curtailing support for the insurgency. By accepting Templer's offer, Ven. Dhammananda was provided with the incentive and the means to reach out to new audiences and increase the demographic makeup of his temple from just a few Chinese families in the 1950s to over 95 percent Chinese in the subsequent decades.

Drawing different groups to the temple gave Ven. Dhammananda fresh areas for development. No longer relying almost exclusively on the Sinhalese Buddhist residents, he began engaging new communities, institutional networks, technologies, and streams of economic capital to address what he and others perceived to be the problems facing Malaysia's minority Buddhists at the time. By preaching alongside Buddhists from other traditions, as well as by asserting that the Buddha simply taught the dharma (and not Theravada, Mahayana, or Vajrayana), he encouraged Buddhists to join hands in propagating the tradition in Malaysia—a country where not only was Islam recognized as the official state religion but also where Christian missionaries were rapidly making inroads among Malaysian Buddhists and Hindus.

Ven. Dhammananda believed that Christian conversion was largely the result of Buddhists' ignorance about their own religion. He realized that in order to prevent young, educated Chinese from being converted to Christianity he needed to provide them with a "proper" understanding of Buddhism. To that end he began an active routine of teaching and preaching at his temple and at other Buddhist societies and institutions throughout the peninsula. He also made extensive use of the print culture. Printing and disseminating Dhammananda's message—in the form of lectures, dharma talks, pamphlets, short books, and the society's periodical (*The Voice of Buddhism*)—was largely the responsibility of his Buddhist Missionary Society, which he established in 1962. By using English as the primary language and presenting Buddhism as a scientific and rational religion, the society tapped into new groups of devotees in and around Kuala Lumpur—namely, English-educated Chinese Buddhists who had been cut off from reliable sources of information related to Buddhism.

Sooja Kim (who often goes by Kimsooja) may be one of the most internationally known installation artists working on Buddhist themes in Asia. In the last ten years alone she has had major shows in North America, Europe, and Asia. Born in 1957, she studied in Korea and later in Paris and now often resides in New York. She creates video shows, photography, mixed media, and other work, but is probably best known for massive installations that occupy large gallery spaces. Her most memorable work has to be *Lotus: Zone of Zero*, which has had many different reincarnations in places like the Samsung Museum in Seoul (2011), Galerie Ravenstein in Brussels (2008), and the Palais Rameau in Lille (2003). In the exhibition she hangs beautiful lanterns from the ceiling in circular patterns she calls Buddhist "mandalas," which patrons can walk under and feel as though they are suspended under a canopy of light while listening to simultaneous playback of Tibetan Buddhist, Gregorian Christian, and Islamic chanting. She wants the three "faiths" to have a "peaceful union" as the "exhibition space is transformed into a place of meditation and contemplation for viewers."

These lofty and ambiguous themes are apparent in *To Breathe: Mandala*, installed in 2011 at the Kunstmuseum Bochum in Germany, as well as other museums. The exhibition features brightly painted walls with large mandalas in the middle of them. As in the *Lotus: Zone of Zero* installations, sound is featured in the space, but here there is a single jukebox playing Kim's own voice performing a spoken-word piece called the "The Weaving Factory." The mandala shape is taken further in one of her most provocative pieces: *Mandala: Chant for Auschwitz* (2010), in which she created a very large mandala made entirely out of suede clothes, shoes, and children's toys. She installed this large piece in one of Hitler's former offices in Poznań, Poland. In the background of the installation recorded Tibetan Buddhist chants were playing. Kim does not practice Tibetan Buddhism, nor does she speak Tibetan. Her Korean Buddhist upbringing has little shape or voice in her art.

The varied activities of Nakazawa, Dhammananda, and Kim illustrate the limitations of approaching Buddhists solely according to sect, teaching, text, country, region, or culture. Nakazawa is a Buddhist temple priest. His faith and propagation of the dharma take a form that render him all but invisible to regnant paradigms of Buddhist studies. He speaks neither of sutras nor of doctrine. When one of the editors of this book, Mark Rowe, tried to pin him down on whether the Pure Land actually exists or is simply a metaphor, Nakazawa smiled at him as if he were a child. His is the knowledge of every inch of his community, of its history, of its people, of its loss. He carries in his head the blueprint of every house that the sea has taken, of every soul it washed away. His work is simply to endure, to provide a bridge to what was before, even as he and his son rebuild an unknown future. Even if the city allows it, the locals may never return to the neighborhood. A temple without people, Nakazawa insists, is not a temple. His Buddhism has little to do with nonattachment or even with teachings of impermanence; it is a Buddhism of connections, of bonds between a temple and its community.

Ven. Dhammananda's interests are similar to those of many other emerging Buddhist nonsectarian groups regarding the need to find a balance between modernity and tradition in order to revive Buddhism. His activities point to the role state policies and concerns about religious conversion play in defining and propagating Buddhism. His story highlights the intense mobility and adaptability of Buddhist monks and laypeople in modern Asia.

For Justin McDaniel, Sooja Kim's work and international profile reveal several neglected aspects of modern Buddhism, and studying them raises new questions. Until very recently, lay contributors to Buddhist art, literature, and doctrine have been ignored or seen as secondary to the ordained. Women, especially, have been relegated to the category of dutiful followers, not active producers of Buddhist teachings and material culture. Kim is hard to classify. She doesn't promote the teachings of any particular sect. She is Korean but does not employ many traditional Korean Buddhist teachings, sounds, or symbols in her work. She sees herself as an international artist, inspired by Buddhism but calling attention to broader global issues like genocide, poverty, labor rights, and oppression. Studying Buddhists in the context of national origin, ethnic makeup, or sectarian affiliation has been standard, allowing figures like Kim to fall through the cracks. Can we call her a Korean Buddhist? A Buddhist artist? A lay Buddhist activist? Kim made McDaniel rethink what counts as a figure representative of modern Buddhism. The profiles throughout this book seek to raise questions like this in the minds of its readers.

The intimate concern with local community seen in the activities of Nakazawa, the ethnically centered work of Dhammananda, and the Buddhist colorings of Sooja Kim's art made us question the very way in which we planned to frame and arrange this volume. We debated dividing our respective sections along the lines of the Mahayana, Theravada, and Vajrayana, or according to the regions of Northeast Asia, Southeast Asia, and South Asia/Himalayas. We approached possible writers who work on these regions and schools, and most leaped at the chance to write about the people who had influenced or inspired them. Initially buoyed by their enthusiasm, we soon realized that stories about Buddhist webmasters in Taiwan, members of international Buddhist women's organizations in Vietnam, internationally known singing nuns in Nepal, Buddhist air traffic controllers in Burma, and alcoholic translators of Confucian texts in Laos were poorly served by section headings like "Mahayana" or "Southeast Asia." It became obvious while reading these profiles that modern Buddhists cannot be defined merely by sect or region. Many travel internationally, regularly use the Internet, speak several languages, and see themselves as part of a global religion.

We then considered dividing them along the lines of "ordained," "lay," and "in-between" Buddhists, but profiles of a former Cambodian monk turned Buddhist lay organizer and processed-chicken-plant worker in New Zealand or of a Korean artist, gardener, and Buddhist sculptor reminded us that many Buddhists are professional ritualists on the weekends but also have families and other careers during the week. Others go in and out of the "robes" at different stages of their lives.

Ways of "Looking"

Similarly to the three figures described above, we saw that the figures who fill the pages of this book were looking in different directions. Through their stories, the editors (Samuels, McDaniel, and Rowe) identified four "ways of looking" as an organizing principle to guide the readers. First, some were looking backward at Buddhist traditions they grew up with or idealized from the distant past. This "looking backward" connected repeatedly to a major aspect of modern Buddhism that we see as "inventing tradition." While the ability to travel great distances in relatively little time and to see and hear other parts of the world through the Internet has been eye-opening for many Buddhists, it has also stirred in many a strong traditionalist reaction born out of competition and comparison. In a world with so many Buddhist practices a short flight or a click away, how can Buddhist teachers or schools define themselves as unique or even superior to the many others? Rather than change with the times or borrow from other Buddhist teachings or rituals, many Buddhists have doubled down, so to speak, on their own tradition—to internally "purify" themselves and reify what they see as a timeless practice. Perhaps not surprisingly, in the effort to reform and renew, they have not necessarily returned to origins but have instead created new practices and philosophies that might never have existed in the past. Inventing traditions has long defined the way many modern Buddhists have tried to express their concerns with the state of their religion. In the nineteenth century, many Buddhist kings, monks, and intellectuals complained that Buddhists had been either corrupted by their dependence on ritual income or infected with "local" beliefs. They wanted to return Buddhism to what they saw as its original spirit. Of course, this idealized Buddhism they longed for had never actually existed outside of texts. Many of the figures profiled in this book have the same approach today. They lament what Buddhism has become and "look backward" in order to cleanse their tradition of the accumulated film of the last two millennia.

Second, this reactionary approach to the anxiety of modernity is only one of the themes to arise out of these profiles. Therefore, we saw that other figures profiled here are "looking forward" to new ways of defining Buddhist ethics, ritual, and labor in their local contexts. Instead of bemoaning what Buddhism has become or competing with other groups over who can be the most "traditional," they embrace new pedagogical methods, new textual genres and mediums, and new ritual and meditative technologies. These Buddhists are not only Internet savvy, but also look to disciplines like psychology, social work, economics, and business/marketing to modernize Buddhist teachings and practices to help the poor, fight against pollution, or care for the elderly. They have embraced what we see as a type of "social-psychological care" for their followers, friends, and neighbors. These Buddhists act as a type of awareness and relief agency that actively reaches out to assist others while providing particular methods to address social and psychological issues.

Third, for many Buddhists, however, social and psychological problems can be overwhelming. We found many Buddhists profiled in this book developing a "new asceticism," retreating from social engagement in order to "look inward." Instead of embracing new technologies and using new methods of social engagement, these Buddhists are developing new meditation methods, retreating from large cities, and reinvesting themselves in ascetic practice. Some are simply trying to get through particularly difficult personal problems like addiction or the loss of loved ones by progressing through different types of contemplative practices or intellectual projects. Some of these new ascetic regimens are based on traditional practices, while others incorporate modern technologies and concepts. It is worth noting, however, that many of these figures, after looking inward, take outward steps to make positive change in the lives of those around them.

Finally, some of our figures are "looking outward" to other religious traditions, other cultures, or other Buddhist ways of being. This new Buddhist "globalism" is a clear theme across numerous profiles. These reformers not only want to improve their own communities through Buddhist teachings and rituals, but also reach out to non-Buddhists both in and beyond Asia. Sometimes they even abandon the very idea of being Buddhist in order to promote an ecumenical world beyond one religion. At other times they have been forced to adapt when moving from their Buddhist homelands to foreign places.

Although it might seem strange to a traditional Buddhist studies scholar not to group our profiles under South, Southeast, Central, and East Asian regional sections, we wanted to respect the voices of the Buddhists we profiled and emphasize that modern Buddhists are learning from each other and crossing boundaries. We realize that no single framework is perfect, but organizing our profiles through gerunds (through process, action, and change), instead of by nouns (through stable traits and consistent characteristics) provokes precisely a reconsideration of existing categories that is much needed in the field. The division of this book into ways of looking is an attempt to bring into focus and explore dynamic Buddhist connections and shifting perspectives—the adaptable stances of individual practitioners toward the worlds they inhabit—rather than by the less mutable divisions of ethnicity, nationality, culture, geography, and sect. By grouping our vignettes in new ways we want to reveal some of the unexpected connections that lie below the myriad of superficial differences and to demonstrate connections across traditions, borders, and practices that might otherwise go unnoticed.

Using "looking" as a guide to categorizing the themes of "invented traditionalism," "social-psychological care," "new asceticism," and "globalism" is not meant as a solution to the perennial problem of classification. Rather, it represents our attempt to embrace the fundamental fact that most Buddhists spill out of the categories we commonly devise to contain them, even those in this book. For example, Irving Chan Johnson is ethnically mixed Asian and European, holds degrees from the United States, teaches in Singapore, works in Malaysia, speaks English, Thai, and Malay, and has trained himself to be a Thai Buddhist muralist. His traditionalist painting has him looking backward, but the modern elements in his murals also have him looking forward. Or consider Olande, an ethnic Dutchman who travels internationally teaching Buddhist ethics while he is also a devout monk in the Sri Lankan Theravada tradition. He looks outward at new communities of potential Buddhists to teach them about techniques of looking inward at their own lives through meditation and discipline.

This book represents one way of exploring Buddhist modernity. Moreover, each of our four categories contains the seed of its opposite. Ultimately, looking inward, for example, can be as effective in mobilizing worldly action as looking outward. Looking backward may not, in fact, lead back to doctrinal purity at all, but forward on a path no less new than that envisioned by those we categorize as looking forward. Such "contradictions" run throughout this volume. They are not a bug in our approach, but rather a feature of it. The fact that a figure could easily represent more than one way of looking demonstrates the need for flexibility in categorizing and a willingness to embrace new ways of bringing stories of individual Buddhists into conversation with each other. We hope the juxtapositions created by our approach will illuminate unexpected connections and surprising differences for the reader and, in doing so, stimulate complex and nuanced understandings of Buddhist modernity.

On Biography

Why profiles? Overviews of Buddhism in Asia in the past helped us a great deal when we were thinking about this book. Usually these are organized around regions, schools of practice and thought, or by the perennially important emic terms: Buddha (teacher), dharma (teaching), and sangha (community of learners).[1] We wanted to move beyond such frameworks and contrast the study of movements and institutions (ecclesiastical, colonial, royal, or governmental) with a focus on individuals who are re-creating Buddhism outside of the various national sangha organizations and political structures. Until recently in our field the agency and creativity of individual Buddhists have often been overlooked, so we were pleased to see a volume edited by Todd Lewis called *Buddhists: Understanding Buddhism through the Lives of Practitioners* (2014). *Buddhists* includes thirty-three profiles of mostly widely known historical and modern Buddhists; more than half of these cover Buddhists located in South, Southeast, Himalayan, and East Asia.

In this volume, we take a different approach. By including approximately seventy profiles, we highlight the rich diversity of modern Buddhism across a broad geographical range. While monks from nearly every corner of the Buddhist world appear, there are also nuns, lay artists, psychologists, social workers, part-time priests, healers, curators, librarians, charlatans, hucksters, profiteers, and rabble-rousers. We did not want only a series of hagiographies of famous Buddhists. We also wanted to give voices to Buddhists in Asia who might be overlooked in other histories and ethnographies and to figures who reflect changes in modern Buddhism but are also shaping the course of those changes.

We are fundamentally concerned with the ways in which individual Buddhists make meaning, display this ever-changing understanding to others, and continually and mutually instantiate society and its explanations. Instead of looking at the commonly accepted characteristics of macro-level culture, overdetermined notions of religion, or the generalized traits of an entire race, here we explore the "practical reasoning and reflexive accounts that people use on a daily basis and that make social life an ongoing practical accomplishment."[2] Our authors consistently demonstrate the value of studying individual Buddhists and their idiosyncratic religious backgrounds and approaches. They also represent the growing regionalization and internationalization of various forms of Buddhism.[3] In the case of Southeast Asia before the nineteenth century, Buddhism in the region scarcely knew national borders. Nation-states with discernible borders, anthems, flags, or public school systems had not fully formed, but nuns and monks already led highly mobile lifestyles. Traveling long distances to study with famous teachers, circumambulate reliquaries, prostrate to powerful Buddha images, and collect and copy manuscripts was considered normal before the colonial period. Electronic communication, the ease of air travel, and the influx of foreign patrons over the last twenty years have led to the formation of international organizations as well as to the opening of meditation retreat centers, new international journals, and even the opportunity for laypeople, nuns, and monks to reach distant audiences through Internet sermons, blogs, and television specials.

There are also regular exchanges of professors and students between Christian and Islamic universities in Asia and their Buddhist counterparts. Today, many urban monasteries even in small cities like Vientiane and Kathmandu have dedicated computer rooms with Internet access. High-ranking urban monks often produce CD-ROMS or construct Web sites to teach their own students as well as students who have access to the Internet globally. New phrases and new rhetoric have been developed to serve new audiences— not merely non-Buddhist or new-Buddhist westerners, but other Buddhists in Asia. High-ranking monks have begun traveling extensively and now can be seen in universities in India and Japan, at Buddhist tourist sites in Sri Lanka, China, Indonesia, and Taiwan, and at international ecumenical Buddhist meetings in Korea, Nepal, and Australia. There are new Buddhist universities with an ecumenical focus like the World Buddhist University in Bangkok (started in Australia) and the International Buddhist College (IBC) located in Songkhla (Southern Thailand), with its parent organization, Than Hsiang Temple, located in Penang, Malaysia. Joint Buddhist publications and Web sites that encourage Japanese Buddhist students to speak to Tibetan Buddhists are being developed. A wealthy class of international Buddhist patrons from Bangkok, Singapore, Hong Kong, and other places are subsidizing publications, conferences, and temple construction throughout Asia. Many of these contacts and initiatives are being made by individual nuns, monks, and laypeople who are reshaping the way Buddhism is taught and practiced. Only by tracing their complex lives can we hope to begin to map out the contours of Buddhism in the region more broadly.[4]

One of the editors of this book, Jeff Samuels, has been conducting ethnographic work in Sri Lanka and Malaysia over the past fifteen years, focusing on the complex lives of lay and ordained Buddhists and the ways in which they make sense of an increasingly connected world. Mark Michael Rowe has been undertaking a large study of "non-eminent" Buddhist nuns, monks, priests, and laypeople in Japan for a decade.[5] They both work with unfinished lives, with people who are reimagining their place in Buddhism and the ways they define themselves as Buddhists. Inspired by their work, Justin Thomas McDaniel, in a forthcoming book on modern Buddhist architects and artists across Asia, wants to question the types of people who are chosen for biographic study by Buddhist studies scholars.[6]

One could assume that any study of individuals, like this book, is purely agent-based. Biographies tend to promote the idea that there is such a thing as an independent entity and in turn make that person, place, or thing an ideal exemplar. Whether we study the five aggregates of Buddhist psychology or basic neurophysiology, there is ample evidence that every person, place, or thing is made up of many parts and dependent on things outside of our control—oxygen, gravity, genetic heritage, farmers, teachers, and the kindness of strangers. We wanted to avoid creating a series of exemplars or reviving the "great man" approach, which posits that history is moved along by certain creative or trailblazing outliers. We emphasize that by looking at individual agents in context we actually see them as part of heterogeneous, process-oriented, and ever-changing synchronic and diachronic networks.[7] They are "in-between" agents. They are not world leaders, spiritual masters, or once-in-a-generation philosophers. In fact, many of them could be called "failures." If scholars focus only on ideal agents, cultural exemplars, profound texts, and timeless creations, then we miss the middling agents, who, despite funding, creativity, and diligence, do not quite make it into the pantheon of greatness. These everyday Buddhists are much more representative than the "great men" of history and teach us what is probable, not simply what is possible. Moreover, biographies have a tendency to focus on outcomes. Instead of studying ideal exemplars who successfully achieve optimal outcomes—great books, paradigm-shifting buildings, revolutionary theories, and inspirational epitaphs—this book looks at "local optima."[8] Most Buddhists profiled here have not created timeless masterpieces of erudition or founded new sects. Instead they have settled on a series of small "goods" and abandoned the optimal "perfects" that they initially wanted to reach in the end. Jeff, in his book *Attracting the Heart,* showed how in rural Sri Lanka great monks were not necessarily lauded for their learning, their ritual expertise, or their leadership, but for the relationships they formed, the manner in which they composed themselves, and the small acts of community building they engaged in on a daily basis.[9] Many of the Buddhists in this book represent those who are often forgotten to history. Many are "non-eminent" Buddhists negotiating between the ideals of their traditions and the concrete realities of their worlds. What follows is not a cleanly bounded, overdetermined "Buddhism," but rather Buddhism as a "sticky engagement."[10] What follows is the point where the rubber meets the road. What follows are lives in progress.

How to Use This Book

Due to our focus on ways of looking among individual Buddhists, we see great advantage to placing the varied and diverse people profiled in this book side by side rather than dividing them by country, region, and/or sect. We hope that readers will experience unexpected comparative possibilities. It might seem strange that the people profiled from India or Japan are not grouped together, but we wanted to treat each person as a series of motivations, hardships, experiences, and aspirations, instead of just a product of geographical and sectarian traits. Some authors focused on how the agents they profiled reflected trends in local Buddhist politics and social relations. Others concentrated on the emotional and affective sides of their interlocutors' lives through intensely personal narratives. See, for example, the stories of former model and new age writer Terry Hu, who is from a political family, is concerned with gender issues, and defines herself by her work with new age healing; or Taniyama, a priest in Japan who fights against the dangers of nuclear power on the one hand and works with elder-care and end-of-life issues within a small community on the other. By reading profiles like these outside of stultifying categories like "Mahayana" or "South Asia" and juxtaposing many different examples, we can suggest new comparative possibilities, as well as significant differences. John Bowen and Roger Petersen, in referring to the struggle between empiricism and identifying patterns in comparative work, write: "the world's complexity demands some respect even as we try to understand or isolate processes and mechanisms . . . we believe that exemplifying is more effective than prescribing."[11] Our own approach to this dilemma was to turn to the model suggested by polyphonic music and novels, where meaning is built out of divergent characters, geographies, and practices. As Michael David Lucas puts it, "Just as polyphonic music combines melodies to create texture and tension, the polyphonic novel collects a multiplicity of distinct, often conflicting voices around a single place, family, object, or idea. Polyphony widens the novel's geographic, psychological, chronological, and stylistic range, while simultaneously focusing its gaze."[12] As editors we wanted to allow the cacophony of voices to be heard while grounding each profile in its local and thematic context.

The profiles are grouped under the four themes of "Looking Backward: Inventing Tradition in the Modern World," "Looking Forward: Social-Psychological Care in a Troubled World," "Looking Inward: New Asceticism in Modern Buddhism," and "Looking Outward: Local Buddhists Becoming Global Citizens." In addition, for teachers and students wanting to read these profiles within course sections based on regional and sectarian divisions, each person profiled is identified by his or her school of Buddhism, country of origin or long-term residence, and dates. The reader particularly interested in Japan or Tibet or Theravada or gender can easily find profiles of people in these categories. In order to further aid readers, we have provided additional tables of contents based on tradition or region. Moreover, the index that follows this volume also shows connections based on key themes such as gender, the Internet, and healing. Thus readers can choose to read all of the Southeast Asian, Theravada, East Asian, or gender-related profiles as a group.[13] As a further aid to readers just beginning to find their footing in Buddhist and Asian studies, each vignette includes a short introductory "blurb" situating that figure in his or her geopolitical and Buddhist context. At the end of the book there is also a Further Reading section for students who want to delve deeper into topics inspired by the profiles in this book. Finally, to spur discussion on issues of categorization and comparison, we also provide short introductory overviews to each of the parts.

We editors are all teachers and respectfully acknowledge the difficulties that teachers confront in trying to find a textbook that will be portable, comprehensive, nuanced, and affordable. We also understand that any single teacher cannot be an expert in every region of Asia or every school of Buddhism. Therefore, we envision this book being paired with a more general history of Buddhist teachings and institutions such as works by Peter Harvey, Rupert Gethin, Kate Crosby, Paul Williams, or John Strong.[14] It could also be used alongside general textbooks on religious ethnography, religious biography, modern religion, or comparative monasticism.

Notes

The editors would like to thank Johan Lindquist for his generous assistance during the early stages of this manuscript. The editors would also like to thank Jean Rowe for reading through countless drafts. This manuscript is greatly improved thanks to her keen editorial eyes.

1. Arthur McKeown outlines three types of Buddhist biography: ordinary, esoteric, and lineage in "The Life and Times of Śāriputra" (Ph.D. diss., Harvard University, 2010).

2. Ilana Friedrich Silber, "Pragmatic Sociology as Cultural Sociology," *European Journal of Social Theory* 6.4 (2003): 429.

3. See a similar approach in the introduction to Justin McDaniel's *The Lovelorn Ghost and the Magical Monk* (New York: Columbia University Press, 2011).

4. For an earlier attempt at this, see Justin McDaniel's "Buddhists in Southeast Asia," *Religion Compass* 4 (2010): 657–668.

5. Samuels developed the notion of "action-oriented pedagogy" to describe the ways in which much of Buddhist learning took place outside of formal Buddhist educational institutions in Jeffrey Samuels, "Toward an Action-Oriented Pedagogy: Buddhist Texts and Monastic Education in Contemporary Sri Lanka," *Journal of the American Academy of Religion* 72.4 (2004): 955–972. Mark Rowe has been working on biographies of over two hundred "non-eminent" monks and nuns in Japan since 2010

through a grant from the Social Sciences and Humanities Research Council of Canada.

6. For more on the study of local optima and complex adaptive systems, see the introduction of Justin McDaniel, *Architects of Buddhist Leisure: Socially Disengaged Buddhism and the Building of Museums, Monuments, and Amusement Parks in Asia* (Honolulu: University of Hawai'i Press, 2016).

7. John H. Miller and Scott E. Page, *Complex Adaptive Systems* (Princeton, NJ: Princeton University Press, 2007), 79. See also S. L. Brown and J. M. Eisenhardt, "The Art of Continuous Change: Linking Complexity Theory and Time-Paced Evolution in Relentlessly Shifting Organizations," *Administrative Science Quarterly* 42 (1997): 1–34.

8. Miller and Page, *Complex Adaptive Systems*, 81.

9. Jeffrey Samuels, *Attracting the Heart: Social Relations and the Aesthetics of Emotion in Sri Lankan Monastic Culture* (Honolulu: University of Hawai'i Press, 2010).

10. Anna Tsing, *Friction: An Ethnography of Global Connection* (Princeton, NJ: Princeton University Press, 2004): x.

11. John Bowen and Roger Petersen, "Introduction: Critical Comparisons," in *Critical Comparisons in Politics and Culture* (Cambridge: Cambridge University Press, 1999), 3–4.

12. http://www.themillions.com/2013/02/a-multiplicity-of-voices-on-the-poly phonic-novel.html (last accessed June 7, 2015).

13. We were inspired by the creative table(s) of contents in Donald Lopez's 1995 edited volume *Buddhism in Practice* (Princeton, NJ: Princeton University Press, 1995).

14. Peter Harvey, *An Introduction to Buddhism,* 2nd ed. (Cambridge: Cambridge University Press, 2013); Peter Harvey, *An Introduction to Buddhist Ethics* (Cambridge: Cambridge University Press, 2000); Kate Crosby, *Theravada Buddhism: Continuity, Diversity, and Identity* (Oxford: Wiley-Blackwell, 2013); Rupert Gethin, *The Foundations of Buddhism* (Oxford: Oxford University Press, 1998); John Strong, *The Experience of Buddhism* (London: Wadsworth, 2001); Paul Williams, *Mahayana Buddhism*, 2nd ed. (London: Routledge, 2007).

LOOKING BACKWARD

Inventing Tradition
in the Modern World

Many Buddhist laypeople and monastics featured in this section have struggled in their attempts to understand what it means to be "authentically" Buddhist. Seeing modern Buddhist practice as corrupt in some way, many have chosen to look back to what they consider was a purer, more traditional Buddhist life, in which the solution to the pressures of modern society (in the realms of finances, family, or career) is to abandon public life and return to the cloister. Oftentimes this yearning to return to what many Buddhists have seen as the traditional life of meditation is actually an exercise in inventing tradition. In fact there is no evidence in Buddhist history that there were ever purely cloistered meditating nuns and monks on a large scale. Most records show that monastics always had to combine a life of public engagement through teaching, ritual, artistic production, or scholarship with the practices of meditation and silent retreat. Even the supposed meditation schools of Chan/Zen/Chogye, the esoteric schools like Shingon, and the strict *vinaya* (monastic precepts) traditions of Theravada have had to balance the practice of meditation and private study with social engagement. However, with the growth of secular education, changing politics, tourism, scholarly curiosity about monastic life, and the rise of public institutions, many monastics feel that they can no longer achieve that balance. In this section, we shall look closely at several Buddhists who are calling for a return to what they define as the ideals of the tradition.

This looking backward at an ostensibly "true" life that the Buddha envisioned has assumed different forms. Some call for a return to a close reading of the earliest Buddhist texts, arguing that scholarship is actually the key to disseminating the true teachings of the Buddha. Some use modern technology and popular art to encourage Buddhist youth to abandon a life of consumerism and hedonism. Others emphasize meditation as a cure for individual and societal woes. For example, in this section we learn about the life of the Sri Lankan monk Kanimahara Sumangala, a university lecturer who abandoned his post to open up a string of meditation schools. He claimed that he was on the edge of full awareness (nirvana) and wanted to return the country to a more spiritual state through his sermons and the insights he gained from his meditation. His claims threatened the monastic establishment and led to him being declared "insane" by other monks and nuns. Kiribathgoda Gnānānanda, another Sri Lankan monk, has taken a more subtle approach in his attempts to help Sri Lankans return to what he sees as a simpler time. Although born a Catholic, he supposedly converted himself and his family as an infant. He practiced meditation as a child and as a young man established a new Buddhist sect aimed at using Buddhist teachings to promote a more mindful society. Although he wanted to return to a simpler time, he nevertheless established a dedicated TV station—Śraddhā (faith) TV—to broadcast dharma sermons on television in Sri Lanka and on the Web around the world. Khedrup Gyatso, a Tibetan monk living in Amdo, is making great efforts to remind those practitioners in his village of their Buddhist roots in the face of encroaching Chinese cultural erosion of Tibetan Buddhism. Through compiling oral histories and serving as a moral exemplar, he hopes to inspire youth to stay true to their heritage. Former banker turned monk, Ashin Bodhinyana of Bangladesh has taken a much more critical view of contemporary Buddhist society, seeing it as rife with charlatan magicians and anti-Muslim profiteers. Sometimes this frustration with modernity is not focused on fellow Buddhists, but on foreigners who try to foist modern liberal values on traditional Buddhist society. Dharma Ratna's complex but seemingly blatant antifeminist views in the guise of tradition are one such example.

Looking backward is not just a practice of men or monks. Women scholars, reformers, and lay artists have also been calling for a return to tradition. A well-known scholar of Chinese Buddhism, Chün-fang Yü, is a devout Buddhist who has spent her career exploring the history of Chinese Buddhism as a scholar at Columbia University. She focuses on revealing traditional Chinese Buddhism to her students and readers through a close study of primary sources. Padma, an anti-alcohol activist in Sri Lanka, saw how alcoholism destroyed her family and links her temperance movement to traditional Buddhist teachings. Soe Naing has also witnessed tragedy as an airport tower controller in Myanmar/Burma. He chants Buddhist texts to safeguard planes in flight and sees this protective magic as equal in importance to proper mechanical maintenance and well-trained air traffic controllers.

The editors of this book were particularly struck by the number of profiles sent to us of modern Buddhist artists. Despite working in avant-garde mediums, many of these artists actually look back towards what they see as the origin of Buddhist teachings and use art to remind their patrons of what has been lost in modernity. One such artist, Sudhir from Pune (India), was initially inspired by the teachings of Ambedkar and now uses art to promote traditional Buddhist symbols and images in the modern world. Jakkai Siributr of Bangkok (Thailand) is an internationally known artist who creatively critiques modern consumerism, social media, and what he sees as charlatan monks and politicians through large installation pieces that contrast traditional Buddhist images with modern materialism and superstitions. Irving Chan Johnson, an anthropologist and artist in Singapore, is trying to revive Buddhist mural painting by creatively using the traditional medium in his painting of a modern temple. He intersperses classical with modern images that work to question the very notion of heritage. Vann Nath of Cambodia was tortured by the Khmer Rouge and since being freed from prison expresses the Buddhist teachings of non-self and compassion in his art with the aim of healing a nation haunted by genocide.

This section also features the profile of a twenty-fourth-generation Shin priest and professor of Sanskrit in Nagoya (Japan) named Toshiya Unebe. In many ways Unebe represents the struggle between living in modernity and longing to maintain traditional Buddhist temple life. He drives his Toyota Prius to teach Buddhist texts and traditional art at a secular university during the week and on the weekend is an active leader of a temple in a farming village on the edge of one of the most modern industrial cities in Asia. He sees his life as characterized by a struggle between traditional Buddhist practice and dealing with traffic on his commute to a university.

YANGON AIRPORT TOWER COMMUNICATIONS WORKER
Soe Naing
JANE M. FERGUSON

Theravada Buddhism is considered the national religion of the Republic of the Union of Myanmar, although Muslims, Hindus, and Christians constitute significant minorities in the country of over fifty million people. Nationalist discourse has perpetuated the archetype: "to be Burmese is to be Buddhist." Soe Naing's (1968–present) practices exemplify how both Buddhism and spirit beliefs are part of his daily work at the airport.

"I have seen *tasay* (ghosts) before, but they moved so quickly *whup-thap*," Soe Naing gestures with a quick flick of his hand, "that I didn't get a good look at them. One flitted by on the concrete apron near where the planes line up . . . but I have heard from others that sometimes they have entered the planes."

Soe Naing, a slight man wearing a plain white shirt and dark-purple *longyi*, animatedly tells about his ghost sighting over a cup of strong tea in a Yangon tea shop. He has worked full-time at Yangon's Mingaladon Airport since 1993 and now has a position in tower communications. According to Soe Naing, news quickly spread around the airport when a pilot reported that he had opened the cockpit door, not yet touched the instrument panel, and the auto-start was already engaged. The pilot continued the flight as planned, and it went without incident, but according to many airport workers this mysterious start was the operation of one such *tasay*. In spite of (or in some cases because of) such incidents, as well as the inherent danger and uncertainty of aviation, many airport workers make daily use of Buddhist texts. "Buddhism has always been with me. When I was a child in Yangon, I remember at new year time, the other kids would be playing, splashing water, but I would have already had my head shaved and be living in the temple compound as a novice monk," recalls Soe Naing.

In the two decades he has worked at the airport, Soe Naing has observed a number of trying situations, not only in airport operations, but also in Burmese Buddhist modernity. "Insight meditation is part of my day, every day. Usually I do it at home, but if there is a gap in my schedule during my work day, I can fit it in," he explains.

He points out that four of the eleven parts of the *Maha Paritta* (The Holy Discourses of Protection) are especially relevant to the challenges of passenger aviation: (1) *Yadana Thoub* (Ratana Sutta)—the sutra that honors the Buddha, the dharma, and the sangha; (2) *Metta Thoub* (Metta Sutta) whereby the recitation of words of loving-kindness effectively neutralize any potential disturbances; (3) *Mawya Thoub* (Mora Sutta), recited to keep families safe; and (4) the *Atanatiya Thoub* (Angulimala Sutta), recited to help a pregnant woman in childbirth, but also to convert a robber to a saint.

While airport workers test the discourses' effectiveness on a daily basis, Buddhist symbolism is also deployed as part of corporate strategy. For example, domestic Myanmar Airways has had Fokker F-27 aircraft as part of its fleet for over five decades, and a number of their crashes prompted concern regarding the airline's safety record. "The Fokker F-27 planes were quite old already. Most airlines would replace their airplanes more frequently than MAW does. Following a few crashes in the late 1980s an airline changed its logo and put a *Padan* (Patthana) symbol on the tail of the planes." The Patthana icon is part of Buddhist symbology for the twenty-four universal causes of relations. The Myanmar Airways Web site for its corporate history shows a name and logo change in 1989, but the corporation does not confirm Soe Naing's theory that the new logo was placed on aircraft tails to prevent crashes or allay fears of flying among the Buddhist traveling public.

When disasters do occur, cosmology offers a karmic "black box" for accident investigation. In December 2012, a Bagan Air flight crashed during its approach to Heho Airport in the Shan State. The airline is already tainted: it is owned by Tay Za, the richest man in Myanmar, often characterized as a greedy tycoon who long exploited his connections with the military regime. Furthermore, as airport workers noted, when that very Fokker 100 aircraft was on a test flight, a small bird was sucked into one of the plane's jets shortly after takeoff. At the time, the pilot was able to return the plane safely and land it, but the bird strike was interpreted as an inauspicious sign for the aircraft, and airport workers like Soe Naing connected this incident to the plane's later crash in Heho.

As demonstrated by its repeated representation in the country's popular media, aviation is an important part of Burmese modernity, even though it is beyond the reach of most of the country's agrarian population. Yangon's Mingaladon Airport was built on an RAF airfield left from the Second World War and established just on the brink of Burmese independence. Although it was once the best in Southeast Asia, and indeed the logistical hub for air travel in the region, economic and political stagnation following Ne Win's coup and his "Burmese Way to Socialism" led to airport disrepair and continued use of outdated equipment and machinery. During the past decade there has been a concerted effort to upgrade its facilities, and 2007 saw the opening of an air-conditioned and modern international terminal. Local folkloristic, Buddhist, and other spiritual practices have been a part of this process every step of the way.

Just as the tower control workers strive to ensure the safe landing of planes onto the concrete of Mingaladon runways, stresses and fears of aviation in Myanmar and modern machines offer Soe Naing specific opportunities to bring Buddhist theories to the concrete realm of everyday practices. As the country's economy is poised to open up to further international investment, Myanmar's logistical infrastructure, particularly its ports and airports, will be tested as never before. Buddhist teachings offer structure, comfort, and protection from danger while workers and passengers navigate these haunted and uncertain airspaces.

THE "INSANE" MONK
Kanimahara Sumangala
DANIEL W. KENT

In recent years, *vipassana* meditation has become almost synonymous with Theravada Buddhism in Sri Lanka. The *vipassana* method, however, is a relatively recent import from Southeast Asia that gained in popularity in the 1950s. Not all Sri Lankans approved of the "foreign" method. While he ultimately failed and was dismissed as insane, Kanimahara Sumangala (1932–1982) represents a voice of dissension, asserting a particular Sri Lankan Buddhist identity and practice against the perceived threat of foreign Buddhists.

In 1981, the head of the Ramañña Nikāya, one of Sri Lanka's three main monastic fraternities, declared the forty-nine-year-old monk Kanimahara Sumangala insane. Earlier that year, Sumangala had begun declaring publicly and forcefully that he was born a stream enterer (the first of four stages to enlightenment), that he had attained the state of stream enterer in a past life, and that he would achieve enlightenment within seven lifetimes. Furthermore, Sumangala claimed that he could deliver a sermon that would transform its listeners into stream enterers who would also be on the fast track to enlightenment. Indeed, he went so far as to point out that if he were allowed to preach five sermons on Sri Lankan radio, he would be able to convert half of the population of Sri Lanka into stream enterers.

Contemporary Sri Lankan Buddhist orthodoxy maintains that one progresses to enlightenment through the gradual development of the "three trainings" of morality, concentration, and wisdom, and that, furthermore, enlightenment is impossible until the arrival of the future Buddha, Metteyya (Skt. Maitreya). Sumangala asserted that liberation actually begins with wisdom, as true morality and concentration are impossible without an understanding of the way things are. Based upon this reversal of the traditional order of the three trainings, Sumangala asserted a model of Buddhist practice premised on listening to Buddhist teachings. Leaders of the Buddhist establishment were threatened by Sumangala's ideas. Despite his death a year later, Sumangala gained a large following of laypeople, who preserved some of his sermons on audiocassettes.

The cassette tapes that record his final sermons reveal Kanimahara Sumangala as stubborn, proud, and not a little combative. He dared to attack the basis of Theravada orthodoxy and for that he was declared insane. Why did he do this? What was it that pushed him to go against fifteen hundred years of tradition? Why did he take such a strong stand against orthodoxy? The answers can be found through the consideration of Sumangala's character as well as the environment in which he was writing. By embracing the power of the Pali canon to transform its listeners, Sumangala attempted to bridge some of the irreconcilable differences between Sri Lanka's rich tradition of preaching and merit making and the active search for enlightenment heralded by the wave of new meditation centers opening around the country.

Sumangala was, first and foremost, a scholar-monk who had served as a lecturer at Vidyodaya University and was published in English in a volume edited by John Ross Carter. In keeping with his scholarly persona, Sumangala based his argument, not on any kind of mystical or meditative experience, but on his mastery of the Pali canon. He argued that he had recovered the original teachings of the Buddha that had been obscured by later commentaries.

While the vast majority of Theravada Buddhists across South and Southeast Asia identify Buddhaghosa's commentaries as the foundation of Theravada Buddhist orthodoxy, Sumangala rejected them and produced his own idiosyncratic interpretation of the Pali canon. He claimed that, in order for meditation to be effective, one must first establish right view and discriminative insight through listening to sermons. Without the right view established by sermons, he argued, there is nothing to develop through meditation. Sumangala illustrated his understanding using the analogy of a prison in which prisoners were forced to act morally. If Buddhaghosa's path was correct, Sumangala argued, enforced discipline would lead to knowledge of the way things are, which it does not. Without right view, morality is of little utility on the path to enlightenment.

In order to appreciate Sumangala's argument, we must account for the religious environment in which he lived. Throughout his monastic career, he was faced with what he considered an invasion of foreign Buddhist ideas from Southeast Asia, particularly in the form of the *vipassana* meditation movement. In the early 1950s, *vipassana* meditation centers based on the teachings of the Burmese monk Mahasi Sayadaw and run by Burmese monks and their Sri Lankan protégés spread rapidly throughout the country. Supported by wealthy, urban Sinhala Buddhist laypeople, including a future prime minister and a future president, the *vipassana* movement made assertions that conflicted with widely held Sri Lankan traditions. They deemphasized the importance of renunciation, claiming that monks and laity alike could achieve enlightenment through the practice of meditation. Kanimahara Sumangala attacked these new meditation centers frequently in his sermons, calling *vipassana* meditators ignorant worldlings who lived lives of leisure based on the alms and sweat of laypeople and appealing to his followers to stop supporting meditation centers.

A strong element of xenophobia runs through Sumangala's sermons and writings. He even argued that Buddhaghosa, the commentator whom he rejected along with a cabal of Tamil monks, had infiltrated the ranks of the Sri Lankan monastic community and had deliberately muddled the dharma in order to prevent Sinhala Buddhists from defending themselves from foreign invasions.

However, while Sumangala had accused Tamil Buddhist confederates of ruining Sri Lankan Buddhist teachings in the past, it was not Tamils but rather false Buddhists who were the true objects of his critique. In 1981, the Sri Lankan civil war had not yet officially begun. There was unrest in the northern regions of the country as militant Tamil organizations began to form but no large-scale armed conflict. Sumangala considered his real opponents the Buddhists from Southeast Asia, who were rapidly establishing *vipassana* meditation centers around the country. His attack on Buddhaghosa, along with his claims that he himself had attained stream entry and that monk and layperson alike could attain similar states, mirror those made by the *vipassana* movement. However, his claim that practice begins by listening to sermons undercut the foundations of this movement, creating space for a uniquely Sri Lankan Buddhist path to stream entry and final release from cyclical existence. By purging these foreign elements, Sumangala hoped to establish an entire society of stream enterers.

Sumangala's rejection of commentaries and attacks on foreign Buddhists in general provide a clear example of a monk asserting a particular Sri Lankan Buddhist identity against the perceived threat of foreign Buddhists.

Theravada Buddhism is a relatively new category that obscures a great deal of diversity in teachings and practices in Sri Lanka and Southeast Asia. The case of Kanimahara Sumangala provides just one example of a monk who resisted the claims of orthodoxy and challenged claims of Theravada Buddhist homogeneity.

THE CHOICES OF A PRIEST ON THE EDGE OF TOYOTA CITY
Toshiya Unebe
JUSTIN THOMAS MCDANIEL

Toshiya Unebe's (1968–present) life as a temple priest, father, husband, and professor is reflective of the life of an average Mahayana Jōdo Shinshū priest in urban Japan. Since the nineteenth century, most Jōdo Shinshū temple priests have held secular jobs, had families, and used their temples as their family homes. Unebe-san's life also reveals some of the problems facing priests of family temples, as the leadership of the temple is tied up with issues of succession, property ownership, and the struggle between maintaining tradition and wanting one's children to have freedom of choice.

I noticed the photograph of the shaven-headed young boy in the kitchen after petting the family's new puppy. "Is this your son?" I asked. "Yes, that is when he was eleven and shaved his head for Shin Buddhist summer camp and undertook ordination. He just turned fifteen recently. He only did it for a couple days, but it was fun." "How about his little sister?" I asked. "Well, she was ordained too when she was nine, but she really likes ballet." He replied as if their extracurricular activities were equivalent and, especially in the case of his son, indeed "choices."

Toshiya Unebe, his wife, and I drank tea in their kitchen and chatted about the difficulties of raising children and sundry on a rainy day in June 2014. This was the first time I had met his wife, who had studied English literature and now does occasional outreach work for foreigners living in Japan. Unebe and I had known each other for a few years, as we both work on Pali and Thai Buddhist manuscripts, but I was now realizing how little I knew about his life outside of his scholarship. As he was just a few years older than I, I had assumed we largely led the same kind of life. We both were lucky enough to be married to wonderful partners, both had a son and a daughter, and both had earned Ph.D.s in Indic studies with a focus on Pali literature and Buddhist history. We met at conferences in Japan, Thailand, and Europe. We helped each other with difficult textual passages and occasionally had a drink together after long days spent with old books. However, looking at the photograph of his son and being in his home, I saw how different we were.

Unebe-sensei is not just a professor; he is also a Shin Buddhist priest (Ōtani-ha [Higashi Honganji] branch of Jōdo Shinshū "sect") who runs his own temple under the tutelage of his soon-to-be-retired father. The temple is attached to his house in Unebe-machi (Unebe's Town). Unlike most Shin priests, his father did not succeed his own father in running the temple. Unebe's grandfather was killed as a young man in World War II, forcing Unebe's great-grandmother to take over the temple until it could be passed on to her grandson, Unebe's father. Unebe-sensei, who will soon be taking over, knows that it is his responsibility to pass the temple on to his son, who might not be willing to take it over. He seems to understand his son's possible reluctance to becoming the next *jūshoku* (head priest). This is not the life Unebe necessarily saw for himself either.

While it might seem that becoming a Buddhist priest is a spiritual choice that involves taking ascetic vows and leading a quiet life of meditation, ritual, and reflection on ancient scripture, in modern Japanese Buddhism it is more of a family legacy than an individual choice. Japanese Buddhist priests are nearly all married, and most have children. They might train for a few days or a few years at one monastery but often return to the temples they grew up in and that are handed down to them. Most of them learn how to be priests by growing up watching and listening instead of through formal training. Unlike Buddhist monks, especially like the Thai Theravada monks Unebe studies as a scholar, Shin priests do not maintain monastic vows. They can drink alcohol, get married, wear robes only for ceremonies, and grow their hair any way they like. Indeed, the only time Unebe's son may ever have to shave his head is for that summer camp. But this does not mean they can do whatever they like. Even without ascetic rules, they have different and often much longer periods of Buddhist dedication and responsibility. They might be able to drink beer and marry the love of their life, but unlike many Theravada monks who can disrobe after a few months or years, they often cannot choose to abandon being a priest. There are thousands of daughters, sons, nephews, and nieces who did not freely choose to become the heads of their temples but are responsible for them nonetheless. This might not be the ordained Buddhist life one first thinks of, but it is the most common life for a Buddhist priest in Japan.

Twenty-three generations is a big weight on anyone's shoulders. Unebe's little brother runs a used-record store in Tokyo, sporting a goatee and listening to old vinyl most days. His sister is the office manager of a small theatrical troupe. They are free of family burdens. Unebe has traveled widely, studied at the famous Pune University in India, and writes on topics ranging from Thai art to Indian philosophy. He has done research at Oxford and Ayutthaya. However, he cannot stay away for long. He would love to travel with his family more, take foreign fellowship and job opportunities, but with his father slowing down and clearly depending on and admiring his son, he must stay in the town named after his family. His commute to Nagoya University is long, but it is the only university with a department in his field within driving distance. He is staying put and putting a lot of miles on his Toyota Prius.

Still, as we walk through Unebe's temple and he proudly points out the various meeting rooms, the lovely tearoom and garden, and the *hondō* (main prayer and ritual room), he is clearly at home. He grew up in this temple, which was founded in 958 CE by the Tendai sect. One of his distant ancestors converted to Shin Buddhism under the influence of the legendary Shin teacher Rennyo in the fifteenth century. There are about a hundred families that are members of the temple. Unebe's town is mostly farms, but now sits on the edge of Toyota City. Toyota is the largest automobile corporation in the world, employing tens of thousands of workers. Many of the people who chant and hold meetings are retired factory workers whose ancestral ashes are enshrined at this temple and others close by. Unebe sees his temple as a retreat for them after many years on the job. His mother even helps out by running a Hawaiian hula dancing class at the temple. The temple might be small, and it certainly cannot move with Unebe's other ambitions and dreams, but his extended family is happy there and are experts at keeping up these old buildings. As we prepared to leave, I joked that maybe his daughter would start a ballet class, following in the nimble footsteps of her hula-dancing grandmother, while Unebe's son chants and gives sermons. Unebe smiled and said, "Hopefully." The choice will be up to them.

A WITNESS TO GENOCIDE
Vann Nath
ASHLEY THOMPSON

Religion and art have long defined the Cambodian state, ranging in function from instruments of social control to vehicles of communal and personal expression. Vann Nath's (1946–2011) life and work comprise the vanguard of an ongoing reconfiguration of relations between the two domains in the wake of the massive social and political upheavals of the twentieth century, with a range of Cambodian artists exploring and exploiting the resources of Theravada Buddhism as a means of contributing to the definition of Cambodia today.

"Keep the artist," the executioner famously ordered. Of the thousands of innocent people held in the Khmer Rouge execution center of Tuol Sleng it was the artist whom Prison Chief Duch did not kill. One would have thought that Duch had everything on his side—shackled, starving prisoners, a terrified corps of workers, a well-oiled killing machine. Yet the artist, because he was an artist and this particular Buddhist one, turned the tables and prevailed, in the end, over the executioner.

Vann Nath grew up in a farming village in Battambang Province, and as most Cambodian boys once did, served some time as a monk. Prior to the Khmer Rouge period he made a living in Battambang town painting commercial placards, private portraits, and, periodically, billboards of King Sihanouk. It was this experience that saved him.

Vann Nath was lifted, skin and bones, from the ranks of Tuol Sleng's prisoners in 1978 at the height of Khmer Rouge terror. He was unshackled, fed, and made to paint. Duch gave him a photograph of a man who had remained nameless and faceless to the vast majority of his countrymen and -women whose lives and deaths he commanded. Vann Nath had three days to prove himself capable of producing an accurate painted reproduction of the photo. With an unflinching acceptance of abuse, he produced a painting whose likeness to the photograph satisfied his henchmen. Painting portraits for nearly one year of the man he came to learn was Pol Pot, he drew strength to defend fellow prisoners then and there and to remember the prisoners' pledge: Whoever survives will bear witness.

Vann Nath was kept on by the next regime in an eerily similar manner, when he became resident painter of the ex-prison transformed into a genocide museum, painting pictures of what he and his prison mates had experienced there. Though he was long a free man, from the liberation of Phnom Penh by the Vietnamese army in January 1979 to the day he died in September 2011, Nath was never freed from this role as prison painter. Made famous in Franco-Khmer Rithy Panh's haunting cinematic portrait of Tuol Sleng, *S21*, Vann Nath became the most visible representative of the victims, speaking through his painting to the international community that was searching for signs of mourning. If his tableaux of torture scenes were to become icons of the genocide, the image of Vann Nath painting them in his prison studio became an icon in and of itself. In representing the genocide he represented art as a means of resistance, time and again fighting oblivion and co-optation by the powers that be. Even as his work was deemed to fall outside the category of "high art," he was framed by an international community as the emblematic artist *en puissance,* a locus of autonomous thought, living proof of the empowerment art can bring. As painting, his work was more than documentation. It was Vann Nath's focused self-mastery as a prisoner-painter in Tuol Sleng that had enabled him to escape execution. The post-1979 paintings rendered as much his determination to overcome as they did the torture experienced there.

Vann Nath's artistic power was profoundly Buddhist. His was a passive resistance of the most enduring sort. Like a master meditator, Vann Nath thoroughly controlled himself. And this self-mastery served to efface the ego, or perhaps more precisely put, to eliminate attachment to the self as a psycho-material entity. Vann Nath's name will be remembered. But the name will always reference a man whose self-affirmation went hand in hand with exemplary retreat. Vann Nath did not paint the Buddha, stupas, or empty thrones. Buddhist icons do not appear reworked in his work. The exploitation of "Buddhism" for ethnonationalist ends characteristic of much modern Southeast Asian art is absent from Vann Nath's world.

One of his paintings shows prisoners shackled together on a floor at Tuol Sleng. Vann Nath is one of them. This painting makes use of the visual alliteration found in Khmer temple mural art. The stylistic tool makes a point about the way in which personal identity was crushed by the Khmer Rouge. If Khmer Rouge effacement of individuality differed radically from that at work in temple murals, through which collectivities are defined, Vann Nath manages, through traditional style, to recuperate a collective identity for the genocide victims. There is no insistence on the affirmation of the individual, either in terms of the artist himself as embodiment of singular genius capable of producing original insight, or in terms of any irreducible uniqueness of the subjects painted. There is no humanist aim by which the artist or the art would claim to speak for humanity. Indeed, the absence of any such affirmation makes Vann Nath the quintessential Cambodian Buddhist painter. If he was prized as such by those looking for Cambodians to take responsibility for their past, and so affirm human agency, he was, at the same time, thoroughly true to himself and the national community he relentlessly served.

Another painting was produced by Vann Nath for a collaborative arts project titled *Mémoire, Archives et Creation,* held in 2008–2009 at Phnom Penh's Bophana Audiovisual Resource Center. The project brought together Vann Nath and Séra, a Franco-Khmer artist, as workshop leaders for a group of young Cambodian art students. Vann Nath named his project painting *The Solitary Man.* He described it as representing a man determined to refuse shelter in order to maintain autonomy. It is a self-portrait of sorts. By this time Vann Nath was quite ill. He continued to survive only, by his own declaration, in order to testify at the Tribunal for Khmer Rouge Crimes. By keeping religiously to himself, Vann Nath forever escaped Duch's deadly hold. His singular self-determination kept the memories of others alive, and continues, across generations and cultures, to model subjectivity.

A MONK BETWEEN WORLDS
Khedrup Gyatso
CHARLENE MAKLEY

Contemporary Tibetan (Vajrayana) Buddhism is a far cry both from westerners' romanticized image of a peaceful, isolated Shangri-la and from Chinese Communists' accusations of monks' feudal oppression of the masses. After major outbreaks of protest led by Tibetan Buddhist monastics and increasing state regulation of monasteries since 1987, Tibetan monks in fast-changing China now must navigate multiple roles in Tibetan communities without running afoul of the state. Khedrup Gyatso's (1970–present) Buddhist scholarship and cultural advocacy work exemplify his successful efforts to combine conservation and innovative outreach to Tibetan youth.

It is a cool June morning in 2011, and Tashi, his bleary eyes nearly swollen shut from partying the night before, is driving me to the monastery on the edge of town to see a respected Buddhist monk, his older brother Khedrup Gyatso. I want to talk with the monk about his recent book chronicling the oral history of their clan villages up the valley. Tashi stops at the gates of his brother's compound in the monastery's expanding complex of temples, lamas' mansions, and monks' homes.

My jaw drops. Rongbo Monastery, the erstwhile ruling seat and cultural center of Rebgong in eastern Tibet (Amdo, Qinghai Province, China), has seen major changes in the shape and functions of its buildings since it was founded in the fourteenth century. The first Shartshang lama built the College of Philosophy when he converted the monastery from the Sakya to the Geluk sect in the seventeenth century. The main assembly hall had even been converted to a reeking fertilizer plant after the monastery was closed and monks and lamas were imprisoned or defrocked under Chinese Communist rule in the 1960s. But what I am seeing is unprecedented. In place of the old one-story wood and adobe courtyard he once shared with other monks, Khedrup Gyatso now lives in a gleaming six-story concrete apartment building, meticulously painted to mimic traditional Tibetan monastic architecture. The state-funded compound, I learn, had been built in 2009, in part to appease young monks and their lay supporters after a brutal crackdown on Tibetan demonstrators in 2008 had landed many of them in prison. Khedrup Gyatso, who had steered far clear of that unrest, had just moved into his comfortable, two-room apartment there.

The monk's young acolyte, a cousin from their home village, ushers us in and prepares tea. Tashi promptly flops down on the cushions in the front room and is soon fast asleep, mouth half open. Khedrup Gyatso looks much younger than his forty-one years. He is short and stout and walks with a slight limp under his maroon robes. His smile can be warm, but his deep voice and discerning eyes have always slightly intimidated me. This time, however, he is eager to discuss his work on the history and ritual traditions of his clan with an interested foreigner (and, perhaps, a potential sponsor). Foreign visitors are rare in the monastery since the 2008 crackdown, and my presence is in fact somewhat dangerous, as it could draw the attention of watchful public security officials. I turn on my recorder as Khedrup Gyatso, sitting cross-legged on his sleeping platform, lays the xeroxed copy of his Tibetan manuscript before him. For the next hour and a half, he holds forth on his clan's history in the serious and elegant speech of a Geluk monastic scholar that is nonetheless tinged with the deep native pride of his rural origins. In this frontier region, however, the irony of stark contrasts is never far away. Our conversation is distracted by the increasingly loud snoring of the hungover Tashi in the next room, until Khedrup Gyatso, with a deep chuckle, tells his young servant to go poke him. Startled, Tashi gets up, mumbles he has to go, and leaves. His older brother tells the servant to fire up his laptop and asks me for the MP3 recording of his lecture. "These will be useful later for our villagers," he says, and, nodding after Tashi, "that kind could really use such knowledge."

Later, I realized that the whole interaction illustrated the extremely fine lines Tibetan monks must walk in China since the 1980s reforms allowed for the enthusiastic revival of Tibetan Buddhist culture and institutions. Khedrup Gyatso, who left middle school to pursue a monastic education at Rongbo in 1986, is one of the rare monks of his generation to successfully (so far) juggle a variety of competing worlds amid the pressures of an increasingly secular and capitalist yet politically tense society. And he did not do it alone. True to the traditional strategies of Tibetan rural households, Khedrup Gyatso's family had risen to local prominence by combining the efforts of his multiple lay siblings, including two brothers living in exile in the United States. Their connections had brought foreign funding for the local Tibetan "cultural center" and library that another lay brother now runs. Khedrup Gyatso, it turns out, acts as both the secular center's figurehead and the family's moral anchor, sharing his time between the center, where he greets visitors and helps run a foreign-funded NGO offering scholarships to rural Tibetan girls, and the monastery, where he offers free teachings about traditional Tibetan grammar and local history.

Khedrup Gyatso thereby epitomizes the hybrid roles Tibetan Buddhist monks must adopt to maintain legitimacy in the face of a crisis of authority among Tibetans and increasing state-imposed limits on the numbers and activities of monks. He lacks the charismatic authority of an incarnate lama, the Buddhist persona historically at the center of Rongbo's monastic polity, now highly compromised under Chinese rule. Yet in his writing projects and advocacy work, Khedrup Gyatso attempts to revive the respected role of the Geluk monk-scholar while participating in the efflorescence of lay scholarship in the valley. As a moral exemplar in the current tense political climate, he must balance his obligations both to his rural home clan and to Tibetans as a whole without running afoul of the state. So, in our conversation, just as in his public interviews, he scoffs at the uneducated "charlatan" monks and lamas he says are destroying Tibetan Buddhism and thus "the very backbone and soul of Tibetans." Yet he himself is not a formal member of Rongbo's assembly, and his own scholarship combines a modernist empiricism with the Geluk monastic reverence for lineage lamas' unassailable dharma. In the preface to his local history book, Khedrup Gyatso expresses ambivalence about the impropriety of a Geluk monk stooping to write about lay affairs. But a sense of impending cultural crisis spurs him on: "Tibetan elders are dying like the setting sun behind the mountain; the shadow will reach to its foot." His hope is that both his scholarship and the center's resources will enable Tibetan youth like Tashi to remember their roots.

A BUDDHIST MEDIA PIONEER
Ven. Kiribathgoda Gnānānanda Thera
STEPHEN C. BERKWITZ

Buddhist monks in twentieth-century Sri Lanka regularly emphasized preaching the dharma to laypeople as part of a larger strategy to reform and modernize Theravada Buddhism. In recent decades, charismatic and entrepreneurial monks have gained sizable followings by addressing cultural and political issues while speaking at rallies, religious celebrations, and on television. Ven. Kiribathgoda Gnānānanda Thera (1961–present), however, breaks new ground by founding a new monastic order that relies on its own media network to spread his vision of the "true" dharma.

In 2013, anyone visiting the Mahamevnawa monastery at Kaduwela in the outskirts of the Colombo district would immediately recognize how it differs from most other Buddhist temples in Sri Lanka. The relic shrine and *bodhi* tree shrine are newly built, and the Buddha image hall is still under construction. There are no shrines to deities or signs of vows that have been made to seek boons from gods or offerings to deflect the effects of harmful planetary influences. The monastic quarters contain a large, tiled meditation hall. And, most strikingly, one finds a sizable television studio and a small radio studio built on the site of the monastery to broadcast sermons on the dharma around the world.

The appearance of this newer monastery with atypical features is symbolic of the larger Mahamevnawa monastic order founded in 1999 by Ven. Kiribathgoda Gnānānanda, and it illustrates something about this monk's efforts to reform the practice of Buddhism in modernity. Born July 1, 1961, into a Sinhala Catholic family, Ven. Gnānānanda (whose monastic name means "the bliss of knowledge") was credited with inspiring the family to convert to Buddhism while he was still an infant. Ordained at age seventeen, he followed the traditional monastic education system and entered a university to continue his studies. However, Ven. Gnānānanda became disenchanted with this course and took up the path of a forest monk to meditate and study the dharma on his own. Having developed his meditation and knowledge of the dharma in concert with a few other ascetic monks, he eventually was given a piece of land in the rural village of Polgahawela, where he built three meditative huts (*kuṭi*) and a simple dharma hall with a thatched roof to found a new monastic order.

Named after the first monastery established in Sri Lanka by the legendary monk Mahinda in the third century BCE, the Mahamevnawa order has been developed by Ven. Gnānānanda to emphasize strict adherence to monastic rules (*vinaya*) and the preaching of the "true" dharma as found in the canonical discourses in a simple style of language. According to Ven. Gnānānanda, many contemporary Sri Lankan monks are involved primarily with cultural needs and nationalistic interests, and thus hardly even observe the Noble Eightfold Path. This monk, however, has eschewed political involvements and focused on teaching the Buddha's own words to as many people as possible. Such an objective has led him to establish the distinctive Mahamevnawa order (*nikāya*), in which monks and nuns are ordained and educated in classes on the canonical discourses and monastic code taught by elder Mahamevnawa monks outside of the traditional monastic educational system. In an effort to promote his goals of illuminating the original teaching of the Buddha and helping people to understand it clearly, his order established its own television station—Śraddhā (faith) TV—to broadcast dharma sermons in Sri Lanka and on the World Wide Web.

Ven. Gnānānanda's work and reputation have earned him a large following among Buddhists in Sri Lanka and globally. The Mahamevnawa order has over fifty branch monasteries in Sri Lanka, as well as four in the United States, two in Australia, and one each in India, Canada, Germany, England, and Dubai. Ven. Gnānānanda's emergence as a leading Buddhist monk in Sri Lanka is the result of several factors related to the modern age in which he lives. Roughly speaking, there are three avenues to fame and influence for Sri Lankan monks: (1) obtaining a leadership position in a monastic order or a historically important temple; (2) participating in politics or entrepreneurial activities to secure patronage; and (3) gaining supporters through a skillful preaching style and a reputation for moral discipline. Ven. Gnānānanda may be counted among the third group of charismatic monks, who employ their preaching gifts in combination with media outlets and appearances to build up a translocal community of followers.

Ven. Gnānānanda's influence is due in part to his persuasive claim that he is helping to spread the Buddha's original teachings as they appear in the discourses. Since the monastic reforms of the eighteenth century, Sri Lankans have largely accepted the notion that familiarity with Pali canonical texts is a sign of erudition. The Mahamevnawa order represents itself as conveying the Buddha's original teachings from the Pali discourses in a form of Sinhala that is easy to understand. Further, Ven. Gnānānanda's criticism of monks in Parliament and his refusal to address political issues serves to distinguish him from many other modern and contemporary Sri Lankan monks, including those who participate in groups like the Jathika Hela Urumaya (National Heritage Party) and Bodu Bala Sena (Buddhist Power Force). This implicit critique of "political Buddhism," along with the rapid growth of Mahamevnawa, elicits a backlash of criticism by more nationalist-minded Sinhala Buddhists.

As Mahamevnawa builds monasteries, broadcasts dharma sermons, and sells books by Ven. Gnānānanda, his version of authentic Buddhism will compete with other forms in the modern marketplace. His emphasis on meditation, simple teachings, and monastic discipline appears tailor-made to appeal to Buddhists across the world who can access his message by visiting Mahamevnawa temples and tuning in to dharma sermons on television and online. This monk and the movement he has founded illustrate that the modernization of Buddhism in Sri Lanka pivots on highlighting so-called traditional texts and practices, and then universalizing them to become applicable and accessible to all. The emphasis on canonical discourses and meditation strips away the culturally determined aspects of Buddhism, allowing an allegedly more authentic core to emerge and be spread worldwide.

EMBRACING BELIEF AND CRITIQUE IN AN ACADEMIC LIFE
Chün-fang Yü
GREGORY A. SCOTT

From Xi'an to Taiwan, contemporary Chinese Mahayana Buddhists have embraced the academic study of Buddhism as part of their religiosity and their engagement with the world at large. Some of the foundations of this field were laid by scholars in China and North America in the early twentieth century, the legacies of whom are still being felt today. Chün-fang Yü (1938–present) represents an example of a nexus point between Buddhist devotion and academic discipline in which personal religiosity and public educational service are brought into balance.

I often met with Chün-fang Yü in her office in a renovated corner of a seminary building leased by Columbia University. I would see her sitting, calmly and elegantly at her desk, which was invariably piled high with papers, articles, and other research materials, and surrounded by gifts and awards from Buddhist associations. One of the largest was a two-foot-tall figure of the Bodhisattva Guanyin, a gift from the Sheng Yen Foundation in Taiwan, the same foundation that had funded the academic chair in Chinese Buddhism of which Chün-fang was the inaugural holder. Scholar, professor, and believer, she embodies the union of the academic and the devotional, and the North American and the Chinese, aspects of modern Buddhism.

Chün-fang was born in China in 1938, and the Sino-Japanese War provided the background to much of her early life, as her family moved first to western China, and then to Taiwan. Her grandmother was a devotee of Guanyin, and her earliest memories of Buddhist practice are not of visiting temples or meditation, but rather of watching her grandmother burn incense, chant sutras, recite the name of Guanyin, and keep a vegetarian diet. She describes how, in Taiwan in the 1950s, Christianity was a much more visible presence in public life and on college campuses than Buddhism. From the 1950s into the 1970s, institutional Buddhism had a very poor reputation among the political elite in the Republic of China, and Buddhist monastics were barred from speaking on campuses.

Coming to New York to pursue a doctoral degree at Columbia University, Chün-fang decided to work on Chinese Buddhism after learning that it was an active and viable subject of study in American universities. She wrote her dissertation under William Theodore de Bary on the late-Ming reformer Zhuhong (1535–1615), but she was also deeply influenced by Master Nanting (1900–1982) in Taipei, and later on by Master Sheng Yen (1930–2009) when she began teaching at Rutgers University. In the 1980s, Sheng Yen established a Chan center in Queens, which she attended, and where a group of Western-born Buddhists were taking on leading roles in Buddhist study and practice. After a long teaching career at Rutgers, in 2004 she returned to Columbia University to take up the newly established Sheng Yen chair in Chinese Buddhism, before retiring in 2013.

Throughout her life, Chün-fang has sought to challenge preexisting approaches regarding the study and practice of Chinese Buddhism. For her dissertation she wrote on an early-modern figure during a time when the mainstream of Chinese Buddhist studies was still largely focused on the earlier Tang (618–907) and Song (960–1279) dynasties. Her 1992 book, *In Search of the Dharma*, provided a rare English-language source describing the experiences of a Chinese Buddhist monk in China of the 1930s and 1940s, while her monumental 2001 work *Kuan-yin: The Chinese Transformation of Avalokiteśvara*, presented a groundbreaking, comprehensive, and exhaustive history of the figure. It is unlikely that she would have been able to conduct such research had it not been for the influence of the modern Western academic disciplines of area studies and religious studies. Buddhist religious groups have increasingly welcomed scholarship that embraces a critical and innovative stance towards the subject, rather than reproducing traditional approaches, as having a positive influence both on their tradition and on their standing in the world of ideas. In her teaching, Chün-fang was careful to balance the introduction of Buddhist doctrine and history with subject-specific lectures on such topics as gender, the visual arts, interactions between Buddhism and local religions, and its historical relationship to the state and to society.

A product both of modern Chinese Buddhist religiosity and North American academe, in her life and work Chün-fang has melded together her personal relationships with Buddhist masters and her academic commitment to produce what she calls a "double vision," a balanced emic and etic perspective that equally informs her written work and her teaching. Her approach has been not to tell readers and students what Buddhism is or ought to be, but rather to show them what there is and to give them the tools to investigate its history for themselves.

At present, Chün-fang sees the discipline of Buddhist studies as facing two major challenges: how to fill existing lacunae in the study of Chinese Buddhism, and how to achieve a balance between the study of doctrine and practice. She notes that while recent studies have continued to explore Buddhism in the Song, Ming, and more modern periods, pre-Tang Buddhism is still largely unexamined, as is the history of Qing-dynasty (1644–1911) Buddhism. Although these eras were neglected by both Buddhist and non-Buddhist writers in the past, they hold a great deal of promise of filling out our understanding of the tradition's historical development. Similarly, while interdisciplinary approaches have contributed a great deal to understanding the cultural and performative aspects of Buddhism, scholars should not lose sight of the need to study its doctrinal and intellectual history. This has traditionally been a focus of academic Buddhist studies and ought to continue to be the core of scholarly inquiry moving forward. In this way, the tradition of historical and philological research can be maintained among a new generation of scholars. This reflects the Janus-faced perspective held by many modern Buddhist academics—namely, recognizing and honoring the legacies of past scholarship but equally aware of the need for new approaches and new ideas to enliven and sustain the field.

KNOWING BUDDHA ORGANIZATION
Master Acharavadee Wongsakon
MICHAEL JERRYSON

The majority of scholarship on Buddhism and globalization tracks the ways in which Buddhists use technologies to enhance the dissemination of the Buddhist teachings (dharma) and the growth of Buddhist transnational organizations. While globalization provides promises, it also provides problems. In Thailand, a country where the majority of the population follows Theravada Buddhism, Acharavadee's (1965–present) Knowing Buddha Organization seeks to redress the global commercialization of the Buddha image, which it considers a desecration of the sacred.

Off one of Bangkok's busy streets is a winding road bedecked with businesses, condominiums, a Christian church, and near its end, the School of Life. It is here that one can find the base of operations for the Knowing Buddha Organization (KBO). Only a few years old, the KBO boasts over two thousand members and has effectively launched campaigns to protect Buddha images in France, Germany, the Netherlands, the United States, and Thailand. KBO is the brainchild of a young Thai entrepreneur-turned-meditation master, Acharavadee Wongsakon.

Acharavadee was born in 1965 to a middle-class family in Bangkok. After receiving a degree in business administration from Sripatum University, she worked for five years until opening up her own store, St. Tropez Diamond. In the midst of her entrepreneurial endeavors, Acharavadee took up meditation as a hobby. Almost by coincidence, her hobby and business patterns collided a few years later when she visited France. During her trip, Acharavadee walked past a bar named "the Buddha Bar." The name puzzled her, so she entered to find a statue of the Buddha placed in the center of the room. People were drinking alcohol, smoking cigarettes, and dancing; this stark contrast to proper Buddhist veneration reduced Acharavadee to tears. Unable to persuade the bar owners to do anything about this inconsistency, she returned to Thailand.

By 2005, Acharavadee's business was flourishing and she had won the annual business award "Boss of the Year." It was during this same year that she attended one of S. N. Goenka's meditation centers in the western province of Kanchanaburi. It was a life-changing experience. After the visit, Acharavadee found that her lifestyle began to change. She remarked, "I began to crave less, I was less greedy, and I became more concerned for other people than before." The gradual shift led her to quit her business and dedicate her life to the dharma. This trajectory led her to another profound experience.

By 2007, Acharavadee had been practicing meditation for seven years. It was at this time that she first experienced an encounter with the famous Thai Buddhist abbot, Venerable Somdej Phra Puttajarn (1788–1872). Despite his having been dead for more than a century, during Acharavadee's meditation she received his mind-to-mind transmission, in which the deceased abbot taught her to cultivate a meditation practice called *Te-cho vipassana*. His teachings led her to attain mastery over the meditation style and to become fully awakened.

After twenty years of owning and operating her own business, Acharavadee sold it to found the School of Life Foundation in 2009. She began to offer meditation classes to young children and adults and published a meditation book that only increased the continual upward surge of enrollment in her classes. The experience at the Buddha Bar in France had had a lasting impact on Acharavadee. She began to discuss the larger issue of the Buddha image with her students. For her, the Buddha offers a unique gift in comparison to other religions. He provides a path out of suffering that is dependent upon each person. She explained to her members: if you cannot protect the Buddha image, how can you hope to protect the Buddhist doctrine? Starting with six students, Acharavadee decided to found the Knowing Buddha Organization on April 17, 2012.

Since its inception, the organization has successfully coordinated one hundred cases to protect Buddha images worldwide. Many of the KBO's campaigns have been quite successful. Buddha images on toilet lids were removed in France, seductive poses in front of Buddha images in *Maxim* magazine were cancelled. In 2013, the Dutch company Boels created Buddha-image toilet boxes in Brunssum, Netherlands. KBO wrote to the embassy on January 25, 2013, requesting that the government take action. The Netherlands responded immediately, ordering the removal of the toilet boxes and issuing an letter of apology.

Acharavadee considers these objects the result of general ignorance about Buddhism. One prominent example found by the KBO is an e-mail they received in 2013. A group of Europeans had inquired about a good way to create a Buddha-image carpet for the Buddha's birthday. The inherent problem with their question is that Buddha images should be placed up high as a sign of respect; the dirtiest and most impolite parts of the body are the soles of the feet.

In a world of mass commercialization that transforms Buddha heads into flowerpots, the KBO acts as a transnational censor. Acharavadee sees Thailand as integral to the larger global problem of disrespecting Buddha images. Though most Thais do not disrespect the images, they still mass-produce and sell these images to foreigners, who take them abroad and use them for various commercial interests. One of the ways to combat this problem has been through protesting the manufacturing of Buddha heads.

Acharavadee's entrepreneurial skills and business tactics have been channeled into artistically powerful productions of the KBO Web site, Facebook page, LCD displays, billboards, DVDs, and booklets. Her efforts have not gone unrewarded. There is wide support of the KBO; in addition to its growing number of members, the organization receives significant contributions from local and national Thai businesses. KBO is comprised largely of educated Thais, the majority of whom are female. Their wide membership also attracts local Thais who occasionally join in their marches, such as the annual protest down the famous backpacker streets of Khao San Road. They post brochures in popular tourist spots like the Grand Palace and have submitted a video campaign for Thai Airways.

In Thailand, Acharavadee is rallying support to make Buddhism the official national religion. Ultimately, the KBO would like the Thai government to implement laws that criminalize the commercialization of Buddha images. On the global stage, Acharavadee and her members argue that people do not need to follow Buddhism to respect its founder. They point out, "There is no prophet in the world who has been oppressively disrespected like this ever before." At their headquarters on June 29, 2014, one of the KBO directors explained that "We are not like Muslims, we do not fight. . . . we just tell people the right way [to treat our sacred images]." Though her global characterization of Muslims is misplaced, her point is quite powerful. Globalization continues to push us closer and closer together; and in the face of this, the KBO offers a civil model for how religious communities can react to the mistreatment of their sacred relics.

EDUCATE, AGITATE, ORGANIZE
Sudhir Waghmare
WILLIAM ELISON

Buddhism has experienced something of a rebirth in modern India thanks to the efforts of B. R. Ambedkar. One of the giants of Indian politics—and political thought—in the late colonial and postindependence years, Ambedkar championed the "depressed classes," the communities stigmatized by upper-caste Hindus as untouchable. In 1956 he led a mass conversion to a distinctively modern, rationalized form of Buddhism. Converting with him that day was Sudhir Waghmare (1937–present), whose subsequent career as a painter has sustained his Buddhist identity at two levels: he produces art for the sangha, and he paints daily as a contemplative practice.

Sudhir is an artist who paints portraits and landscapes. His palette emphasizes ochres, and many of his compositions are based on a ground of earth tones, lending an organic look and texture to his painting. He has worked with the image of the Buddha, visualized in a realist idiom, and also with a figure that appears no less iconic in the context of Buddhism's Indian revival: the bespectacled and suit-clad Dr. B. R. Ambedkar, the movement's architect, who died (or, within the tradition, attained *parinirvana*) in 1956. Sudhir's landscapes, on the other hand, focus on the immediate. He paints views of his own neighborhood in the western Indian city of Pune, New Modikhana—a place whose dusty streets and walls are dominated by shades of ochre.

These days Pune is a boomtown, one of the urban engines of the economic growth that has seemed to vindicate the policies of India's political and business elites over the past two decades. But among the city's middle-class

SINHALA BUDDHISM AND ALCOHOL CONSUMPTION
Padma

MICHELE R. GAMBURD

People's identities reflect what they eat and drink. How do Theravada Buddhists in Sri Lanka think about the effects of alcohol consumption on gender, caste, ethnicity, and nationality? Padma (1921–2015) provides one example from a Buddhist-majority area on the island's southwest coast, where social pressures encourage men to drink but religious sanctions condemn them when they imbibe.

Padma was a proud old woman from a high-status family who lived in a village near the beach. Before retiring twenty years prior, she had worked as a school principal. Despite her respected position in the community, she faced multiple challenges at home. Padma's late husband had drunk heavily. In addition, two of her son were alcoholics, and Padma regularly fought over money with her son who lived down the street. Risking the wrath of local distillers, she actively encouraged police presence near illicit liquor taverns. I learned to admire Padma's deep knowledge of Buddhist teachings and texts and to recognize in her conversation elements of the Sinhala-Buddhist nationalist rhetoric that pervaded Sri Lanka during its long-standing ethnic conflict with the insurgent Liberation Tigers of Tamil Eelam (1983–2009). One warm afternoon, my research associate and I spent several hours speaking with Padma about alcohol consumption and Buddhism.

In Theravada Buddhism, the Five Precepts set out basic rules for conduct, directing laypeople not to kill, steal, be unchaste, tell lies, or take intoxicants. Observing the Fifth Precept by abstaining from mind-altering substances allows a Buddhist to act mindfully and follow the other precepts more easily. Avoiding intoxication also helps with meditation and the development of wisdom. In contrast, the desire and craving associated with substance abuse lead to perpetual suffering. Theravada Buddhism also condemns livelihoods dependent on producing and selling liquor. Right Livelihood, one of the principles of ethical conduct that makes up the Noble Eightfold Path, suggests that Buddhists should not make their living through professions that harm others, including trading in weapons, poisons, or alcohol; killing animals; and cheating. But despite religious prohibitions on making, selling, or drinking alcohol, many village men drank regularly. Local women, in contrast, avoided and disapproved of liquor.

In our interview, Padma emphasized the superiority of her family by discussing their diet. She said: "In my childhood home, we didn't even have eggs or chicken, let alone alcohol. Once when my grandfather got sick, the

Ayurvedic doctor told him to take a medicine made with alcohol. My grand-father said, 'No. Even if I die, I don't want that medicine.' He said he wouldn't take any more medicine from that doctor. This was because of Buddhism, Sinhala Buddhism." She had fed her children a vegetarian diet when they were young, and she herself had not eaten fish or meat for thirty years. If her sons drank to excess, it had nothing to do with their upbringing. She associated meat eating with people from untouchable castes. Dietary choices correlated closely with religious identity, gender, and caste status.

Although written records document the use of intoxicants in South Asia for over three millennia, many Sri Lankans credit European colonizers with promoting high levels of alcohol manufacture and use. Padma asserted: "The ancient kings drank, but only toddy. The normal people didn't drink. This is what the history books say. Then the Portuguese came. They ate bread and drank alcohol. The local people thought that the wine was blood." Padma associated the island's loss of independence to poor leadership and alcohol use. She noted, "The last king, who was a Tamil [and a Hindu], was a drunk-ard. The British caught him and took him to Bangalore in India, where he died." Padma's portrayal of these historic events reflects Sinhala-Buddhist resistance to both European colonialism and South Indian domination.

The colonial powers and local business elites both profited substantially from the liquor trade. Economic transformations brought about by merchant capitalism and the plantation economy created a large working class that formed a ready-made market for arrack (a distillate made from fermented palm sap).

Historians tell us that in South Asia a widespread temperance movement formed part of the Indian subcontinent's drive for independence from Brit-ish rule. In Ceylon (as Sri Lanka was then known), a temperance movement of the early 1900s accompanied a revival of Buddhism in the late 1800s. Tem-perance rhetoric suggested that the colonizers were converting people to a foreign lifestyle by promoting alcohol use. Begun by urban Christians, the movement gradually came under control of Sinhala-Buddhist rural elites; by the early twenty-first century, the Christian origins of the movement had been largely forgotten. The movement sought to spread middle-class ideas, raise moral standards, and promote thrift. By imposing these values on the lower classes and calling the values "Sinhala," the temperance movement made alcohol consumption an issue of Sinhala-Buddhist cultural, national, and religious identity.

Nationalist beliefs about Buddhism, ethnicity, and alcohol extend from the nineteenth and twentieth century into the present. When I asked Padma whether alcohol use had increased in the village since she was a child, her response offered clear-cut distinctions between past and present and Sinhala and Tamil ethnic identities. She said, "When I was small, only one person in the village drank. He didn't cause any trouble. After drinking he would recite some poetry and go to sleep. People just laughed at him. Since then, alcohol consumption has gone up. Now boys as young as fourteen are drinking illicit liquor in this village." Although she disliked the local situation, Padma compared it favorably to practices in Jaffna, a Tamil city in northern Sri Lanka, saying, "I have heard that in Jaffna, school kids are given a toddy for breakfast." Echoing the anti-Tamil sentiment prevalent in the Sinhala media, she critiqued Tamil parents' core values.

Consumption choices marked clear distinctions between "us" and "them." Padma associated purity, merit, and political legitimacy with vegetarianism, abstinence from liquor, Sinhala Buddhism, and people of her own family, caste, and ethnicity. She associated impurity and moral turpitude with eating meat, drinking alcohol or blood, and being from an untouchable caste. On the impure side of the scale fell the Portuguese and British colonists, Sri Lanka's last (Tamil Hindu) king, and parents who served toddy to children for breakfast in the Tamil heartland. Abstinence from alcohol plays a large role in Sinhala-Buddhist identity construction, and has for at least a century.

THE BUILDER OF TEMPORARY TEMPLES AND GOLDEN CORPSES
Jakkai Siributr
JUSTIN THOMAS MCDANIEL

Modern Buddhist art has been largely ignored by scholars of Buddhism, but it is one of the fastest growing parts of both the fields of installation art and modern painting. Modern Buddhist artists living and working in Thailand are leaders of this new movement in the arts. Jakkai Siributr's (1969–present) work creatively critiques modern Thai Theravada Buddhist attitudes towards wealth, magic, and individualism.

Jakkai Siributr and I share two interests: Philadelphia and corpses. I teach in Philadelphia, and he studied at Philadelphia University (one of the oldest industrial arts and fashion schools in the United States). Now he is a modern artist who creates provocative installations that comment on modern Buddhist practice and belief, especially in Thailand. I had written a book about ghosts, corpses, and magic in Thai Buddhism that focused on a particular monastery known as Wat Mahabut. This monastery has a famous shrine honoring the mummified corpse of a child who is believed to bring those who worship there good luck. Jakkai's interest in this monastery inspired him to create an installation that explored the very idea of powerful corpses that are a part of Thai Buddhist practice.

These corpses are commonly called *kuman thong* (golden child). *Kuman thong* are the mummified corpses of stillborn children and aborted fetuses, and some are children who die in their first few days or even years of life. These corpses are mummified (bled, desiccated, and stored in camphor oil) and then usually covered in gold or blackened by roasting them slowly. More often than not, *kuman thong* are actually not mummified fetus corpses but small golden wooden or plastic statues of infants. They are held by some practitioners of Thai Buddhism (as well as Cambodian and Malaysian Buddhists) to be sources of protective power and often fetch a great deal of money in the religious markets of the region.

Jakkai's work generally looks at these seemingly superstitious and commercial practices. Like many modern Buddhist artists trained in the West, he is concerned about the "commercialization" of Buddhism. *Kuman thong* could certainly be seen as a particularly gruesome commercialized product, but Jakkai's thinking on this subject is complex. He does not simply condemn these specific practices as unfortunate products of modernity or religious greed, but wants to make Thai Buddhists (his main audience) aware of the practices that they do every day but rarely reflect upon. He does not believe that the use of *kuman thong* is merely superstitious. He believes that human aspirations, whether they are for money, fame, safety, a good next life, healthy children, and so on, create a type of energy that pools around certain sacred sites or objects like *kuman thong*. He is not sure if that energy is just his imagination or is real, but he "feels" it, and his art explores these practices that cannot be explained rationally, despite our attempts to do so. He wants his audience to be aware and in that awareness learn to be honest with themselves and even occasionally laugh at themselves. He laughs at himself often because, despite the uncertainty of his belief, he engages in these practices out of habit and a strange compulsion that he finds hard to explain. In our interview in Bangkok and through subsequent follow-up conversations, I was impressed with his candor about his struggle with belief in and skepticism over certain Thai Buddhist practices. For him, being modern is not a simple choice of giving up superstition but of reflecting deeply and deciding to believe anyway—deciding consciously not to always make sense.

Jakkai's agenda is not to change Buddhist practice but maybe to understand himself. He is increasingly finding space to present his reflective installations. Exhibitions of modern art with a heavy emphasis on installation pieces have become better known since the opening of several new public and private gallery spaces in Bangkok over the past ten years, along with the success of artists like Thawan Duchanee, Hathairat Maneerat, Montien Boonma, Khemrat Kongsuk, and others. In a recent exhibition at Chulalongkorn University in Bangkok, Jakkai made himself part of his installation by creating a statue of himself sitting in meditation in the center of the room while texting on his cell phone. There was also an elaborate piece called *Shroud,* which the viewer could stand under, becoming enveloped in the piece. The shroud is made of dozens of small, handwoven Buddha images. The fabric (crocheted hemp) and the way the installation was set up allowed the viewer to "wear" the Buddha-like clothes. The installation also featured a statue of the artist as a walking Buddha statue holding a shopping bag. This piece was particularly resonant as the university's gallery is very close to the largest shopping complexes in the country.

Jakkai might be the most active contemporary artist in this Bangkok art scene, but he also takes his work outside of Thailand to Western galleries. For example, in one installation called *Temple Fair* (2008) in New York City, he made dozens of fabric images and whimsical creations that the audience could walk around, thus showing that Buddhist temple life is not merely about monastic training and ritual but about festivals and leisure. Similarly, he told me of a show in Miami in which he made religious "lottery tickets" so that gallery viewers could see how Buddhist monasteries are places where both spiritual and material aspirations converge. In San Francisco, he had an interactive piece called *Reciprocity* in which viewers could write down their own aspirations as part of the exhibition. In a large solo show called *Karma Cash & Carry* in New York in 2010, he created large textile compositions alongside installation and video works. The exhibition was organized "around his conception of a karmic convenience store, where merit can be bought and sold." Although he speaks to larger themes of religion and commercialization, his art is decidedly local. For example, he set up a spirit house (*san phra phum*) on the street where he lives in Bangkok and wrapped the trees in monks' robes. It was designed to make the street sacred, with the specific goal of stopping people from discarding trash and parking illegally. He also wanted to stop city officials from widening the street and cutting down the adjacent trees. He said it has worked, but now he worries that the spirit house will become popular and more crowds will come to make offerings to it! In many ways this project perfectly encapsulates Jakkai's struggle between producing objects of devotion and questioning the very motivation that lies behind his and others' devotion.

A RAKHINE MONK FROM BANGLADESH
Ashin Bodhinyana
JACQUES P. LEIDER

Bangladesh, a predominantly Muslim country, has a small population of Buddhists living in its southeast part near the border of Myanmar. Ashin Bodhinyana (1958–present) is a Rakhine Theravada monk, a member of an ethnic group whose cultural survival has been increasingly threatened by the hegemonic Muslim environment. After the conquest of the Rakhine kingdom by the Burmese in 1785, many Rakhine fled to the southern part of the Chittagong District and were resettled by the British in Cox's Bazar.

I met Maung Than Aye for the first time in 1993 while I was doing field-work in Cox's Bazar, now a busy Bangladeshi sea resort. He was not yet a monk, and I was a Ph.D. student trying to get in touch with the local Rakhine (or Arakanese) community. Good luck brought me to the Mahatheindaw-gree temple (founded in 1799) where we met. We have been in touch ever since.

In Bangladesh, Buddhists are a minority of about one and a half million that splits into several ethnically and linguistically different communities, including the Barua, the Chakma, the Marma, and the Rakhine. Rakhine come from western Myanmar, or Rakhine State, which used to be an independent kingdom until 1785. Many fled the oppressive conditions under the new rulers and took refuge in the Chittagong District. The descendants of those who did not return to Rakhine after the First Anglo-Burmese War of 1824–1826 still live as a tightly knit community in Bangladesh and keep regular contact with their homeland. Like other traditions, the *shinpyu* ceremony for boys and young men when they are ordained and spend a short period of time at a monastery is preserved in high regard. But the path of monkhood is not a tempting choice as a lifelong, "professional" career. As Ashin Bodhinyana (Maung's higher ordination name) puts it, parents discourage their sons from renouncing the worldly pleasures of a consumerist society. Ashin thus counts as a rarity.

Venerable Bodhinyana became a monk in 1997, around the age of forty. Inspired by the teaching of Ven. Buddhadasa Bhikkhu, the choice to take the robes marked the completion of a spiritual path that required two years of self-study and multiple stays in meditation centers in Myanmar and Thailand. But Ven. Bodhinyana's earlier life showed little sign of his monastic vocation. Like his father and five brothers, Maung Than Aye studied at St. Placid's High School, a well-reputed missionary school in Chittagong.

After enrolling at Chittagong's Government College, he went on to study at Chittagong University, where he earned a master of commerce degree in management. He became a banker for eight years until he obtained what he calls "a much awaited visa to travel to the US." But barely three months after coming to America, he dumped the green card, returned to Bangladesh, and announced his decision to live as a monk. In fact, things did not happen in a rush. The idea had been germinating in his mind since the time he worked at the bank. Today when he visits Cox's Bazar or Chittagong, he calls occasionally at the bank branch where he was employed, and his former colleagues, who by now "hold high posts and draw high salaries," call him "a happy man." Still he wonders, "Am I really so?"

Although the monastic rules observed by a Theravada Buddhist monk are the same in Bangladesh as anywhere, there is a greater freedom for deviant monks to go unchecked, as there are no state authorities to exercise control and restrictions as in Myanmar or Thailand. Ashin Bodhinyana's criticism of fellow monks in Bangladesh, "so-called monks" as he would say, is not limited to those who pretend to have supernatural powers, to the scandals they provoke, or to their corruption. His own view of Buddhist teaching has little patience for the popular religion, the one that scholars call "practical Buddhism," where ceremonies and ritual acts take up the better time of monks and laypeople. He sees the true teaching of the Buddha little honored by the masses bent on seeing earthly wishes fulfilled. So he wonders, "Is, then, Buddhism so delicate, refined, and subtle that it is unable to take root and prosper in a people of rugged, unrefined, and coarse nature?" He criticizes Rakhine Buddhists who do not uphold the ideal of their religion, unlike Islamic radicals who place their religion "at the topmost, high above their community, ethnicity, and nationality."

Ashin Bodhinyana's strongest criticism is reserved for his own folk. It is not the Muslim radicals who threaten to wipe out Rakhine Buddhists, as some fear, but the Buddhist Rakhines, "rotting socially as well as religiously" who are the real threat to their own survival. It should not be the task of monks to take a leading role in politics when communities clash, as they did in the ghastly violence that spread through Myanmar and Bangladesh in 2012: this is the task of the laypeople. "I don't feel at all threatened by Islamic extremists," he writes me. But while walking through the countryside, he would prefer a lay companion. In the cities no ugly words would be raised against him, because educated and "even secular Muslims have high regard towards the monks."

Within the orbit of Bangladeshi Buddhism, Ashin Bodhinyana's scathing criticism of divisions among the monks and the cunning management of credulous devotees by business-minded monks reveals a rectitude that borders on moral rigorism. But the truth is also that he looks at the world with utmost frankness. The rhetoric of "true" versus "false" monks is not something new in the history of Buddhism, but his particular attitude and his ability to live independently of the monastery and the ritual and social duties of a monk certainly are. As he says, "I saw many monks leading a luxurious life, drifting away from the core element of Buddhism—simple living." Uncompromising about what he believes the true teaching implies, to purify one's body and mind, Ashin Bodhinyana has ultimately chosen to stay aloof from social requirements and even from teaching, for which he feels no inclination. He would rather, as he puts it, "share his thoughts" with the likeminded who are "prepared to take them." Today, after years spent in various monasteries, he stays in his mother's home in Moheshkhali, where he moved from Teknaf when his mother passed away. He lives off the revenue of his mother's landed property and with the support of close family members.

REBUILDING TEMPLES AFTER WAR
Grandfather Pait
JUDY LEDGERWOOD

Should impoverished communities trying to recover from revolution and war use their small incomes and food stores to rebuild religious institutions, stage elaborate rituals, and feed monks, or should they save money, send their children to school, and buy new technologies? Grandfather Pait's (1914–2004) life highlights these tensions in postwar Theravada Buddhist Cambodia.

In 1994, I saw Grandfather Pait filling potholes with a hoe and a woven basket near Sabbay village as a Buddhist form of community service. He had on a big floppy hat, a shirt, and a traditional Cambodian *kroma* (checkered scarf) around his waist. The previous three years had been rough for Pait; Noch, his wife of forty years, had died in 1992. Pait had remarried, and talk in the village was critical, not of the new wife, but of the way that Pait treated her. He was accused of being stingy, a serious if common criticism in postwar Cambodia. This accusation, whether true or not, reveals tensions in modern Cambodia between efforts to rebuild Buddhist networks ideally centered on giving, selflessness, and communal bonding and the efforts of people to accumulate money, protect their immediate families, start businesses, and become part of the global capitalist community after decades of war and violence. For Grandfather Pait, Buddhist merit making was at the heart of this tension.

Born in 1914, Pait had lived through French colonialism, the years of rel-
ative stability during Norodom Sihanouk's reign in the 1950s and 1960s, and
the American-backed Lon Nol administration during the years of civil war
(1970–1975). When the war came, Pait and his family fled to Phnom Penh as
the region south of the city became a battlefield. His daughter was married
with three children, and Pait struggled to help support an extended family
of eight in a city full of war refugees. Swept up in the radical Khmer Rouge
Marxist revolution, they were driven out of the city in 1975. The entire urban
population was sent to the countryside and organized into communal work
teams by age and sex. In the communist-era work camps, Pait herded cattle
and Noch wove mats on elder work teams. Noch's mother and one of the
grandchildren died of starvation in 1975. Pait's daughter, her husband, and
two surviving children were sent to Battambang, where her husband and
both children died. His daughter eventually escaped across the border into
Thailand and resettled in the United States. "The Khmer Rouge horrors
forced one to commit *baap*" (selfish/malicious actions), Pait said years later,
"lying, stealing—whatever one needed to do to survive."

After the collapse of the Khmer Rouge regime in 1979, Pait and Noch returned to Sabbay village, where he did some fortune-telling. As an elder in
the 1990s–2000s, he wore white and was addressed as *achar* (Buddhist lay of-
ficiant). The couple did not hear that their daughter was alive until 1987.
She remarried and had three daughters in the United States. Though she was
poor by American standards, Pait's daughter would regularly send them
small amounts of money (US$100–300), especially at holidays.

It was this flow of money that became the source of the accusations of
stinginess against Pait. Two other households in Sabbay also had relatives
in the United States, and over the course of the 1990s they built fine newly
elevated wooden houses. They bought new oxen and eventually motorcycles.
But Pait and his new wife continued to live in a thatched hut on the ground
with a dirt floor. Noch's surviving sister complained of not receiving what
she thought should be her share of money from her niece abroad. Pait must
be hoarding money, people speculated. Many analyses of post–Khmer Rouge
Cambodia argue that in the wake of the social devastation family ties were
weakened, and a loss of social reciprocity is thought to have characterized
this period.

But Pait was not hoarding the money, or at least not most of it. In fact he
was astonishingly generous. He was giving his relatively limited money to
the surrounding temples. The Khmer Rouge had systematically destroyed
Buddhist temples and other religious buildings. The buildings at nearby Wat
Samnang were completely destroyed, and the large trees that shaded the

temple complex were cut down for firewood. At Wat Sabbay the Khmer Rouge had attached mines to the temple walls and blown it up. The monks' quarters, riddled with bullets and scarred by shelling, were used as a makeshift clinic.

When we conducted research on the dramatic rebuilding effort at temples in the area in the early 1990s, we found that Pait was a major donor at Wat Samnang, the temple where he had ordained in his youth. The head of the temple committee pointed out to me construction projects undertaken and trees planted through the generosity of Grandfather Pait. Pait had me take pictures of the plaques that bore his name as donor. He showed me that they said "and daughter" to point out that he was also making merit for her. In 2003 I gave Pait, then eighty-eight, a ride into Phnom Penh so he could call his daughter; along the route he pointed out other temples where he was a donor. He said that, in all, he had contributed to the rebuilding or refurbishing of fifty-two temples. The phone call was to try to convince his daughter to send cash to him directly; lately she had begun sending the money through a nephew in the city, who then brought him rice and only small amounts of cash, apparently to curb his giving.

In donating much of the money his daughter sent him to help rebuild temples, Grandfather Pait was performing one of the most meritorious acts a Buddhist can undertake. In Cambodia, as across the countries of Theravada Southeast Asia, old age is the time to turn to Buddhist merit making. This pattern is all the more important given that Khmer Rouge survivors, including Pait, report having committed *baap* in order to stay alive. By wearing white, taking precepts on holy days, taking on the title *achar,* giving donations, and quietly filling the potholes near the temple, Grandfather Pait was earning merit. He chose generosity and renunciation but had to suffer the criticism of his neighbors. Pait passed away in 2004. His ashes are interred in a stupa (Khmer: *chedey*) with those of Noch at Wat Samnang, a temple shaded by rows of mango trees that his donations paid to plant.

SCHOLAR, REFORMER, AND ACTIVIST
Dharma Ratna
DAVID N. GELLNER

The Buddhism of the Kathmandu Valley, Nepal, is the last remnant of the Mahayana and Vajrayana Buddhism of north India, which preserves rituals and liturgies in Sanskrit that are in many cases around a thousand years old. There has been continuing contact with Tibetan Buddhism and increasing influence, with some Newars from Nepal adopting Tibetan forms of practice. From the 1930s, however, a Theravada revival movement, deriving first from Burma, later from Sri Lanka, and lastly from Thailand, with many monks and nuns from within and beyond the Newar community, has been more influential. Dharma Ratna (1930–2007) is part of that revival movement.

Dharma Ratna "Trishuli" was a scholar and a reflective, self-aware Buddhist: he was dedicated to research and clear exposition in the name of Buddhism. He always struck me as a very wise man, who used his time well, never wasting a minute (he preferred scholarly production to speechifying and meetings). I had the impression that he understood the society he came from quite profoundly. He was not educated in English, and so did not form part of the small group of jet-setting Buddhist activists who benefited from government patronage to represent Nepal at international meetings in the 1980s and 1990s. The memorial volume in his name lists forty-five books published in Nepali, another forty-five in his mother tongue (Newari/Nepal Bhasa), and a further ninety-three unpublished works. Very many of these were translations from Pali, but some were collections of hymns, plays on Buddhist themes, or local histories.

One day, in January 2000, I ran into him by the Bagmati River and we spent some time discussing the Theravada movement, and in particular the thorny issue of the ordination of nuns, which I was researching at that time for the book that I later published with Sarah LeVine (see also LeVine, this volume, on Dhammawati). Dharma Ratna's opinion was that the *anagarikas,* the local Theravada nuns, were wrong to have taken the *bhikshuni* or full nun's ordination from the Chinese Fo Guang Shan sect. "They can stay as *anagarika* and still be *arhats* (enlightened beings)," he said. "They've taken the Sarvastivada Vinaya [Mahayana rules of monastic conduct], but kept the Theravada *siddhanta* (teachings)." I tried to point out that the ordination tradition was one thing, and the philosophical teachings another, which led to the following exchange:

DHARMA RATNA (DR): Look, they've just taken the bits they wanted. Chinese nuns don't eat meat, but the nuns have all been in Burma and Thailand and so they do [eat it]. Chinese nuns work, they don't.

DAVID: What sort of work do the Chinese nuns do?

DR: They teach, work in hospitals, and do all kinds of development work. If I were an *anagarika,* I'd just stay as an *anagarika.* There are different words [for being a nun] in different countries. It's only in Nepal and India that they are called *anagarika.* The Buddha said [when the earliest nuns came to him], "Are you ready to bow down to the youngest monk?" They said that they were, and he said, "Very well, but [because I have permitted women to be ordained] the teaching will now last only for five hundred years [instead of 5,000]."

DAVID: But if you say that women cannot be equal, how can that be the Buddha's teaching?

DR: How can we say that it isn't?

DAVID: Western Buddhists will be angry if you say this.

DR: Being angry is one thing, but it doesn't affect the facts. You can't be a Buddha, an Indra, or a Cakravartin as a woman. You can be a Buddha's mother, or you can be reborn in the Brahma world where there are only men. . . . But look, all this is just my opinion. I'm just a householder. I have to say *namaskar* to them, whether they are *anagarika* or *bhiksuni, bhiksu, fakir,* or whatever!

With that, he smiled gravely, got up, and continued on his way to Lalitpur.

This discussion reminded me of another we had back in 1989 when we discussed Newar life-cycle rituals. He told me that he wasn't really in favor of the girls' mock marriage ritual for which the Newars are famous. He did not think it really had much point: "But what to do? We have to live in society." I countered, "But by that argument you could get rid of first rice-feeding and all the others as well." He disagreed: "The marking of the end of the period of birth impurity has a point, but mock marriage rituals do not."

Despite what might be seen as quite conservative and distinctly unmodern attitudes, Dharma Ratna was an important and highly respected figure in the revival of Buddhism in Nepal in the second half of the twentieth century. He was a Pali scholar and played a key role, with Bhikshu Buddhaghosh, in the establishment of the Pariyatti Siksa in 1962. This was the Buddhist curriculum and system of study that is so instrumental today in teaching Buddhism and spreading it to young Nepalis or groups that have not traditionally been Buddhist (see Letizia, this volume).

Dharma Ratna was not only an activist and organizer but wrote many of the key popularizing, didactic texts for laypeople. He supported Theravada monks and nuns as much as he could. Yet he was no Theravada fundamentalist, simultaneously believing in and practicing the traditional Vajrayana Buddhism he had inherited as a Sakya and a member of Kwa Baha, the famous "Golden Temple." Unlike many supporters of the new Theravada movement, he did not disparage and run down Vajrayana Buddhism. Rather, he saw the new stress on knowledge of Buddhist doctrine and learning as a way into a complex hierarchical structure that would still have room for the traditional forms of practice based on Sanskrit liturgies and mantras.

Dharma Ratna's example shows that it is possible to believe that the values, teachings, and history of Buddhism should be imparted to laypeople using modern methods and textbooks, without thereby embracing a modernist critique of all ritual or all non-Theravada forms of Buddhism. One can be a moderniz*ing* Buddhist without necessarily being an aggressive modern*ist* out to consign all traditional Buddhist practices to the dustbin.

A THAI MURAL PAINTER IN SINGAPORE
Irving Chan Johnson
IRVING CHAN JOHNSON

Irving Chan Johnson (1971–present) is an associate professor in the Department of Southeast Asian Studies at the National University of Singapore. He has been painting traditional Thai Buddhist art since he was a child. His current project (begun in 2013) involves painting the walls of the chapel at Wat Uttamayanmuni, a Theravada Thai temple in Singapore. His life reveals a tension found among many Buddhist scholars between being a practitioner and an academic.

Deep in the recesses of Thai Buddhist hell, in an immense cauldron of boiling oil, Osama bin Laden glares cheekily at the monk Phra Malai hovering above him. In front of the celebrated face of international terrorism, Adolf Hitler frowns, his brown eyes staring at the flames that seem to engulf him. Behind him, a naked Thai couple—man and woman, their ethnic identities inscribed by their distinctive nineteenth-century hairdos, scramble up the trunk of a *ngiu* tree. The tree's razor-sharp thorns peel away at their soft flesh. A skeletal arm grabs the woman's ankle. Perhaps it is a desperate plea for help or a sinister desire to drag her back into the flames. Once upon a time, the couple had engaged in an adulterous affair and now they have to pay for their karmic misdeeds. As they cling to the *ngiu*'s thorny branches, they are pecked at by vultures with beaks of iron, forcing them to lose their grip and fall into the gaping jaws of a prehistoric wolf and saber-toothed tiger. Death is no relief for the damned, and on being reborn into this terrifying world of fire and pain, they are forced to make their way up the *ngiu* again and again until their karma runs its course.

I painted this vivid image on a heavy concrete slab in the grounds of a Thai Buddhist temple in Singapore, one of five Thai monasteries on the predominantly ethnic Chinese island. I began my painting project in August 2010. What started out as a casual artistic endeavor to decorate the backrest of a cement statue of a Brahmanic ascetic soon became a social and ritual commitment to materializing a traditional Thai Buddhist narrative. My painting took a year to complete and was an artistic trigger that soon had me painting the main doors to the temple's large shrine (*wihan*) and, more recently, a fifteen-year project of painting all the inner walls of the building. I was never paid for my work, save for occasional donations I received from well-wishers to purchase brushes, paints, and gold leaf. I have always viewed my paintings as my contribution to the aesthetics of the temple as well as an exercise in anthropological thinking. At a deeper and more personal level, I believe that my work as a mural painter generates a large amount of karmic merit.

Born the children of a Thai mother and a Caucasian American father, my siblings and I grew up as Thai Buddhist children. The temple was not just a religious site where we celebrated birthdays and mourned the departed, but also a social venue where we met friends, gossiped, and played. Furthermore, Wat Uttamayanmuni was part of a Kelantanese Thai religious landscape that had spread beyond the confines of the Malaysian state of Kelantan. My mother's natal village was in Kelantan, a predominantly Malay Muslim state where ethnic Thais make up no more than eleven thousand individuals. Having a Kelantanese Thai Buddhist temple in Singapore reminded us of our identity, not only as Thais and Buddhists but also as a minority community living at the furthest extremities of the Thai Buddhist world.

In my mural of Buddhist hell, I was always conscious of the connections I had between the space in which the work appears—a wall in a Thai temple in Singapore frequented by Chinese worshippers—and the dialogue between my artistic self and those around me. This constant awareness reminded me of my professional training as an anthropologist. The wall was not only my canvas but also an anthropological field site. Men, women, and children would watch me as I painted, often standing silently from a distance, at other times talking, joking, advising, and criticizing. Sometimes they would even try their hands at the job itself, making a mess on the wall before I politely pulled the brush from them. These encounters shaped the scene I painted, and I soon noticed that the painting had its own agency. What I painted was determined by the social and temporal situation I found myself in. I did not work with a fixed visual template, as do some Thai painters who copy the works of more established artists. Rather, I worked with the overall composition in my head, recalling what I had seen in Thailand's temples, in books, and the stories I had heard from my maternal grandmother. On most days I worked in silence, save for the Thai country songs that blasted through my iPhone's tiny speakers.

Chinese Singaporeans, who made up the majority of temple goers, were largely unacquainted with the tale of Phra Malai. I had to be constantly aware that, for many in my audience, this was a new visual experience—one that was a combination of aesthetic spectacle and moral learning. Artists and anthropologists work within the rigid structures of their society and of the society they write about and tell stories of. Their position is one of interstitiality. They attempt to break from the structures that confine them in their recollection of narrative moments either as writing or painting but are inevitably constrained by their own interpretations of what constitutes the ethnographic experience.

The painting of Phra Malai's journey to the netherworld represents a celebration of artistic egoism (I signed the painting in the bottom righthand corner, unlike the Thai Buddhist painters of yore, whose works remain largely unnamed), a reflection of modernity's tussle with Buddhist traditionalism and of my own struggles with cultural representation. The mural resembles what George Marcus and Michael Fischer have termed "ethnographies of experience," where the ethnographic gaze is focused "on the person, the self, and the emotions—all topics difficult to probe in traditional ethnographic frameworks." Thinking about how I painted the mural is akin to fieldwork and the indigenous artist's involvement in a reflexive process of "culture making." Thai mural artists are engaged in the lives of their audiences and are both affected and effected by the images they churn out. Their magnificent creations represent an evolving bricolage of silent emotions, reflections, histories, and ideologies.

LOOKING FORWARD

Social-Psychological Care
in a Troubled World

Rather than looking backward in the hope of returning to "tradition," the figures featured in this section actively engage with discovering ways of making Buddhism relevant to contemporary society and thereby seek a life of greater meaning and significance. They engage in activities and reinterpret what it means to be a Buddhist in ways, to quote John Nelson's contribution, "that may not always align with established social and cultural norms." These Buddhists seek to engage the world and in so doing challenge, and sometimes even break down, traditional boundaries, not only by drawing on multiple traditions, but also by reinterpreting Buddhism in ways that justify their activities.

The most evident characteristic of the Buddhists described in the vignettes that follow is their high level of mobility. Traveling across different sites in a single country to care for victims of a natural disaster or across multiple countries to seek an education or ordination or to extend the reach of social service may allow practitioners to reinterpret the contours of Buddhist ethics and, in the process, challenge traditional sectarian boundaries as well as ideas of practice. Travel invariably opens people to different doctrines, liturgies, Buddhist traditions, and even other religions. The international ties and networks of these mobile figures of Buddhist modernity result in an indirect and sometimes an overt challenge to the divisions and boundaries that have traditionally defined the field of Buddhist studies.

For instance, while the Nepalese nun Dhammawati identifies herself, in some ways, as a member of the Theravada tradition, she nonetheless challenges the very concept of sectarian affiliation by receiving higher ordination from the Taiwanese Fo Guang Shan monastery and, in turn, by encouraging her students to travel to and study in Thailand, Sri Lanka, and Taiwan. In a similar manner, the Chinese-Malaysian Theravada monk discussed in Corey Bell's article not only believes that "Mahayana, Hinayana, northern and southern [lineages] are merely designations" but also actively attempts to downplay Buddhist sectarianism in the name of humanitarian and liberal pragmatic pursuits such as organizing business camps and hosting "one of the largest and most thematically diverse Buddhist Web portals in the world."

Sectarian boundaries are further challenged by the ways in which some Buddhists have responded to natural disaster, ways that may act as a centripetal force drawing together members of disparate communities and traditions. Consider the Japanese priest Kaneta Taiō, who sees his post-tsunami work as a counselor as the direct outcome of being a member of the local community rather than a member of the Sōtō Zen sect. Similarly, even though Taniyama Yōzō could have replaced his father as head priest of a local Buddhist temple, he chose instead to downplay any sectarian affiliations in favor of a more pan-Buddhist and pan-religious humanism that fuses religious, biomedical, and social welfare activities (such as creating Buddhist hospices and centers to train people in becoming "clinical religionists").

Engaging the world challenges the division that is sometimes used in discussions of monastic vocation. No longer being seen as either falling on the side of studying (*granthadhura*) or meditating (*vipassanadhura*), the efforts expended by the figures in this section have largely been redirected from teaching about Buddhism or Buddhist meditation to a plethora of other activities. Along with providing physical and psychological relief in the wake of the 2011 tsunami and nuclear disaster, the men and women monastics and laypeople represented here have used Buddhism as a vehicle for treating drug addicts and alcoholics (Luang Por Yai), for aiding both national and international victims of radiation fallout (the Reverend Takahashi), for bridging the gap between older and younger generations (Nakanishi), for helping the terminally ill through the creation of Buddhist hospice centers, as well as for empowering Nepal's low-caste Tharus by convincing them to embrace their religious heritage and identity through the creation of Buddhist Awareness Camps (Vasudev). Indeed, many of the monastic and lay figures found in this section have transformed themselves into aid workers and, as a consequence, Buddhism into a type of NGO.

The traditions of Buddhism, in turn, are used by several of the figures to challenge cultural biases and injustices. For example, Chunda, a Newar woman who pursued a Ph.D. in Nepal, has sought to reduce the number of women and young girls who fall victim to sex trafficking and sexually transmitted diseases by reinstituting a Newar Buddhist menarche ritual that, she believes, would provide the necessary space for a girl to realize her full potential as a woman. Further afield, we find Terry Hu, a Taiwanese actress who draws on a wide range of religious and spiritual writings to critique male chauvinistic tendencies in contemporary Taiwanese culture. Traveling farther northeast, the vignette of Nakanishi Eiko—the seventy-nine-year-old wife of a temple priest—illustrates how the creation of a Temple Women Liaison Group was used to lobby her own Buddhist sect to enfranchise temple wives.

The process of reaching out in the hope of creating a more equitable and just society sometimes necessitates reinterpreting, reenvisioning, or simply overlooking what might be labeled as Buddhist ethics. We see such a move in the life of Achan Chahn Ly, a militant monk living in Thailand who sought to bring down communism in the Lao PDR and Thailand through spreading anticommunist propaganda and supporting anticommunist insurgents. Though he did not go so far as to say, as some before him had, that it is not a sin to kill a communist, many felt that his support of the insurgents went too far. Further afield, we see how the Tibetan Buddhist figure Khandro Tāre Lhamo has become a symbol of epistemic resistance by answering the prayers of those imprisoned by the Chinese Communist government as well as providing them with hope and protection through an affirmation of faith.

Reinterpreting Buddhism in ways that may not always align with established social and cultural norms also necessitates various processes of modernization. The Nepalese nun Dhammawati, the Chinese Malaysian monk Dhammapala, and the Taiwanese monk Houguan all believe that the content of Buddhist education—for monastics as well as laypeople—needs to be expanded beyond Buddhists doctrines and meditative traditions to include foreign languages (particularly English) and secular subjects (e.g., business, leadership and communication skills, and accounting). Beyond modernizing what counts as Buddhist education, several lay leaders and monastics have discussed the need to reenvision how best to reach out to laypeople, especially given their busier lives. Such methods of propagation include a variety of electronic media (Facebook, Web TV, e-comics, temple-run cable networks, and e-books), as well as methods that resonate with the laity's interests (e.g., creating Buddhist jazz cafés where monks act more as counselors than ritualists). For some forward-looking Buddhists, it also includes the creation of virtual spaces wherein laypeople could perform devotional activities (including sutra copying and virtual lamplighting). Such modernizing tendencies may force a reconceptualization of what a Buddhist temple is and how it should function as a site that draws on the expertise of a much wider range of contributors, not only by downplaying the centrality of a spiritual leader or abbot, but also by transforming how the physical space itself is used.

STABILIZING THE RHYTHMS OF LIFE AFTER THE TSUNAMI
Kaneta Taiō
TIM GRAF

Buddhist responses to the March 11, 2011, earthquake and tsunami disasters in Japan have elicited notably favorable media coverage, especially when compared to portrayals of Buddhism after the Kobe earthquake of 1995. Buddhist professionals have contributed to this shift by deemphasizing the role played by sectarian affiliation in multireligious and interdisciplinary relief collaborations. Kaneta Taiō (1956–present) became well known for setting the stage for recreational activities in the disaster zone. His mobile counseling café has since become an important training venue for a new generation of "interfaith chaplains."

It was a windy day in early May 2011, eight tumultuous weeks after the March 11 earthquake, tsunami, and nuclear disaster in Japan. I was on my second tour to the tsunami-stricken areas, interviewing priests for a documentary on Buddhist responses to 3/11. I had met Sōtō Zen priest Kaneta Taiō earlier at a conference on religion and disaster relief in Sendai, but now that circumstances allowed for a longer conversation in front of a camera, I found myself hesitating. Was it appropriate to capture an unfolding catastrophe on film? Ever since I had first entered the disaster zone, I wondered about the effects of my fieldwork both on the people of Tōhoku and on myself. I tried to suppress my nervousness, but when startled by the slightest aftershock, I nearly jumped out of my seat. Kaneta, unshakable as ever, relieved the tension with a laugh. The "aftershock" I felt, he assured me, was just the wind.

Within the first two months of the 3/11 crisis, Kaneta had participated in almost two hundred funerals for tsunami victims. He volunteered at a local crematorium in Kurihara city, fifty kilometers away from the coast, as a lack of heavy oil forced survivors to bring bodies inland for cremation. He chanted sutras in the midst of destruction, mobilized others to volunteer, organized prayer vigils, and conducted spirit-pacifying rituals for the dead and the bereaved. He shared his food supplies with neighbors and opened the doors of his temple to people seeking shelter. He took care of his mother-in-law and her traumatized dog after they had lost their house in the tsunami—all of this while it was yet unclear how many of his friends and colleagues were among the nearly sixteen thousand dead who were found in the debris, buried, or floating along the coast for days and weeks. The impact of the March 11 earthquake was so overwhelming that, according to Kaneta, "in the end, there was no distinction between those who were killed, those who suffered because of the disaster, and the rest of us."

More than two years after 3/11, nearly 2,700 people are still reported missing. Many of the 300,000 displaced are still living isolated in crowded temporary housing units. Kaneta visits the shelters on a weekly basis. He fights depression with jazz, offers counseling sessions over coffee and cake, and coordinates a radio show with practical hints for life after the tsunami. To him, being a priest has little to do with intellectual reflections on Buddhist orthodoxy. His teaching derives from practice; his self-understanding as a Buddhist professional is that of an engaged local community member. What characterizes a priest, according to Kaneta, is his or her ability to respond to the needs of the local community by performing a variety of roles in society, roles that require a wide-ranging set of skills, regardless of sectarian affiliation.

Café de Monk, the mobile counseling service he initiated, puts Kaneta's ideas into practice. Every time Kaneta drives his bus towards the hardest-hit areas, he takes with him relief goods, motivation, and a handcrafted "Café de Monk" sign made of debris. A track by Thelonious Monk marks the café's opening with jazz. Everyone is welcome to let go of stress and "complain" to a monk for free. Playing on a pun in Japanese, Café de Monk can mean "complaining at a café" as well as "Monk's café." Listening carefully to the stories of survivors in face-to-face conversations is, according to Kaneta, the key to counseling in post-disaster situations. The prospect of "spiritual care," however, does not motivate people to show up and start talking about their problems with strangers. It is cake, rather than Buddhism, that first brings them together. The actual counseling develops after that, though many of the local fishermen would prefer to talk with him over *sake* and beer rather than tea. In any case, ludic elements provide the arena for serious conversations about experiences of loss and depression, or, by request, for prayers and rituals in commemoration of the dead. In rare cases, even exorcisms for those haunted by the spirits of tsunami victims are provided.

Kaneta's form of Buddhism is by no means distinctly modern. The ways in which recreational practices are currently multiplying within transreligious relief projects, however, are unprecedented. Collaborations between Kaneta and medical doctors, social workers, scholars, and religious practitioners on a relief project called Kokoro no Sōdanshitsu (Spirit Counseling Center) illustrate this point. Because volunteers are urged to deemphasize sectarian distinctions to allow for collaborations between different religious organizations, transformations of the Buddhist message are bound to occur. The fact that religious practitioners have not pressed the religious aspects of any particular organization has contributed to a notably more positive picture of Buddhism in the Japanese media. This trend has not only worked to balance pejorative, reductive descriptions of rituals as "funerary Buddhism," but it has also marked a turn away from widespread descriptions of religions as dangerous cults. Negative images of religion have prevailed ever since 1995, when members of the religious organization Aum Shinrikyō committed a series of violent crimes, most notably the sarin gas attack on the Tokyo subway.

The framework that allows Kokoro no Sōdanshitsu to communicate its goals and formulate a transreligious agenda compatible with contemporary social norms can only be fully understood through the lens of the psychologization and clinicization of Buddhism and death-related practices in modern and postwar Japan. Since the 1990s, both trends have strongly influenced the hospice movement and the institutionalization of spiritual care. Kokoro no Sōdanshitsu has led this development by training "clinical religious specialists," often described as "chaplains," in "practical religious studies" since 2012. The training Kaneta offers as one of the teachers in this program at Tōhoku University involves transreligious qualifications, competence in local religious culture, and practical skills acquired in the Café de Monk that may not necessarily be described as "clinical."

The perseverance necessary to stabilize the rhythms of everyday life after major disasters can hardly be overstated. Following our interview back in 2011, Kaneta showed me around his temple. Massive family graves, built to last for generations, were lying in ruins. I resisted the urge to lift them back up, realizing that such work was best left to survivors working through grief. But Kaneta had no immediate plans to reassemble them; he knew that the next large-scale aftershock would just knock them over again.

PRESIDENT OF THE THERAVADA NUNS' ORDER OF NEPAL
Dhammawati
SARAH LEVINE

As a teenager, Dhammawati (1934–present) ran away from home to ordain as a Theravada nun. Encountering hostility from the monks' order on her return after many years' training in Burma, she fought to raise the status of both Buddhist nuns and laywomen in Nepal. As preacher, scholar, educator, meditation teacher, and campaigner for full ordination for women, she has become a leading Theravada feminist.

Before dawn one February Monday in 1998, more than three hundred Newar Buddhists pile into buses in Kathmandu and head to Lumbini, the

Buddha's birthplace, for the inauguration of the International Bhikkhuni Sangha Gautami Temple. On their arrival many hours later, they are welcomed by Dhammawati Guruma, a bright-faced woman of sixty-four in pink and orange nun's dress, who shepherds them into the courtyard where a lavish lunch is laid out. During the meal she chats with devotees, serves the elderly, offers young children tidbits; and, once lunch is over and the travelers have retired to their quarters to rest before the evening's festivities, she starts the cleanup. While the younger nuns and laywomen work in the kitchen, she quietly gathers dirty tin teacups and, after washing them at the courtyard pump, sets about collecting discarded biscuit wrappers, which she stuffs into a sack.

For many years the Theravada Monks Order of Nepal talked about building a pilgrim guesthouse at Lumbini until, noting no progress, Dhammawati announced her plan to build a conference and retreat center to honor Mahaprajapati, the Buddha's foster mother and the first ordained Buddhist nun. Now, after three years of fund-raising and dealing with contractors, her dream of dormitories, dharma hall, and stupa is an impressive reality.

In 1949, Dhammawati, who today is a celebrated preacher, scholar, translator, author, meditation teacher, and the abbess of Dharmakirti Vihara in Kathmandu, ran away from home to "shave her head." Determined to study the dharma about which she had learned a little from a Theravada missionary, fifteen-year-old Ganesh Kumari Shakya, as she was then known, made her way to Burma, where she received ordination as an "eight-precept laywoman" and given a monastic name. In 1963, as the first Nepalese monastic to attain the Dharmacarya, the highest level in the Burmese Buddhist educational system, she returned home to fight the "Asian disease"—namely, the male conviction that, regardless of proven talent, all females are inferior to all males. "And in those days," she recalls, "Nepalese monks had a very bad case of the disease." With the help of family members and admirers, she established her own nunnery for "virgins" (as opposed to widows and divorcées, most of whom lived in monasteries, where they cooked and cleaned for the monks). Once she was financially independent of the monks (*bhikkhus*) and thus effectively free from their interference, with the assistance of a small team of nuns who like herself had trained in Burma, she set about teaching Theravada Buddhism. While she welcomed people of all ages and both genders to the nunnery, her focus was on women, whom the *bhikkhus* largely ignored.

While from the outset Dhammawati worked towards gender equality in her native Newar society, gender equality within the Buddhist sangha was not as yet her goal. As an "ordained laywoman," she accepted that *bhikkhuni* (nun's) higher ordination had died out long ago and, once dead, could not to be revived. She only began to question her conviction in 1987 when, during the first conference of Buddhist women at Bodh Gaya, she heard the Dalai Lama encourage nuns to take higher ordination, a rite which, contrary to her belief, had survived in China to the present day. Soon after, some nuns from Fo Guang Shan Monastery in Taiwan, who had learned of her work as a community leader, visited her in Kathmandu and invited her and some of her colleagues to take higher ordination from Chinese monks and nuns on the occasion of the inauguration of Fo Guang Shan's temple complex in Los Angeles. On the return of the newly ordained nuns to Kathmandu, the senior monks refused to acknowledge their elevated status. Moreover, though several dozen Nepalese nuns have since taken full ordination abroad, the monks continue to address them as *anagarika* (ordained laywoman) rather than *bhikkhuni* and to exclude them from meetings of the monastic sangha. Dhammawati is sanguine about their intransigence. Those old *bhikkhus* will pass away, she says, and the younger ones will have a different attitude.

Ever since Theravada Buddhism was brought to Nepal in the 1930s by missionaries aiming to reform the laicized Mahayana Buddhism practiced by the Newars of the Kathmandu Valley, most Nepalese monks have received their religious training in monasteries abroad. They have learned to speak foreign languages fluently, become comfortable in other cultures, and developed extensive support networks. By contrast, Dhammawati is one of very few older nuns who trained abroad. From the 1960s, when the generals were firmly installed, Nepalese monastics could no longer study in Burma. This is in part why, for decades, other than for occasional short visits to Buddhist sacred sites in north India, nuns rarely left Nepal.

This custom began to change after the Bodh Gaya conference when Dhammawati started sending young nuns to study in Thailand, Sri Lanka, and Taiwan through contacts she was making in the newly established International Association of Buddhist Women. These days she is convinced that a modern secular education and fluency in English, which she never had the chance to acquire, are as essential to a nun as it is to a laywoman. She encourages young nuns to go as far as possible in school. Furthermore, in the belief that before fully committing themselves to the celibate life, they should be exposed to the opposite sex, she insists they attend coeducational schools and colleges.

When Dhammawati ran away to Burma more than sixty years ago, there were only a few—socially marginal—nuns in Nepal. Now, due in large part to her leadership, there are more than two hundred nuns, including many well-educated, multilingual, fully ordained *bhikkhuni* whom laypeople hold in the highest regard. Their daughters, meanwhile, read and absorb the lessons of *Beloved Daughter,* the story of a Newar girl named Ganesh Kumari who overcame extraordinary challenges to become a Buddhist nun and a leader of women.

THE RISE OF THE "CLINICAL RELIGIONIST"
Taniyama Yōzō
LEVI MCLAUGHLIN

The earthquake, tsunami, and nuclear disasters that devastated northeast Japan on March 11, 2011, inspired a wave of religious-aid responses. Some of the most well-publicized and well-funded of these initiatives are being led by Buddhist priests who are formulating new types of chaplaincy that combine pastoral care with clinical expertise. Taniyama Yōzō (1972–present) is a Mahayana priest who has been offering practical training to religious caregivers in post-tsunami Japan.

Until he graduated from high school, Taniyama Yōzō (b. 1972) followed the path of a typical temple son. Everyone he grew up with in Kanazawa, a picturesque city on the Japan Sea, shared his sectarian affiliation, and he could have followed a predictable route to replace his father as a temple priest responsible for their ritual needs and pastoral care. He is thoughtful and soft-spoken, a big bespectacled man with an affable smile. It is easy to see how he would be a reassuring presence in a local Buddhist temple.

Taniyama talks about his youth as we sit on a chartered bus packed with religious studies academics and the Buddhist and Christian priests they study—almost all of whom are also Ph.D.s who teach at universities—en route to a reception at a hotel in Shinjuku, central Tokyo. This June 2013 weekend is typical for Taniyama. He has traveled from Tōhoku University in Sendai, where he is in the middle of a three-year professorial appointment at the university's newly founded Department of Practical Religious Studies, to present in Tokyo at a national Buddhist studies conference on the project he helms—that is, training Buddhist priests, Christian ministers, and a variety of other practitioners as *rinshō shūkyōshi* ("clinical religionists," or chaplains).

Taniyama has come a long way from his local temple roots. Over the last decade, he has attracted national attention for his leading role in proposing Japan-specific fusions of religious, biomedical, and social welfare approaches to the country's most immediate social dilemmas. These include Buddhist-led initiatives to reduce Japan's sky-high suicide rate and to aid a rapidly aging population that is increasingly likely to die in hospital. Most recently, he has numbered among Buddhist activists seeing to the needs of thousands of ordinary residents in northeast Japan who are living with trauma and bereavement in the wake of the 2011 disasters. Since 2013, he has gained renown in religious studies circles, and in the popular media as well, for his role in fostering a trans-sectarian community of religious care-givers with practical training in counseling and other types of "spiritual care" intended to serve the needs of survivors in northeast Japan still reel-ing from the earthquake, tsunami, and nuclear disasters of March 2011. Japa-nese scholar-priests are nothing new, and Buddhists have cared for the dying and provided solace to the bereaved since the religion took hold in Ja-pan more than fifteen centuries ago. However, the *rinshō shūkyōshi* project represents a new phase, the latest development in a trend that has acceler-ated in recent years: Japanese Buddhism reformulated as a type of clinical expertise based in scientific inquiry, not sectarian tradition, intended to appeal to a populace that is enthusiastic about medical treatment but mostly unwilling to accept explicitly "religious" help.

Tōhoku University's new chaplaincy initiative emerges as an aggregate of the secular academic education, volunteer experience, fieldwork outside Japan, training in palliative care, and professional cooperation with medi-cal practitioners that Taniyama has undertaken since he left Kanazawa to pursue Buddhist studies at Tōhoku University in the early 1990s. Taniyama's first publications in 1995 and 1996 on interpretations of *jihi* (compassion) in social welfare and on views of the disabled in early Indian Buddhist *vinaya* texts reflect the tenor of this time. He was swept up in Japanese enthusiasm for volunteer service that followed the 1995 Hanshin earthquake disaster, and he sought to apply text-based study of Buddhism to help people *now*, not in future existences. He completed his master's-level research on Buddhism's attitudes towards the disabled while he volunteered as a caregiver for dis-abled people. For his doctoral research he looked beyond Japan, undertak-ing four years of fieldwork in Bangladesh, where he investigated ways in which various *pūja* (ritual devotions) take shape within interactions between monks and lay Buddhists. Taniyama views his years spent honing partici-pant ethnographic skills as his most important preparation for the vocation he took up as soon as he finished his Ph.D. at Tōhoku University in 2000. From April of that year, he undertook training as a Vihāra monk at Nagaoka Nishi hospital, Japan's first Buddhist hospice.

Vihāra is the Sanskrit and Pali word for monastery, and it is the term that the hospice founder Rev. Tamiya Masashi applied to the Buddhist version of cooperation among doctors, nurses, social workers, and chaplains that he established at Nagaoka Nishi in 1992. As a Vihāra chaplain, "my training as a Buddhist priest was worth nothing," Taniyama tells me; learning how to run a local temple did not prepare him to provide care for the terminally ill, and he received only the most elliptical instruction from Rev. Tamiya, the head Vihāra priest on the ward. He credits his fieldwork in Bangladesh for giving him the confidence to elicit conversation from patients by listening without passing judgment. His ethnographic experience, more than his Buddhist clerical training, helped him attempt reconciliations between children and dying relatives with whom they were too distraught to speak.

In the spring of 2011, Taniyama was called back to Sendai in order to contribute his mixture of Buddhist, academic, and clinical expertise following the compound disasters. What started in March 2011 as an ad hoc combination of ritual intercessions for thousands of corpses extracted from the debris performed in tandem with emergency counseling for survivors led to the 2012 founding of Tōhoku University's Department of Practical Religious Studies and its affiliated programs. These include Taniyama's bid to train chaplains who will continue to work in the disaster-afflicted region and in other parts of Japan. At present, just under twenty participants join the *rinshō shūkyōshi* program's regular training sessions, and Taniyama tells me that, while he considers it irresponsible to conclude this program with a formal chaplaincy license that may extend beyond the lifetime of the training program itself, the Japan Spiritual Care Workers Association (JSCWA) has agreed to license those who complete all of the sessions and pass a qualifying examination. Taniyama is also working with clergy and influential religious studies academics to secure support from the Japanese Association of Religious Organizations (Nihon Shūkyō Renmei) and other national bodies to transform the clinical religionist bid into a Japan-wide endeavor. Clinic-based chaplaincy may only be a fledgling initiative in Japan today, but persistent work on the part of innovative and well-connected practitioner-academics like Taniyama could see Buddhist practice melded with clinical treatment find an enduring place in institutions across the country.

ACTIVIST TEMPLE WIFE
Nakanishi Eiko
JESSICA STARLING

Temple priests in Japan have been publicly permitted to marry since the early twentieth century, but Buddhist institutions have been slow to recognize the role of temple wives. Even in the case of the Jōdo Shinshū (True Pure Land School), which has embraced a married clergy for some seven centuries, temples follow a patrilineal model of inheritance and the position of temple wife/mother has been largely neglected in official regulations of the sect. Nakanishi Eiko (1930–present) represents the educated, activist contingent of temple wives in Japan who seek to harness the power of modern Buddhist networks and the language of democracy and liberalism as they advocate for a greater recognition of the role of Buddhist women.

Nakanishi Eiko, seventy-nine, was waiting for me in the bright September sun outside the train station. Her dark-colored lay clothes (black slacks and a patterned blouse) conformed to the unofficial "uniform" worn by most temple wives, but their elegance belied the physical labor that would occupy her for most of the day. During the fifteen-minute drive to her small temple in rural Shiga Prefecture, she briefed me on the nature of the event I would be observing that day. It was a combination elderly association meeting and Sunday school event, intended to encourage more interaction between these two generations in the community. Despite the aging demographic in her rural village, Nakanishi explained, the temple used to draw a large number of children to its Sunday school events. In the end, extracurricular activities rather than depopulation had recently begun to drain participants from the temple's children-focused events. These days most of the village's children have sports or music practice on Saturdays, and there is scarcely time for socializing at the temple.

When we arrived, Nakanishi introduced me to volunteers belonging to the temple's women's association. These five women in their sixties had already been buzzing around the temple kitchen for a few hours, preparing the midday boxed lunch for participants. Next she led me outside and pointed out her two grandchildren, who were playing with the other elementary school–age children by using a low wall surrounding a statue in the middle of the grounds as a balance beam. In one corner of the gravel parking lot, beneath the steps of the main hall, was a row of children's bikes; in another was a cluster of walkers and rolling grocery carts. The members of the village's elderly association had made their way up the temple steps and were resting on chairs in the shady main hall.

I had previously met Nakanishi in a quite different setting, near the ostensible center of Jōdo Shinshū (True Pure Land Buddhism, the sect to which her temple belongs). At the sect's central conference facility in Kyoto, Nakanishi is an impressive presence. Organizing, educating, and spurring to action the nearly five hundred members of the Temple Women Liaison Group that she helped found, Nakanishi works to shape the future of women's status in her religious institution. With her tireless petitioning of the sect's administration, Nakanishi has pressed for the recognition of temple wives, known as *bōmori* or *jizoku fujin,* as a distinct category of Buddhist practitioner who should be represented in the sect's governing body. So far, she has seen no changes in official policy, but her tenacity is unflagging. "I have learned to be more subtle, though," she admitted. "When I first got started with this issue, I did not realize how conservative people in the administration were, and I think I stepped on a few toes. Now I've learned more indirect ways." Even her fellow temple wife network members sometimes need their arms twisted, however. Some are resigned to the belief that the administration will never change, while others prefer to spend the two days of their annual gathering in Kyoto practicing new styles of Buddhist liturgical performance involving operatic singing rather than engaging with political matters.

While Nakanishi, who was born in 1930, is a unique package of elegance, intelligence, and tenacity, she represents a generation of temple wives who have benefited from numerous waves of women's movements in Japan. Her four-year college degree was earned from Kyoto Women's University (Kyoto Joshi Daigaku), which was founded as a Jōdo Shinshū–affiliated school with the support of Buddhist women's associations across Japan. Further, the networks that emerged within twentieth-century Buddhist institutions have made it possible for Nakanishi to connect with a community of Buddhist women that extends throughout Japan. Indeed, she moves back and forth between local and national contexts and sees herself as an agent of change in both.

The building of a national association of Buddhist women's groups (*Bukkyō fujinkai*, originally called *nyoninkō*, or female confraternities) began in the late nineteenth century. In the early twentieth century, networks of temple wives began to form alongside those for laywomen. However, in Nakanishi's sect, the local and regional associations have never been consolidated into a national group. Having met her peers—leaders of local temple wife associations from all over Japan—at a major event in Kyoto twelve years ago, it dawned on Nakanishi that she belonged to a larger category of Buddhist practitioner that had not been recognized adequately by the institution, perhaps because of the somewhat invisible work that they often perform in the domestic realm of individual temples. Convinced of the necessity for collective action, she set about organizing her new temple wife friends into a national network, the Temple Women Liaison Group. Once it had been organized, Nakanishi mobilized the group to collectively lobby the Buddhist sect to enfranchise temple wives.

Back at her tiny temple in rural Shiga Prefecture, Nakanishi was busy making other kinds of connections—between her Buddhist temple and her small rice-farming community, between local residents old and young, and between the Buddha Amida and the villagers. The activist temple wife waved to her two grandchildren to stop playing and sit down at the front of the main hall, where the elderly attendees were already seated in chairs to accommodate ailing backs and knees. She handed out liturgy books to all present and made sure the children had turned to the right page. Her son, currently the temple's acting resident priest, began the day's events with a reading of a religious text, in which all of the participants joined. Next they rearranged chairs to play a trivia game, run a relay race, and sing songs. Then Nakanishi and the volunteers brought in low folding tables and everyone sat down to eat the lunch they had prepared.

MODERNIZING BUDDHIST PROSELYTIZATION IN HONG KONG
Dhammapala
COREY L. BELL

Buddhism in Hong Kong, long associated by younger people with superstition and a narrow preoccupation with reciting sutras, is witnessing the beginning of a renaissance. Its new vitality is particularly manifest in its increasing intersectarian harmony and efforts to be relevant to contemporary urban life—factors that reflect the cosmopolitan and hypermodern flavor of this global city. Ven. Dhammapala (1970– present), a Sri Lankan–trained, Malaysian Chinese Theravada monk who teaches at the University of Hong Kong, has defined important new parameters in this trend.

Hong Kong is a densely crowded yet imposingly ordered metropolis—a place where spaces are tightly parcelled, ruthlessly demarcated, and oppressively prescriptive; they dictate behavior and brand themselves in the identity and subjective experience of their residents. Against the backdrop of Hong Kong's overburdened spatial semantics, however, there has been a public yearning for more amorphous and malleable spaces—true "spaces" free from hyper-densities of signification. Such spaces, their advocates hold, are sources from which true creativity can emanate, providing a facility for resisting the dictates of material society, reorienting the self, and realizing new possibilities.

The Tung Lin Kwok Yun (TLKY) Buddhist charity foundation's Wong Fat Ching She facility (WFCS) appeared, on my first visit, to be such an amorphous space. Across from the towering Belvedere Garden estate in the New Territories' Tsuen Wan District, its entrance lay at the corner of a small cul-de-sac marked by a concrete gate engraved with both Buddhist and Confucian motifs. As I headed up a narrow track, the landscape suddenly opened

into a broad, gated concrete plain populated by several nondescript buildings, an old basketball court, and a Chinese-style pagoda. The main building,
situated in the middle, presented itself as a modest, quasi-classical structure
with both British colonial and Chinese architectural features, indecorously
colored in a faded-pink hue. Through its wide wooden gate, Buddha statues could be vaguely discerned, seated serenely in a dimly lit dharma hall.
Yet upon closer inspection, it could be seen that they were lightly bathed
in the strange yet familiar blue luminance of computer screens. This modest and relatively unkempt building was also home to a vast, amorphous
virtual space: the high-tech brain center of the TLKY-sponsored Buddhistdoor Web site, one of the largest and most thematically diverse Buddhist
Web portals in the world.

The energy behind the transformation of this humble facility has come
from a monk who is dedicated to realizing TLKY's vision to modernize Buddhist proselytization and pursue a broader humanitarian ideal through
philanthropic activities. That monk is the Malaysian-Chinese Theravadan
monk Dhammapala. In his mid-forties, with a Ph.D. in Buddhist studies from
the University of Hong Kong, this bespectacled, softly spoken man is steeped
in the scholasticism of non-Mahayana Abhidharmic traditions. Yet as a
foreign-born, ethnic Chinese monk in a strongly secular and cosmopolitan
society, Dhammapala prefers not to be bound by the constraints of sectarianism and religious dogmatism. This flexibility is reflected in WFCS's constitution and activities. Unlike a traditional monastery, it does not have a
regular sangha. However, Dhammapala has welcomed an eclectic array of
monks to reside there, many of whom have come to study in the University
of Hong Kong's Buddhist studies program. Often he leads Pali chanting sessions in the evening in front of Chinese-style statues of Amitābha,
Mahāsthāmaprāpta, and Avalokiteśvara. Yet he has also opened the hall to
traditional Chinese Buddhist dharma functions. "Mahayana, Hinayana,
northern and southern [lineages] are merely designations," he states smil-
ingly, sipping tea under an ink painting of a circle—the Zen symbol of tran-
scendental emptiness.

Yet under Dhammapala's supervision, WFCS has also hosted and promoted
a range of other less distinctly "Buddhist" activities. For example, it has
hosted "Leadership and Communication" camps for youths, and even public talks on diverse social issues by prominent authors and intellectuals, such
as Dhammapala's friend and the prominent journalist and cultural critic
Leung Man-tao. Dhammapala has also overseen the rapid growth of its education program, with classes now ranging from scholastic Buddhist theory
courses, to taiji and qigong, to "Little CEO" training classes for elementary

school–aged children. Dhammapala also often opens facilities for the free provision of services from Chinese medicine to counselling, as well as the collection and distribution of goods for charity.

This multifariousness has come to be largely because Dhammapala does not see himself as the face or spiritual leader of the WFCS in the mode of a traditional abbot. As he points out, the temple adopts a more modern organizational structure in line with that of its parent organization, TLKY. Yet it also reflects his philosophy that "participation . . . is far more rewarding than mere obeisance" and reflects his desire to tap the "diverse experience and specialist knowledge" of those within the Buddhist and indeed the broader community. This is also the case with the Buddhistdoor Web site. Not only does Dhammapala minimize his own presence on the portal, but the great majority of its content draws from the expertise of a wide range of contributors, including monks from various lineages, professional writers, artists, community group representatives, and health-care professionals such as psychologists. The Web site's content ranges from audiovisual recordings of Buddhist teachings and culture, to art therapy, articles on self-esteem and interpersonal communications, radio programs on the conundrums of pet breeding, and promotions for the "Oh yes, it's free" movement—a group dedicated to reducing materialism by facilitating non-monetary trade. Through Dhammapala's open and consultative editorial approach, Buddhistdoor has had the space to morph into a truly vast and multifarious resource for Buddhists of different denominations as well as others interested more generally in self-improvement, contemporary social issues, or charity.

Dhammapala's approach stems, in part, from his religious proclivities. His Ph.D. thesis focused on the spiritual path of the ancient Sarvāstivāda school. This lineage held that enlightenment is nothing other than the cultivated absence of the various defilements. As reflected in the vast proofligacy of their literature, progress in their path comes through adopting a variety of methods suited to subdue or eradicate these defilements, one at a time if need be. Faced with the difficulties of proselytizing in a fast-paced and complex cosmopolitan urban setting, for Dhammapala this philosophy has translated into not only a more liberal pragmatism but also a disinterest in traditional sectarian tendencies to narrowly define and prescribe formulaic remedies for our individual and collective spiritual ills.

Dhammapala's perspective on modernity is both refreshing and sober. For him, it is in part the "context and something that shapes the difficult challenges" of proselytizing and doing pastoral work in hypermodern Hong Kong. But he also sees modernity as a resource and a receptacle for new possibilities. "Buddhistdoor helps us connect to a global audience in ways that were not possible before," he states with proud earnestness, adding that he does not "see its [modern] vision as necessarily antithetical" to his Buddhist beliefs. Under his guidance, Buddhistdoor and WFCS have become creative spaces that are intended to give all who venture through them the room and freedom to shape—both drawing from or through their struggle with modernity—their own path towards emancipation.

MODERN MIRACLES OF A FEMALE BUDDHIST MASTER
Khandro Tāre Lhamo
HOLLY GAYLEY

The two decades leading up to and including the Cultural Revolution (1966–1976) were a period of turbulence and devastation for Tibetans under Chinese Communist rule and for Buddhist institutions on the Tibetan plateau. Khandro Tāre Lhamo (1938–2002) was a female Buddhist master credited with numerous miracles benefiting her local community during those decades. Thereafter, in the post-Mao era, she helped to spearhead the revitalization of Buddhism in the Tibetan region of Golok.

An aging Tibetan doctor, Pema Garwang, sat by the wood-burning stove in his home above the monastery and, in a halting voice, sang a prayer he had composed during his eighteen years in a Chinese prison. Like other religious leaders and elites, Pema Garwang had been imprisoned during the socialist transformation of Tibetan areas in the late 1950s, following their forcible incorporation into the People's Republic of China. By his own account, he survived while so many perished due to the blessings of Khandro Tāre Lhamo. The prayer that he composed for her begins:

Oh! From Tārā's pure and spontaneous realm, Yulo Köpa,
Arises a magical emanation of noble Tārā, mother of buddhas;
I supplicate the holder of secret mantra, Tāre Lhamo.

From this prayer, it is apparent that Tāre Lhamo was no ordinary Tibetan woman. Born in 1938 as the daughter of a well-known lama (Buddhist teacher), she became identified with female figures drawn from Buddhist cosmology, such as her namesake, the female bodhisattva Tārā mentioned in the prayer. From her youth, Tibetans in her local community of Padma County in Golok considered Tāre Lhamo to be a *khandroma,* which literally means "sky-goer" and serves as the title given to a revered female tantric master. Pema Garwang wrote this prayer after one of numerous visionary encounters with her while in prison. As he poignantly put it, "At that time, we could not meet during the day, so we met at night in dreams."

While starting to research the life of Tāre Lhamo, I visited Pema Garwang with his grandniece, a college student in Xining who wore a sweater and jeans and helped me understand his thick Golok accent. Pema Garwang told us that he was protected by two items given to him by Tāre Lhamo: a lock of her hair that he had stitched into his coat and a gold ring that, miraculously, the prison guards were never able to remove (now the ring slips on and off easily). As my research progressed, friends and disciples of Tāre Lhamo were eager to show me items she had given to them, like the *zi* stone worn by a close friend, or a set of rings ornamented by a bell and scepter prized by a prominent government official. As relics of contact, such gifts function as talismans and tokens of her blessings.

During regular visits to Golok between 2004 and 2007, I heard numerous tales of Tāre Lhamo's protective powers and miraculous feats similar to Pema Garwang's account. Her miracles were grassroots in scale and concerned the immediate needs of her local community. When a childhood friend lost a herd of yak, Tāre Lhamo performed protection rituals and the herd returned two days later. During widespread famine linked to the failed policies of the Great Leap Forward (1958–1961), Tāre Lhamo would sometimes appear as if dead and then return from visionary journeys with sacred substances to nourish the people around her. In miracle tales, both oral and literary, she is credited with rescuing the recently deceased from the torments of hell, circumventing imminent danger such as preventing a rock slide from falling on a road crew, and facilitating the release of more than one lama from prison. These are just a few examples that reveal the dire conditions of the times and how Tāre Lhamo served as a beacon of hope for her local community.

What makes such miracles modern? To address this question, let us consider the social nature of miracle tales. As a dialogic practice of constructing narratives, miracle tales portray how a particular community interprets an event within a shared episteme or worldview. For Buddhists in Tibet, rainbows and flowers blooming out of season are regarded as auspicious signs, a prophecy uttered by a tantric master is considered efficacious, and gifts bestowed by one are imbued with blessings and protective powers. In line with this, Tāre Lhamo's hagiography presents an account of her miracles as the "common perception" of eyewitnesses rather than objectively verifiable events per se.

Miracles take on new meaning in the context of the Maoist era in which tales about Tāre Lhamo first circulated. Starting with the socialist transformation of Tibetan areas in the late 1950s and lasting through the Cultural Revolution (1966–1976), this era witnessed the systematic destruction of Buddhism on the Tibetan plateau. Monasteries were demolished, sacred texts burned, high-ranking lamas imprisoned, and public religious observances banned. In these turbulent decades, miracle tales served as a mode of epistemic resistance, by which I mean the assertion of Buddhist systems of meaning in the face of ideological and practical challenges. In recounting miracles, Tibetans affirmed their faith in Buddhism despite communist propaganda and policies that demonized religious elites in struggle sessions and suppressed religious practice for nearly two decades.

For Tibetans, miracle tales affirm that the buddhas and bodhisattvas did not abandon them during this devastating period and continued to live in their midst and work tirelessly for their benefit. For the outside observer, such tales attest that Buddhism was never wholly effaced, despite its suppression. Not only did it remain alive in masters like Tāre Lhamo but also in the ordinary Tibetans who maintained faith in them and shared tales of their miraculous deeds. Pema Garwang insisted on this point: that during this period local Tibetans respected Tāre Lhamo, viewed her as kind and compassionate, and maintained faith in her as a *khandroma*.

THE TEMPLE IS A PLACE OF SOLUTIONS
Takahashi Takushi
JOHN NELSON

Takahashi Takushi (1948–present) epitomizes the kind of priest who will usher Japanese Buddhism into the twenty-first century. Fearless, innovative, self-confident, and yet compassionate, he has pioneered new institutional dynamics that bring together diverse constituencies. He represents the vanguard of "experimental Buddhist" responses to the demographic and social shifts that are confronting institutional Buddhism in contemporary Japan.

It is not unusual for a Buddhist priest in Japan to lead a workshop for elderly temple members about the inevitability of death and the choices they can make that will facilitate leaving the world peacefully. It is unique when the priest uses a coffin as a lectern, then opens the lid and lies down inside the silk-covered container. "Ah, how relaxing! What a relief! You really should try it and discover for yourself there is nothing fearful about the end of our lives." Before long, several members from the audience have come to the front of the room and taken their turns lying in the coffin. Each one comments afterwards to the television reporter present for this workshop that Rev. Takahashi Takushi has helped them understand and accept this natural part of the life cycle.

Rev. Takahashi's Rinzai Zen temple Jingūji is perched in precisely the spot from which the entire valley of Matsumoto (in central Japan) can be seen. In a number of ways, the view from the temple is emblematic of the expansive and visionary perspectives of its head priest. A foundational experience of his career, recounted in his 2009 book *Tera yo! Kaware!* (Hey temples! Change!), describes how in 1978, Rev. Takahashi (born after the end of World War II, in 1948) accompanied a group of parishioners and local veterans to New Guinea in an effort to locate the remains of Japanese soldiers. They searched primarily in jungle settings, focusing on a number of caves where many soldiers hid to avoid capture or execution. For those who were gravely wounded, ill, or otherwise debilitated from a lack of food, these caves became their tombs.

Takahashi wrote that nothing in his life or training as a priest prepared him for the grim reality of discovering and reclaiming human bones. He was so profoundly moved by the suffering of these soldiers, as well as the anguished sadness of the family members in his group, that he could not even chant sutras. He says his "comfortable Buddhism" was shattered, with the bones of the dead seeming to call out to him, "Well, Priest, what are you going to do about it?" From that point forward he thought of his role as a priest in new and strategic ways. Instead of a never-ending cycle of lucrative funerals and memorial rituals, he was now committed to giving people resources that could help them alleviate suffering in their own lives as well as encouraging them to help others.

After the incident in New Guinea, Takahashi became sensitive to the ways in which authority exacts compliance, whether through laws, intimidation, coercion, bribes, or violence. Always critical of how Japan's military had dominated life during World War II, he was now convinced that the authorities had cared little about the tragic loss of life. He witnessed the student demonstrations of the 1960s, the Red Army violence of the same period, and the Lockheed Scandal of 1976, all during a time when Japan's leaders were pushing for rapid economic expansion in a global context. In his own Rinzai Zen (Myōshinji) denomination, he saw authority figures vying for power and prestige, the traditional senior-junior relationship (*senpai-kōhai*) dominating professional interactions among fellow priests, and women marginalized both as temple wives and as priests. But what could a single priest in the countryside do?

The mid-1990s were pivotal years that deepened Rev. Takahashi's social and religious activism. In 1995, shortly after the Kobe earthquake and the Aum Shinrikyō gas attacks in Tokyo, he established a monthly gathering that invited noted academics, entertainers, writers, musicians, and journalists to attend. Although the initiative was halted in 2006, by November 2005 "Asama Gakuen (campus)" had convened eighty-six times with an estimated thirty thousand attendees. For Rev. Takahashi, the initiative demonstrated that people would gather at a temple to pursue mutual interests not necessarily related to Buddhism. Instead of emphasizing rituals as the purpose of a temple, as was typical for most if not all Buddhist denominations in Japan, the Asama Gakuen events expanded the range of possibilities for what a temple could be.

Buddhism has always emphasized "healing" both body and spirit via a variety of methods. As Rev. Takahashi's temple was located near a hot springs resort, it was logical that he do whatever he can to help alleviate physical suffering. In 1996, he received a letter from a friend in Moscow alerting him to the high rate of thyroid cancer among rural children caused by the 1986 Chernobyl disaster in the Ukraine. He raised money to bring twelve young patients to Japan for treatment. With cooperation and donated equipment from nearby hospitals and universities—an effort later recognized and funded by the Japanese Ministry of Transportation—an NGO set up by Rev. Takahashi and several physicians developed a thyroid screening program that has since been taken over by local hospitals in Russia. During the seven years of his involvement with this project Rev. Takahashi made some thirty-five trips (averaging about five a year) to a site in the Ukraine that required four hours additional travel from the nearest airport. Back home in Matsumoto, his parishioners came to believe that no one would die (and thus require funeral services) while their primary ritual specialist was traveling abroad to help others. He is now extending this same expertise to NGOs working with individuals exposed to radiation in the March 2011 Fukushima nuclear reactor meltdown.

If modernity can be characterized in part by an emphasis on the individual and a search for a life of significance that may not always align with established social and cultural norms, then Rev. Takahashi stands out as a progressive, late-modern Buddhist priest. He has taken his Rinzai Zen heritage and applied it in ways that resonate with secular concerns about death, healing, institutional accountability, and social activism. At funeral services, he breaks with tradition to give an overview of the sutras he chants to both funeral participants and the immediate family. He promotes temple-NGO affiliations whenever possible so that regional and global networks inform local perspectives and increase possibilities that may contribute resources for a person's life or a community's social support systems.

For Rev. Takahashi, the temple is a place where, "No matter what kind of anxiety or problem a person is facing, he or she can find some kind of solution. We want people to feel they are cared for by the temple, and that they can't get this kind of service elsewhere," he says. Whether collecting the bones of soldiers in the caves of New Guinea, helping battle thyroid cancer among Chernobyl (and Fukushima) victims of radiation, or making his temple a kind of community clearinghouse of services and information, Rev. Takahashi represents a new and progressive model of what a determined and innovative priest can achieve.

MAITREYA'S IT GUY
Cide
JUSTIN R. RITZINGER

Buddhism in Taiwan has flourished in recent decades. Following the "economic miracle" of the 1970s and 1980s and end of martial law in 1987, new Mahayana organizations such as Fo Guang Shan, Tzu Chi, and Dharma Drum Mountain have established operations across the island, and even across the globe, to promote and implement their reformist vision of the dharma. Yet in the shadows cast by these large religious multinationals labor numerous smaller groups throughout Taiwan. The layman Cide (1972–present) is a key figure in one such group that reflects Taiwan's religious vitality, economic development, and technological sophistication.

Posha Shan Faming Temple is not a place one finds by accident. Tucked away in Zhonghe, just across the river from the bustle of Taipei, it stands in a nondescript neighborhood of warehouses and businesses. This is no coincidence. In a former life, the temple had been the warehouse of a trading company that flourished during Taiwan's economic miracle. Today, the owner of that company has retired, not just from business but from worldly life. Arriving on an autumn day in 2008, I walk up the broad stairs to the open rooftop courtyard. At the top is the main hall, where an image of Maitreya is enshrined in place of Shakyamuni. Off to the left is the guest hall, where I find the former businessman and current abbot, Chanjing (1949–present), chatting with a few laymen over tea. I have already visited several times for my research, and he waves me in with no formality and pours me a cup. The tea is good and the conversation pleasant, but it is not the abbot whom I have come to see.

The true driving force of the temple is not the pious retiree enjoying his tea but a layman in his mid-thirties who goes by the dharma name Cide. The name alludes to the object of his devotion, Maitreya (Cishi), the next Buddha of our world. Cide is a proponent of the Maitreya School, founded in 1924 by the Chinese activist monk Taixu, a key figure in the reform movement known as Humanistic Buddhism. Although he is often said to have rejected such things as devotion to bodhisattvas, Taixu found in Maitreya a figure who exemplified the values of his movement. In Taixu's vision, Maitreya's descent and attainment of Buddhahood would come in the distant future through the gradual purification of this world brought about by engaged individuals working to create a pure land on earth. This progressive and utopian vision formed the basis of his personal practice and a prominent part of ritual and academic life in his seminaries. After the tumult of war, revolution, and Taixu's death in 1947, however, his new vision of Maitreya was largely forgotten.

After ten or fifteen minutes Cide arrives. A self-effacing man of medium build with a youthful face offset by salt-and-pepper hair, he is dressed like many Taiwanese professionals in a short-sleeved dress shirt and slacks. It is in large part Cide who has made the temple what it is. Cide is Chanjing's son and, like the trading company it replaced, Faming Temple is a family enterprise. Cide was instrumental in converting both his father and the temple, first from Daoism to Buddhism, and then from Pure Land to the Maitreya School. Although pivotal, Cide's role in all of this has been nearly invisible: in the temple's literature, Chanjing is the central figure; Cide's role is almost entirely behind the scenes. This choice may reflect ambivalence with lay initiative as well as the close partnership between a man who has renounced home and family and his son, the sort of irregularity in monastic discipline not uncommon in smaller temples but not found in larger, more prestigious organizations.

Cide leads me back down the stairs and into the first floor of the building. Below the temple halls, the main structure is devoted mostly to the more practical side of the temple's operation. Here we find the true heart of the temple and Cide's attempt to propagate the Maitreya School: a desktop computer. The Internet has played an essential role in the contemporary revival of interest in the Maitreya School. Much like the emergence of print culture in Taixu's day, the Internet has allowed isolated proponents of minority viewpoints to form networks through which to share resources and offer encouragement. Faming Temple presents itself as part of a broader wave of interest in Taixu's Maitreyan teachings across the Chinese-speaking world. Their literature often refers to exchanges with individuals and groups in the People's Republic. Yet these exchanges, I was surprised to discover, were entirely virtual. None of the principals had met one another.

At the PC, Cide shows me his latest project, a preliminary clip of a digitally animated cartoon of the Sutra of Maitreya's Ascent. The clip pans through the geometric splendors of Maitreya's heavenly palace—row upon row of computer-generated balustrades, gates, and fountains painted in bright gold, soft purple, and midnight blue. The medium is a little jarring, but appropriate to a text that enjoins its readers to visualize the wonders of Maitreya's palace. Although the film was planned in Taiwan, the temple found it more cost-effective to outsource production to China. Both economically and religiously, Taiwan is becoming ever more closely tied to the mainland.

Under Cide, the temple's online presence has only grown since our meeting. There is a site devoted to the temple itself that includes extensive information on its history, activities, and plans, as well as opportunities for online devotions such as sutra copying and virtual lamplighting. Another site, Maitreya Web TV, is devoted to the multimedia propagation of the Maitreya School. Here one finds the now completed cartoon, along with Buddhist sermons, music, webcomics, and e-books. A third site is devoted to Buddhist vegetarian cuisine. According to the online temple gazetteer, as of 2013 the temple site has had four hundred thousand views, while Maitreya Web TV has broken three and a half million. This expansion is mirrored offline, where temple attendance seems to be increasing at its expanding roster of activities.

Thus, in his unassuming way, Cide embodies a number of key developments in contemporary Taiwanese Buddhism: the resources derived from economic development, increasing ties to the mainland, and the growing but ambivalent role of lay leadership. He also represents the potential of the Internet to foster diversification by facilitating networks of isolated groups and disseminating minority viewpoints. Cide, at least, will continue to work towards this end. Once his young sons are established in life, he intends to leave home and succeed his father as abbot of Faming Temple.

A FEMALE MONK AND THE HMONG
Mian Parnchand

IAN G. BAIRD

Within Theravada Buddhism in Thailand, women are not officially allowed to become fully ordained nuns; rather, they are only allowed to become white-robed nuns. Thai Buddhist monks also rarely develop special relationships with ethnic Hmong people. Mian Parnchand (1910–1970), or Luang Por Yai, the cofounder of Wat Tham Krabok temple in Saraburi Province, was therefore a highly unusual person, being among the first Thai women to become a "monk" and to develop a particularly special relationship with the Hmong people.

Mian Parnchand, although born to humble circumstances in the central Thai province of Lopburi in around 1910, was already recognized as special at birth. Already at two years old she was reportedly administering high-level Theravada Buddhist sermons. Some thought she was crazy, but as a young girl she claimed to be able to remember her past lives, communicate with spirits, and predict the future. For unknown reasons, however, at around the age of twelve she apparently lost all her special abilities. Later she experienced extreme poverty, married, and had two children, both boys, before her husband abandoned her after she plunged into extreme alcoholism in the Klong Toey slum in Bangkok where she had moved. She ended up living on the streets, in miserable conditions, without anyone respecting her. Then suddenly, for unknown reasons, she again remembered her past lives. Ashamed at her own behavior, she stopped drinking and apologized to her grown children, who supported her in 1949–1950 while she ordained as a white-robed Buddhist nun, or *mae chee,* at the Buddhist temple at Khong Mao, in her home village in Lopburi.

In 1957, while conducting a long ascetic walk (*thudong*) together with her two nephews, Chamroon and Charoen Parnchand, who had both ordained as monks, the three established Wat Tham Krabok temple in an area surrounded by impressive limestone mountains, near the district capital of Phraphuttabat in Saraburi Province, central Thailand.

Chamroon, who prior to ordaining had been the "righthand man" of the chief of the Thai police, Phao Sriyanond, but was forced to flee Thailand after Field Marshal Sarit Thanarat ousted Plaek Phibulsongkhram in a coup d'état in 1957, became the first abbot of the temple, although all the teachings of the monks there came from Mian Parnchand, who declared herself to be "Luang Por Yai Khetmarajja." The title "Luang Por Yai" is unusual, as "Luang Por" is a respectful prefix added to names of senior male monks in Thai.

"Yai" means "large." Thus, "Luang Por Yai" means "Respected Founder Father," an odd title for a woman. Although one could say that she was among the first *bhikkhuni*, or female monks, in Thailand, she probably never ordained as a monk, although she started to wear brown robes like other monks at Wat Tham Krabok and apparently considered herself to be a *phra* (monk). Moreover, according to an interview with Luang Por Chamroon, she apparently "didn't feel like she was a woman." Due to her unorthodox circumstances and teachers, she was not accepted by the Buddhist hierarchy, and as a result Wat Tham Krabok is not, even now, accepted by the Sangha National Council (Thai: Mahathera Samakhom). It is instead officially considered to be a sangha residence (Thai: *samnak song*).

Wat Tham Krabok is now best known for having treated over 105,000 Thai and foreign drug and alcohol addicts since 1959, and it was this work that resulted in Chamroon Parnchand becoming the recipient of the prestigious Ramon Magsaysay award in 1975. The herbal concoction used to detoxify addicts was developed by Luang Por Yai.

Although Luang Por Yai passed away at the age of sixty in 1970, her teachings are still taught at Wat Tham Krabok. Apart from the 227 precepts typically followed by Theravada Buddhist monks, she taught that monks should abide by ten additional precepts, or truths (Thai: *satcha*). These include specifying how long one will ordain upon becoming a monk; eating only one meal a day; not causing division among group members, creating factions, or doubting the group's leadership; not receiving gifts or money for personal accumulation; committing to meditate and chant for specific periods of time based on how many incense sticks have burnt down; conducting walking journeys (*thudong*) each year; and never traveling by vehicle, aircraft, or boat.

Luang Por Yai's teachings are based on *Laktham Lokuttara* (the foundations of the supramundane existence), and she is considered to be an earthly manifestation of Lokuttara. Although too complicated to explain in detail here, Lokuttara is considered to be a highly enlightened state of mind. Thus, Luang Por Yai, as an embodiment of this state of mind, is believed to have been the pinnacle of all religious thought.

Luang Por Yai had a particularly important relationship with ethnic Hmong people. Many Hmong deeply admire and respect her, and they refer to her as "Luang Mae" (or the Great Mother). Many Hmong believe that Luang Mae was a reincarnation of Niam Nkauj Ntsuab (or simply Nkauj Ntsuab; Princess Choua in Hmong), the female of the cognate pair who created the world by separating land from sea and creating mountains and valleys. According to one version of the story of how the Hmong and Luang Por Yai first met, Luang Por Yai was apparently meditating in a cave near the present temple when local Thais tried to coax her to come down. She refused, stating that she would do so only with "her people." After great efforts, it was determined that these were the Hmong, and once some Hmong were brought to the cave, she agreed to descend with them. Although Luang Por Yai had regular contact with the Hmong beginning from at least the early 1960s, she died before Hmong people from Laos started coming to Wat Tham Krabok. However, three years prior to her death she predicted that large numbers of Hmong would arrive from Laos after 1975.

Beginning in the late 1970s and continuing into the 1980s and 1990s—at least until Luang Por Chamroon died in 1999—Wat Tham Krabok provided considerable support to ethnic Hmong insurgents fighting against the communist Lao People's Democratic Republic government. In addition, tens of thousands of Hmong eventually came to live on the expansive lands of the temple in the 1990s and early 2000s. In 2004–2005, over fifteen thousand Hmong living there were accepted as political refugees by the United States.

Luang Por Yai or Luang Mae has profoundly influenced a large number of Thai and Hmong followers since Wat Tham Krabok was founded in the 1950s, and even now large numbers of Hmong in Thailand and in the United States, including those who never visited the temple, continue to prize medallions of her. Over one hundred thousand have also benefited from the addiction treatment she invented.

THE GLOBALLY LOCAL PRIEST
Sato Masaki
DANIEL G. FRIEDRICH

Historians have long recognized the role played by Jōdo Shin Buddhists in the transformation of Japan's northernmost island from the peripheral territory of Ezo to full inclusion in the Japanese state as Hokkaido early in the Meiji era (1868–1912). At present, nearly 46 percent of Buddhist temples on the island are affiliated with the True Pure Land sect. Problems confronting temples across Japan, such as rural depopulation, the graying of society, and concerns that Buddhist teachings and practices no longer hold meaning for the majority of the Japanese population, are especially acute in the rural regions of Hokkaido. Drawing upon knowledge of practices both international and domestic, Sato Masaki (1931–present) established a monthly Sunday service at his family temple in an attempt to encourage lay involvement in temple activities and instill an understanding of the sect's history and teachings in temple members.

It is the third Sunday of the month, which at Nembutsuji, a True Pure Land Buddhist temple in northeastern Hokkaido, means that anywhere from forty to eighty people are gathered for the monthly Sunday service. Arriving early to claim a seat in the back, I am greeted by Sato Masaki, the former head priest of Nembutsuji, who is busy with the final preparations for the service. Although eighty-two years old, Sato is still actively involved in temple activities. The monthly services, held since April 1978, are one of the most representative aspects of his work as a priest. Speaking to no one in particular, Sato expresses his displeasure that no one is there to greet temple members on their arrival as they sign the record book. Sato asks that I greet people and hand out prayer books.

Sato's inspiration for this service reveals how global and local forces shape the practice of Shin Buddhism. Upon receiving his priestly license in Kyoto in 1953, Sato returned to work as an assistant at his family temple, Nembutsuji. Members of the regional Rotary Club asked him to establish a Boy Scout troop at the temple and, seeing this as a new way of involving preteens in temple activities, he readily agreed. In 1967, he and the troop traveled to the United States to take part in the twelfth World Boy Scout Jamboree and tour the western United States. While in California, Sato was invited to preach at Pasadena Buddhist Temple's Sunday service. Returning to Japan, he assembled a group of lay leaders to explore the possibility of holding a regular Sunday service at Nembutsuji.

Two years after becoming head priest of Nembutsuji and eleven years after his trip to America, Sato presided over the first Sunday service. Relatively unchanged from the one he had attended in Pasadena, the service begins with a welcome from the master of ceremonies, an elderly man in his seventies. His intonation and pattern of speech are reminiscent of a hotel wedding hall's MC. Following this welcome, while the temple wife (*bōmori*) plays a series of soft chords on the electric piano, a member of the temple women's association presents a lit candle that Sato places on the right side of the altar table before offering incense. Sato then leads the congregation in reciting the *Essentials of Jōdo Shinshū* (*Jōdo Shinshū no kyōshō*).

Originally, the *Jōdo Shinshū* pledge (*Jōdo Shinshū no seikatsushinjō*) had been read, but Sato and his son—the current head priest—decided to use the *Essentials,* hoping to instill a better understanding of the sect in temple members. Sato credits a visiting teaching priest with the idea of chanting the *Essentials.* Unlike the *Shinshū* pledge, in which temple members affirm taking refuge in Amida Buddha's vows and working to spread the Buddhist teachings for the betterment of humanity, the *Essentials* lays out the sect's official name, founding figures, and main texts. The penultimate section explains that followers practice Buddhism by listening to the call of Amida Buddha and eschewing the need for prayers. The *Essentials* concludes by stating that the goal of the sect is to share its teachings throughout the world. For Sato, the benefit of chanting the *Essentials* is clear: it succinctly instructs the congregation on the sect's history and practices. Although this information figures largely in dharma talks and sectarian publications, it is usually not discussed in funerary practices, which have traditionally been the impetus for lay engagement with Buddhism in Japan. Once the *Essentials* are finished, the *Shōshinge* is chanted. The service then concludes with a dharma talk and the singing of *Shinran's Hymn of Benevolence* (*Ondokusan*).

On this particular Sunday, the handout Sato prepared in advance and distributed before the service indicates that his dharma talk will be part of an ongoing a series in which he discusses the twelve lights of Amida Buddha. However, rather than discussing Amida's twelve lights, Sato engages the congregation in a conversation about the challenges of aging and his own goal of presiding over five hundred Sunday services. As part of this discussion, Sato reports on an active member of the temple who, due to failing eyesight, has decided to scale back his level of involvement in temple activities. Then, addressing recently retired members of the congregation, he describes how the baton must be passed to the next generation. At various points in his dharma talk, Sato directs his remarks to specific individuals, gently reminding them of their parent's commitment to the temple and, in the case of one, his participation in Boy Scouts. These reminders, though at times entertaining, serve a strategic purpose as well. The relationships Sato evokes are not to Shinshū teachings, or even Buddhism more generally, but individual and familial bonds within the temple community. After the service, Sato makes a special effort to greet first-time attendees or those who have been away for some time. This month, immediately after the service, Sato approaches Nishi, a man in his sixties, who since retiring from the financial services branch of the local agricultural cooperative, has, at Sato's urging, become more involved in temple activities. Nishi's participation, Sato later explained, confirms the success of the Boy Scout troop in creating bonds between the temple and temple members. Sato elaborated by noting that the current leader of the scouts is a lay member who had been part of the troop as a youth.

In the face of drastically changing demographics and increased competition in the religious marketplace, temple priests have been challenged to find new ways of making Buddhist teachings and temples relevant to Japanese at all stages of life. Sato responded by establishing a temple-affiliated

Boy Scout troop and seeking ways to expand lay roles in temple services. His efforts reveal an overlooked aspect of contemporary Japanese Buddhism's globally local character: the ways in which new ideas and practices spread through Buddhist communities as a result of personal contact, often bypassing sectarian centers entirely.

RAISING THE POWERFUL GIRL CHILD
Chunda Bajracharya
CHRISTOPH EMMRICH

The urban Kathmandu Valley is an arena of passionate debates about which kind of Buddhism should help define modernity as represented by the imagined future woman. Between a modernizing traditional Newar Buddhism and a variant of Nepalese Theravada that emerges readily modernized, both of which have equally come to shape contemporary women's religious lives, it is Chunda Bajracharya who best embodies and articulates what is at stake in the present moment.

She waved to me, inviting me to join her and her students gathered around the large seminar table at the Newar Language Department of Tribhuvan University's Patan campus. I had come to ask her to elaborate further on a position she had taken in an article dealing with an old Newar menarche ritual and its significance for raising girl children in Nepalese society today. Chunda, looking at me with her deep-set eyes under that tall forehead of hers, with an almost imperceptible smile on her pencil-thin lips framed by a resolute jawline, tidied the loose end piece of the pink chiffon sari she was wearing and made sure her hair, firmly tied back in a bun, was in place. Born into a family of *vajrācāryas*, a Buddhist Newar caste in which the paternal lineage qualifies men to perform Tantric priestly functions within a householder-run monastic setup, Chunda's most likely contribution to Newar Buddhist religious life would have ranged from marrying and assisting a priest, to conducting rituals within the extended family, to donating to Buddhist institutions. Instead, she chose to pursue a doctoral degree at Nepal's leading university, where she has become a renowned academic teacher—a landmark event in the history of Newar Buddhist women's education.

In elegant Newar, insistently punctuated by *Makhu la* (Is that not so?), she began to explain how the ritual I was interested in introduced Newar Buddhist women to the modalities of sexual reproduction, thus making them less likely to fall victim to girl trafficking and sexually transmitted diseases.

In contrast, in her view, the relatively novel and increasingly popular practice of sending one's daughters to monasteries or meditation centers, where they would wear a robe, learn to meditate, and listen to stories from the Pali canon during school holidays, scantly prepared them for anything, least of all for a life as an adult laywoman. Chunda's stance is itself a reaction to a critique of traditional Newar Buddhism as failing to empower women, a critique that blames what it would identify as Hindu or Buddhist ritualism, instead promoting alternative forms of female religiosity shaped by Newar religious specialists trained in Burma.

Over the last forty years or so, the practice of *r̥ṣiṇī*, known by the Pali term *isinī* (literally "the female sage") in Burma, an ascetic format redesigned for Nepalese girl children, has successfully established itself as a prominent coming-of-age ritual that replicates or integrates many forms of the traditional Newar menarche ritual. According to Chunda, these newfangled performances do not deliver what they promise. The empowerment of ordinary girl children cannot take place in a nunnery. It must happen at home through the mentoring of fellow senior laywomen who enable adolescents to navigate their world. Most of all, empowerment cannot emerge from an exercise that shuts out the emerging woman's sexuality. It is only possible by making her aware of the role her informed sexual conduct plays in protecting her body, in standing up to Newar men, in safeguarding the Newar family, and in promoting the Newar nation. In that sense, Buddhism's contribution to the making of the contemporary Newar woman cannot come through a return of the celibate nun, but by recapturing one of the things that is truly Newar about Buddhism: the ritual enablement of the girl child to realize her full potential as a woman.

The importance of the mother tongue, the Kathmandu Valley as a place of primordial ethnic belonging and entitlement, and a historical narrative of integrity lost to the colonizing forces of the non-Newar Nepalese state are all part of an indigenism that Chunda shares with other Newar intellectuals across the Hindu-Buddhist divide. It is thus not surprising to find her playing a leading role in the influential Newar Language Women's Association, founded in 1979. In the current language of NGO activism prevalent in Nepal, Chunda's agenda foregrounds "capacity building," "leadership training," and, in her case, ethnically defined "individual solutions to individual problems" rather than equality and social justice. What she shares with some of Margaret Ward's Irish "unmanageable revolutionaries," Kumari Jayawardena's global "third-world feminists," or V. Geetha's Tamil "women of the Hindu right," in other words, what allows her feminism to be nationalist, is that she deploys argumentative strategies developed in the anticolonial struggle and the early waves of the women's liberation movement. Her primary interest lies in power.

One of the recent public exchanges in which Chunda's voice was heard most clearly is the controversy over whether or not the tradition of the Royal Kumari, involving a girl child to be chosen from a Buddhist family to ritually protect the Nepalese monarchy, was in conflict with the United Nations Convention of the Rights of the Child. The discussion has revolved around the kind of education the (now formerly royal) Kumari should enjoy during her tenure to ensure that she leads a successful adult life after her term ends. But it has also raised much larger questions regarding the status of old institutions requiring the now deposed king as a ritual agent in a new federal state. Chunda has taken up the challenge, vigorously arguing in favor of the Kumari's homeschooling, the transferring of the role played by the king to democratically elected representatives, and the cautious modernization of an institution that preserves the claims to Newar Buddhist participation in national leadership as represented by state ritual power.

Towards the end of our meeting, Chunda encouraged her students to introduce themselves. I met some highly motivated and creative young researchers promising to produce some fine new work in Newar studies. None of them saw their future in academia. For my own work on that menarche ritual, Chunda recommended that I consult a book written by one of her brightest female students, Gyani Maiya Maharjan, an extraordinary study that greatly advances our knowledge of the tradition. Gyani Maiya, too, as her fellow students are likely to, found her place outside academia in a world very different from the one in which Chunda grew up—a world in which one need be neither a male nor a *vajrācārya* nor a professor to contribute to public debates on what constitutes Newar religion. Gyani Maiya works, as she herself states on the back cover of her book, as a beautician at the Mijala Beauty Parlor, just across from the monastery where Nepalese girl children briefly live like nuns during their school holidays.

BUDDHA WAS THARU
Vasudev Choudhary
CHIARA LETIZIA

The synergy between Theravada Buddhist modernism and the ethnicization of politics in post-1990 Nepal caused the propagation of Buddhism as a tool of ethnic revival and claims against the Hindu state. Tharu ethnic leaders, reversing two centuries of Hinduization, presented Buddha as the Tharus' common ancestor and the adoption of Buddhism as a return to their true ancestral religion. Vasudev Choudhary

(1949–present) is one of the lay activists engaged in diffusing Buddhism in his own group, searching for evidence of a Buddhist past in Tharu customs, organizing Buddhist awareness camps, and celebrating new Buddhist life-cycle rituals.

Vasudev Choudhary made it his life's mission to teach Buddhism to the Tharus, his own ethnic group inhabiting the Tarai, the plains of South Nepal. At every public gathering he delivers the same message: Tharus are descendants of the Buddha and were originally Buddhists, but think they are Hindu because they have been lied to for two centuries. Tharu traditions reveal their true history: the earth mound at the entrance of Tharu houses resembles a Buddhist *caitya;* Tharu traditional artifacts look like Buddhist objects in the Lumbini museum, and so on. Vasudev visits Tharu families, urging them to stop asking Brahmans to perform "costly and superstitious" rituals and to call him instead, a Buddhist ritual specialist who is one of them.

He admits that his mission is difficult but remains undaunted, saying that Buddhist teachings on self-reliance, learning from experience, and doing what is good have changed his life. Since 1996 he has organized Buddhist awareness camps aimed at young Tharus in many districts. His last wish is to build a monastery near his village and have a Tharu monk live there.

Vasudev is president of the Youth Buddhist Awareness Committee of Udayapur District and one of many local Tharu pandits, activists, and performers of Buddhist rituals. The roots of this Buddhist activism can be found in the reaction of Nepalese ethnic groups to the former Hindu monarchy's rhetoric of national unity, which stressed the primacy of the Shah monarchs, Hinduism, and the national Nepali language, while denying the enormous diversity among the population. This diversity found a voice in the 1990 People's Movement, where ethnic groups demanded a greater recognition of cultural and linguistic differences and denounced the domination of high-caste Hindus. Ethnic intellectuals have also been rewriting the history of their previously Hinduized groups now in search of identity. Renowned Tharu intellectuals proposed a new history for Tharus, affirming a Buddhist past.

The activism of ethnic leaders converged with that of Buddhist Newars in Kathmandu Valley, who since the 1920s had been experiencing a revival of Buddhism in its modernist Theravada form. Newar monks and laypeople had a key role in the campaign for a secular state in 1990, which sought the recognition of religious diversity. Their activism also involved missionary work to spread Buddhism among other Nepalese groups, in part to increase the number of Buddhists in the national census.

This synergy led to the organization of Buddhist Awareness Camps for ethnic groups, where elements of Buddhism with a modernist flavor mixed with ethnic and political activism. The Tharu Welfare Society created a Buddhist committee and took charge of such camps among the Tharus from 1995 onward. These were five-day residential camps held in villages. Around fifty participants—preferably young people—were requested to not smoke or drink and to follow a series of lectures given by Theravada monks and Newar and Tharu laypeople. Every morning, after worshipping Buddha, participants were taught the Five Precepts, the Three Refuges, the Four Noble Truths, and the life of Buddha. Other lectures demonstrated the historical link between Buddhism and the Tharu community in the Tarai (where Lumbini, the birthplace of Buddha, is located) and presented Buddhism as an instrument of progress. The participants were asked to organize identical programs in their own villages. From these camps emerged the first generation of Tharu Buddhist activists.

Vasudev's experience exemplifies this process: he participated in the first camp in Kathmandu in 1995 and then organized several camps in his district, inviting Kathmandu monks and lay activists as well as renowned Tharu intellectuals. At these camps Vasudev and his colleagues lectured on Buddhist funerary rituals and marriages. The ethnic message was omnipresent: dominated by Hindu Brahmans as a lower caste until that point, Tharus could count on Buddhism to improve their quality of life. An intense activism followed, which led to the construction of local monasteries, attempts to offer substitute life-cycle Buddhist rituals performed by lay officers, and efforts to find further evidence of a Buddhist past in Tharu traditions and artifacts.

The Buddhism promoted by activists such as Vasudev mediates modernist elements, traditional values, and political strategy. These activists see Buddhism as a rational and modern system of values, discarding superstition and "blind faith" (features they attribute to Hinduism). They link the soteriological message of Buddhism to social commitment, seeking to free Tharus from exploitation and their position of inferiority in a religiously defined hierarchy. These activists emphasize Buddhist education, viewed as a tool for the development of their "backward" group. Their homes often house a Buddhist library, and they send their children to Theravada monasteries in Kathmandu Valley for temporary ordination.

Tharu Buddhists were connected from the outset with an Asian Buddhist network, thanks to the foreign contacts developed by Newar activists at the World Fellowship of Buddhist Youth's conferences. Taiwanese funds, including the Fo Guang Shan monastery, financed the Buddhist camps. More generally, financial support for the development of Buddhism in Nepal, including the education of Nepalese monks and nuns overseas, is provided by Buddhist institutions from Burma, Sri Lanka, Taiwan, and Thailand. In the Tharu pandits' houses and Tharu small monasteries, books and ritual objects of Malaysian, Taiwanese, and Thai origin can be found.

These modernist and globalized aspects contrast with the emphasis placed on rewriting the group's history, inventing a Buddhist past and a common prestigious ancestor, the Buddha, for the group: one has to be originally Buddhist in order to justify the present adoption of Buddhism. The Buddhist modernist idea of individual responsibility and autonomy of choice contrasts with the national Tharu organization's collective adoption of Buddhism and the affirmation that Tharus are "naturally Buddhists."

Buddhism contributed to the Tharus' effort to constitute a single ethnic identity, which the several groups scattered in the country using the same ethnonym had never shared. Affirming their descent from Buddha, Tharus rooted themselves in the Tarai—the land where Buddha was born—thus claiming their indigenousness.

Vasudev's activism tells us about some particularities of Buddhism in contemporary Nepal: laypeople are increasingly involved in teaching and spreading the doctrine; the Buddhist global network and East-East connections are growing in importance; Buddhist life-cycle rituals have been developed along with the mythology of an original Buddhism; and the propagation of Buddhism, coupled with ethnic activism, has connected with activism for a secular state. Buddhism, perceived as egalitarian and rational, is portrayed as the right religion for a democratic and religiously pluralist state out of the Hindu fold.

A MODERN TAIWANESE EDUCATOR
Houguan
STEFANIA TRAVAGNIN

The identity of Taiwanese Buddhism is rooted in the fifty-year occupation on the island (1895–1945), the practice of mainstream Chinese Mahayana Buddhism implemented by monks who moved from the mainland to Taiwan in the early 1950s, and the media and digital transformation of the local religious landscape in the past two decades. The monk Houguan (1956–present) exemplifies all these factors, which he is developing further in his career as preacher and educator.

Locally and internationally, Buddhist modernity in Taiwan after the Japanese occupation was seen as rooted in the figure of the monk Yinshun (1906–2005), who was a theorizer and promoter of modern Buddhism for the Human Realm. However, it is Yinshun's best-known disciple, the nun Zhengyan (b. 1937), and her Tzu Chi Foundation that now provide the most popular and best-known images of the modern face of Buddhism—and of Buddhism for the Human Realm—in Taiwan. Often labeled as a Buddhist NGO, Tzu Chi was established in 1966 in Hualian through the joint efforts of a few Taiwanese women who were inspired by Zhengyan's teachings of compassion and charity; only twenty years afterwards Tzu Chi inaugurated its first general hospital. Through the years, Zhengyan's followers increased in number, and Tzu Chi started establishing offices elsewhere in Taiwan and abroad; right now the foundation counts more than forty countries and nearly four hundred branch offices. In 2011, *Time* magazine included Zhengyan on its list of the one hundred most influential people in the world.

Less known to the public sphere is Yinshun's disciple Houguan, who is nevertheless the real embodiment and promoter of the so-called modern Taiwanese Buddhism in a specific area: the education sector. The upgrading of the curricula of Buddhist seminaries, the adoption of the new media to teach monastics and laity, and the efforts to arrange and participate in cross-strait symposia on pedagogic matters are among the highlights of the role that Houguan has played in Buddhist education.

Houguan was born in 1956 in Miaoli County. At the age of eighteen he became interested in Buddhism while reading the *Da zhidu lun* (The Treatise of the Great Perfection of Wisdom), one of the main texts of the Chinese version of the Madhyamaka School, and a cardinal scripture for Chinese Buddhism. He enrolled in the Chung-Hwa Institute of Buddhist Studies and conducted most of his studies directly under the supervision of Yinshun. Houguan was thus trained in the most modern institutions for Buddhist learning that Taiwan could offer. This newly defined modern education is based on reforms that Taixu (1890–1947) implemented in Mainland China in the 1920s. Taixu's new system of learning included the study of secular subjects (such as English, Japanese, biology, psychology, Western philosophy), a philological and historical approach to the study of Buddhist texts, a different system of examination, and the classification of degrees that mirrored public schools and were approved by the central government.

In the late 1980s, at Yinshun's suggestion, Houguan enrolled in a Ph.D. program at Tokyo National University, with a research project that addressed philological and doctrinal aspects of *Da zhidu lun*. Buddhist monks in Taiwan and Mainland China were all aware at that time that Japanese Buddhist academia offered the most advanced and best structured Buddhist education in East Asia. In fact, the history of Buddhist academia in Japan started in the early Meiji (1868–1912), and had already gone through the process of curricula update and recognition by the central government by the time Chinese Buddhists started carrying out reforms in the area of education. Japanese institutions then became not only the ideal schools for Chinese and Taiwanese sangha from the very beginning of twentieth century, but also the main reference model for Chinese and Taiwanese Buddhists in their own reforming of Buddhist schools.

In 1997 Houguan decided to withdraw from the doctorate program and assist Yinshun in his reforms of sangha education back in Taiwan. Aside from a few years at the Huiri Lecture Hall in Taipei, Houguan has spent most of his time as dean and teacher of the Fuyan Buddhist Institute. He is also president of the Yinshun Buddhist Cultural Foundation, an organization that promotes the understanding of Yinshun's thought and practice, provides students interested in pursuing Buddhist studies with scholarships, and organizes national and international symposia on Buddhism—especially Yinshun's Buddhism.

As part of his mission as dharma educator, Houguan was involved in the updating of the curricula of the Fuyan Buddhist Institute, and he distinguished himself by adopting technology in his educational initiatives. For example, the institute started a Web site that narrates its history, including all the notes of Houguan's and other teachers' lectures as downloadable files. Even its Buddhist academic journal, where students of the institute and other scholars of Buddhism publish, is available online. Houguan also opened evening and weekend courses for the public. His lectures have all been recorded and distributed on CDs, together with his notes in digital form. Fuyan also has its own channel on YouTube, where videos of Buddhist lectures— including talks delivered by Houguan—are uploaded regularly. This online teaching enabled Houguan to reach a wider audience in Taiwan and abroad, and created new modalities of dialogue and exchanges between teachers and students of Buddhism. Houguan has also been involved in the digitalization of the entire oeuvre of Yinshun and Yinshun's teacher, the reformer Taixu. Most important, Houguan made available Yinshun's unpublished notes on *Da zhidu lun* in digital form, through the reproduction of the notes in jpg format along with transcriptions in pdf. All these CDs are now among the most important tools for Chinese and Western scholars of Chinese Buddhism.

The very first conversations I had with Houguan back in 2002 were all about Buddhist principles and textual history, and his comments were always framed in scholarly terms rather than those of a believer. Houguan had a perfect command of Sanskrit and Pali terminology, and an impressive knowledge of Buddhist history and scriptures. We discussed contemporary scholarship in the field, and he talked me through the special collections in Fuyan's library. In our subsequent e-mail correspondence, he referred often to Western scholars and drew parallels between his and Yinshun's interpretations of *Da zhidu lun* and Lamotte's work on the same scripture.

Houguan's life and mission mirror the narrative of modernity that has characterized Buddhism in Taiwan during the second half of the twentieth century. The establishment of worldwide Buddhist organizations such as Fo Guang Shan and Fagushan, the opening of Buddhist charities like the Tzu Chi Foundation, sanghas' interventions in political debates and engagement in social welfare, the foundation of Buddhist seminaries and Buddhist universities: these are key aspects of Buddhist modernity that started to take shape in postcolonial Taiwan and developed rapidly after the lifting of martial law in 1987.

INVENTOR OF A BUDDHIST ALPHABET
Pema Rinzin Takchungdarpa
KALZANG DORJEE BHUTIA

Buddhist studies has long been dominated by the study of texts, most of which are considered part of the classical literatures of Asia. However, scholars must also consider the development of vernacular literatures in Buddhist communities, as the case study of the eastern Himalayan Sikkimese Bhutia language demonstrates. The vocabulary developed by the pioneers of this literary tradition, such as Pema Rinzin Takchungdarpa (1946–present), not only allows for the preservation of this language, but also manages to capture the rapid changes that are reshaping Sikkimese society.

In the summer of 2012, it seemed that every jeep in the small Indian Himalayan state of Sikkim was playing the same tune. The song " 'Dzum segs segs" extols the beauty of a blushing young woman and was eagerly downloaded on phones and MP3 players throughout the state. Its popularity was in part due to its being sung by local Sikkimese talents, two schoolteachers from Yoksam, but also because it was written in Bhutia or *Lho skad* language, the unique dialect related to Tibetan spoken in Sikkim. Despite the uniqueness of the song, its popularity is representative of a wider movement in contemporary Sikkim to revitalize and promulgate Bhutia language and culture.

The man at the forefront of this movement is Pema Rinzin Takchungdarpa, a retired schoolteacher from western Sikkim who previously served as

Deputy Director for Language and later Joint Director for Education in the state government. For over forty years, Pema Rinzin has worked hard to develop Bhutia language and literature, publishing during his career multiple textbooks, grammatical texts, dictionaries, and poems, and participating in multiple community interest groups, all designed to promote Bhutia literature. When I visited him in his home in Gangtok in 2012, he explained to me the challenges behind these activities. He explained that, historically, Bhutia was not a written language. Its spoken form is held to have been introduced to the area by the Bhutia community when they migrated from Tibet in around the thirteenth century. Unlike other local languages such as Lepcha and Nepali, for many years Bhutia was not taught in schools; instead, classical Tibetan became its approximate in the state educational curriculum. The authority accorded Tibetan was largely due to its status as the classical language of Buddhism, the religion of the Bhutia and Lepcha communities of Sikkim that remains the central element of Sikkimese culture and politics.

Buddhism was also a central part of Pema Rinzin's early life. Born in west Sikkim in 1946 to a father who was a renowned lama from the royal monastery of Pemayangtsé (*Pad ma yangs rtse*), Pema Rinzin received his first education at Pemayangtsé. His family represented west Sikkim's *ngakpa* (*sngags pa*) tradition, wherein many of the men took admission in their local monastery and trained in monastic ritual and liturgy using Tibetan-language texts but remained non-celibate and were also responsible for farming their ancestral properties. However, Pema Rinzin was also born at a time of great transition for Sikkim, when the small state was still an independent kingdom but was slowly opening to the world. Like a number of his peers, rather than remaining at the monastery, after he completed his education at a monastic educational institution Pema Rinzin became a teacher. Equipped with a comprehensive knowledge of classical Tibetan language, grammar, and astrology, he started teaching in 1966. However, Pema Rinzin's background in Sikkimese cultural traditions left him with vexing questions about the relevance of teaching young, ethnically Bhutia people Tibetan language, and in the 1970s, when the opportunity to create a Bhutia-language curriculum for the state arose, he leaped at the chance.

Pema Rinzin decided to tackle the tricky issues of spelling and orthography in a controversial manner. He retained the Tibetan alphabet but removed the pre- and postfix particles that make spelling in Tibetan so difficult. He advocated for writing Bhutia as it sounded, rather than as according to Tibetan rules. Local monastic scholars, *khenpos,* and lamas all deplored his approach, stating that the departure from tradition was not only incorrect but also fundamentally disrespectful to local culture. Pema Rinzin laughs as he recalls debates he had with old teachers and friends but explains that he could understand their reservations regarding changing the spelling of Tibetan words due to the link between the Tibetan alphabet and Buddhism. He states that without Buddhism there would be no language. Historically, the Tibetan written language developed around the same time as Buddhism's entry into Tibet, and the vast corpus that makes up Tibetan literature had, until the twentieth century, been mostly religious. The written word thus has a special significance in Tibetan cultural areas, and modifying its spelling was thought to have religious as well as cultural impact. Ultimately, however, Pema Rinzin managed to appease the *khenpos,* who have all become supporters of Bhutia language and literature.

Bhutia has made great progress as a written language and is now taught at all levels of the state curriculum. Pema Rinzin laments that this is still not enough. Bhutia is rarely spoken in Sikkim's urban areas, and it is not taught in the private, often missionary-run schools where many Bhutias send their children in order to learn English and secure much-coveted government jobs. Language choice and education in Sikkim have socioeconomic implications that leave many young Bhutias illiterate in their native language. As a result, Pema Rinzin sees his mission as one that goes beyond language curriculum to broader issues related to cultural preservation and the construction of Bhutia tradition in contemporary Sikkim.

For Pema Rinzin, Buddhism is inextricably intertwined with these concerns. When I visit the home he shares with his wife and university student son, he shows me his beautiful shrine room, where he begins and ends his day performing the prayers and rituals he was taught at Pema-yangtsé. Though he is frequently asked to return to the monastery due to his expertise, he prefers to divide his time between Gangtok and rural west Sikkim, where he remains engaged in his language promulgation activities. The inspiration for these activities is his sense of tradition learned from his elders, the monastery, Tibetan texts, and his daily ritual practice. As I prepare to leave his home, Pema Rinzin reemphasizes this connection, stating that, "Without Buddhism, we Bhutias would have no written language; and as we owe our language and tradition (*bstan pa*) to Buddhism, I owe anything I have achieved in this life to *künchoksum* (*kun mchog gsum;* the Three Jewels)."

TRADING IN THE BUDDHIST LIFE FOR DRUGS
Former Novice Ai Kham
ROGER CASAS RUIZ

Contemporary economic and educational development in Sipsong Panna challenges the cohesion of local Tai Lue communities and the authority of Theravada Buddhist monasticism as a vehicle of socialization for Lue males. Youth in former peasant-urban and peri-urban areas in the region are particularly vulnerable to this challenge, as is highlighted by the example of Ai Kham (1989–present).

After a first visit in early 2004 to one of the ethnic Tai villages in Jinghong City, the capital of Sipsong Panna (China), I became friends with the novices and the abbot monk living in one of the city's main temples, a favorite place of recreation for boys and young men in the village. When they were not working in the fields, they would go there to play cards, cook, and eat the occasional fish freshly caught in the pond nearby. For several years I spent a lot of time hanging around with them. In spite of the proximity of the city, at that time the pace of life in the village was pretty much that of a rural environment: villagers still worked their lands on the banks of the Mekong and its tributary, the Nam Ha, and lived in old wooden houses raised on stilts. Many Han Chinese migrants already lived in the village, dwelling under the houses of the Tai.

One of the lads frequenting the temple was a boy of around fifteen whose loose attire and meaningless tattoos expressed a devil-may-care attitude. Soon enough, other youngsters at the temple described him to me as a troublemaker. Ai Kham had actually been ordained at the same time as the two young novices (*pha noi*) in the temple, but before a year had passed, he had been defrocked, together with another village boy, when they were caught stealing a hen from a fellow villager. He had also quit school during his first year of education.

After being disrobed, the boy went back home to help his family, one of the poorest in the village, as his little brother was still too young to do labor. But Ai Kham disliked working. He preferred to be away from home, roaming the streets of the village and beyond into the city. While he did not get involved in big business, he would sometimes steal a thing or two and sell it in order to indulge in the infamous *ya ma* (cheap methamphetamine pills). Taking *ya ma* made Ai Kham even lazier, and relatives and villagers alike regarded him as someone who does not listen to elders and is hard to deal with.

Around 2009, the Chinese government cracked down on drug users. Ai Kham, having pushed his luck for too long, was finally paid a visit by the local police and taken to a rehabilitation center around five hundred kilometers away from Sipsong Panna. He spent two years in this facility, working without a salary and being allowed to call his family only once a month. After he was released, it took him less than a year to get caught again. This time it was on the Burmese side of the border, where he had been sent by someone in China to collect a stash of pills. He spent only a few months detained there, though, as his parents paid some money to get him out. But Kham remained difficult to deal with, sleeping during the day and going out with "undesirable" company at night.

Among these companions were also other kids and young men in this village, who after working hard in the fields during the day would eagerly embrace the nocturnal modernity offered by the city at their doorstep: discos, karaoke rooms, alcohol, and prostitutes. Very often unable to satisfy their desires and become proper urban consumers/citizens due to their lack of money, smoking *ya ma* was perhaps just a way for them to fill the gap—not one that was taken lightly by the powers that be in China, though. Many of the village's youngsters ended up spending time in prison or rehabilitation centers.

As Ai Kham entered his twenties going in and out of institutions, the transformation of his village gained momentum. In 2010, things started to change drastically: an offer by a tourist company to buy agricultural land and develop the village into an ethnic site for Han tourists ended up creating dramatic internal strife in the community, pitting households and even family members against each other, and ultimately, as had happened before with other Tai villages in Jinghong, accelerating the transformation of the village into a suburb of the city. A new road, completed in 2014, literally paved the way for Han migrant workers to flock in, which dealt the last blow to the old community.

The transformation also affected the temple. Already in 2005 the abbot, fed up with petty disputes among villagers, resigned and returned to his native village in the south of Sipsong Panna. Soon afterwards, the novices who ordained with Ai Kham disrobed, and since then no village boys have been ordained. The few fellows occupying the monastery of late have come from Tai areas in Shan State or northern Laos. As the old ties of kin and friendship have been shattered by drugs and internal strife, boys and young men do not gather there anymore. Outside of annual village festivals and occasional ceremonies, the temple is deserted.

Ai Kham's parents have rebuilt their old house into a seven-story building and are doing better now. But he has yet to see it. During the Tai New Year of 2012 I was invited to eat with the family. Ai Kham was also there, but soon after that he was once again caught by the police. No one really knows how long he will have to spend being "rehabilitated" this time. His parents are no longer interested in paying money to facilitate his release. When he is home, he reverts to the old ways and, despite the sacrifices they have made for him, remains the "ungrateful son." They think keeping him in jail will finally teach him a lesson. Chances are it will not.

TWO SELF-SACRIFICING BUREAUCRATS
Iizuka and Akabashi
LEVI MCLAUGHLIN

Soka Gakkai, literally the "Value Creation Study Association," was founded in the 1930s as an educational reform movement but transformed thereafter into a lay Buddhist organization following the teachings of the medieval Japanese reformer Nichiren (1222–1282). From the 1950s into the 1970s, Soka Gakkai's membership exploded from a few thousand adherents to millions of member households, and though the Gakkai now dominates Japan's religious landscape, comparatively little is known about the lives of its members. A glimpse into the lives of Soka Gakkai's rank-and-file administrators, such as Iizuka (1969–present) and Akabashi (1981–present) reveals how the organization's salaried employees regard their occupations not simply as jobs but as religious vocations.

Mr. Iizuka (pseudonym) and I became friends more than a decade ago, shortly after I began ethnographic research on Soka Gakkai in Japan in 2000. He approached me in his capacity as a representative of the *kanbu*, "executive" or "administration," as one of the thousands of salaried employees who dedicate their lives to service within Soka Gakkai's massive bureaucracy. An intelligent and compassionate man in his mid-forties who listens to others carefully and chooses his own words with equal care, Iizuka seems perpetually conscious of his responsibility to represent Soka Gakkai's reliable, professional face to the outside world. Dark suit, shiny black shoes, crisp white shirt no matter the weather, sharply parted hair, and never a hair out of place—he is a bit of an anachronism, a throwback to Japan in the immediate postwar years, when Soka Gakkai was anxious to overcome its image as a religion of the poor and socially marginalized. At every encounter with

fellow Gakkai adherents, Iizuka provides them with a behavioral and sarto-
rial model that implicitly urges conformity to a rigidly disciplined ideal. I
have seen a member of the Young Men's Division jerk to attention and run
to put on a tie when he saw Iizuka coming, and an older Gakkai man apolo-
gize reflexively to him for his "slovenly appearance" when he was really just
wearing casual clothes.

Every weekday morning, Iizuka wakes before dawn at his home in western Tokyo to make the first train to the center of the city. He travels for well
over an hour to arrive at Shinanomachi, the neighborhood in the center of
the capital where Soka Gakkai, Japan's largest lay Buddhist organization, is
headquartered. Beginning at 7:00 a.m., Iizuka joins thousands of his fellow
Soka Gakkai employees and ordinary adherents in morning *gongyō,* the
devotional chant that makes up Soka Gakkai's Nichiren Buddhist practice:
Chapter Two, "Expedient Means," and sections of Chapter Sixteen, "Life
Span" of the Lotus Sutra, the putative final teachings of the historical Buddha. This is followed by repeated incantations of *namu-myōhō-renge-kyō,* the
title of the Lotus known as the *daimoku.* Iizuka spends at least an additional
hour every morning chanting *daimoku,* focusing his attention on the continued success of his son, a talented biology student who has just started university; on his elderly mother, who is descending into dementia; and on the
two young children of his younger sister, who died suddenly of cancer at the
age of forty several years ago.

Like all devout Gakkai members, Iizuka also chants for the health and
well-being of Ikeda and Kaneko Daisaku, Soka Gakkai's honorary president
and wife. For decades, Ikeda Daisaku has towered over Soka Gakkai as its un-
questioned authority in all matters, and since Soka Gakkai split from its
parent temple Buddhist sect Nichiren Shōshū in 1991, everything associated
with Ikeda's life and person has taken on an even deeper significance for the
group's devotees. Shinanomachi began as a nondescript administrative hub,
but today it functions as a sacred space. Millions of Gakkai adherents make
pilgrimages to Shinanomachi from all over the globe each year to connect
directly with Ikeda by engaging in devotional activities at the site associated with his person. Iizuka, like other intensely devoted headquarter employees, regards his daily commute as part of this pilgrimage ritual.

Born in Sasaki, a working-class port city in Nagasaki Prefecture that is
dominated by a U.S. military base, and raised in grinding poverty by parents who converted to Soka Gakkai, Iizuka confronted two stark choices as
he finished high school: drop out of school and work in menial jobs to support his mother, who was teetering on the brink of divorce from his father;
or seek to study at Soka University. Iizuka did not apply to any other

universities, as he considered study at the school founded by Honorary President Ikeda as the only meaningful alternative to giving up postsecondary education to care for his parent. When Soka University accepted him, he was overcome with gratitude, and when he made it through the competitive hiring process to gain a position in Soka Gakkai's salaried administration, his commitment to the organization hardened to an indestructible core.

For Iizuka, the entire world, even nature itself, makes sense to him in Gakkai terms. During a long car trip through Fukushima Prefecture in June 2013, Iizuka talks about how he has spent the last ten years learning to identify the types of flowers, trees, insects, and animals that thrive on Soka University's capacious grounds. "If it's a plant that grows at Sōdai, I know it," Iizuka says to me and our driver, Mr. Akabashi (pseudonym), as he reflects on how he strengthened his bonds with Soka University and its founder by memorizing seasonal changes at the campus. For members of the *kanbu,* the dedicated inner circle within Soka Gakkai's already rarefied sphere, all things in the world, from the minutiae of nature to daunting personal challenges posed by the organization itself, reveal their meaning when viewed through Soka Gakkai's fusion of Buddhist and modern rationalist perspectives. Mundane phenomena and life-altering decisions alike acquire heightened significance as they are woven into Soka Gakkai's narrative, and each one provides the organization's employees with another opportunity for self-sacrifice through service, another chance to demonstrate dedication to Ikeda Daisaku and Soka Gakkai.

Iizuka and Akabashi have never met before, but they quickly adopt an attitude of easy familiarity thanks to their shared *kanbu* culture. Soka Gakkai's administration casts a net across Japan, overcoming regional distinctions by binding its adherents together within a rationalized bureaucratic hierarchy. The institution clearly departs from earlier Buddhist examples: instead of taking its cue from Japanese temple Buddhism or earlier types of lay organizations, Soka Gakkai models its organizational apparatus on the administration of a modern nation-state. Honorary President Ikeda soars atop a hierarchy of thousands of paid *kanbu* employees and many thousands more unpaid volunteers who continually guide members—organized and monitored according to location, sex, age, occupation, and many other quantified criteria—in a perpetual process of fusing personal interests and aspirations with Soka Gakkai's institutional goals. Some of Soka Gakkai's unprecedented success in dominating Japan's religious landscape can be attributed to the efficiency of the administrators who keep the wheels of its bureaucracy turning—administrators who are willing, even eager, to martyr themselves in service to a mission they regard as far greater than themselves.

Like all modern bureaucracies, Soka Gakkai's administration depends upon a steady supply of reliable human resources prepared within a standardized educational system. Akabashi graduated from Soka Gakuen, the organization's high school in Tokyo. Since the 1970s, the organization has relied increasingly on its private school system to staff the ranks of its bureaucracy; most of the younger *kanbu* have attended at least one Gakkai school, and not a few have spent their entire lives in Gakkai institutions. As we approach the barricades that bar entry to the radioactive zone less than ten kilometers from the Fukushima Daiichi nuclear plants, Akabashi tells us that he, like Iizuka, was recruited right after university into the Gakkai administration, in his case to the Systems Bureau, the Shinanomachi headquarters IT department. In April 2012, a decade into his career, the administration transferred Akabashi to Iwaki City, Fukushima, to assist Gakkai communities situated closest to the Daiichi plants that are blighted by nuclear fallout. Before he left Tokyo, friends and family held emotional farewell gatherings "as if I was going off to war," he chuckles quietly. He also received a personalized written message of encouragement from Ikeda on the morning of his departure to Fukushima, urging him to take care of his health. I ask him how he feels about being an unmarried thirty-two-year-old living in an area notorious for its dangerously high radiation levels. "This transfer was my destiny," Akabashi states immediately, obviously accustomed to answering questions along these lines. "It is my mission during this human existence to contribute to the recovery, even in a small way."

A FACEBOOK BUDDHIST
Nara
TONGTHIDA KRAWENGIT

Nara (1986–present), an only child, attends the activities at Dhammakaya Temple in Pathum Thani with her family. They attend the temple regularly to listen to the abbot's teachings and practice the form of Dhammakaya meditation originally taught by Luang Phor Wat Paknam Pasi Charoen. Like many young people in contemporary Thai society, Nara enjoys the way the Dhammakaya temple uses modern technology—its official Web site with dharma media, the YouTube channel, and Facebook—to present traditional teachings.

Nara is an only child, born in Bangkok in 1986. She lives with her family in Ayutthaya Province, where her parents run a business. Both her parents are devout Buddhists. Educated in private Christian schools and sent to high school in New Zealand, she is bilingual in Thai and English. Because she attended Christian ceremonies with her classmates, she respects Christianity and is interested in learning about other cultures and religions, but she has never wanted to change her own religion. Her family has always been Buddhist. Her maternal grandmother was ordained as a nun and lived in a temple in Ratchaburi Province. As a little girl she often visited her grandmother and stayed overnight with her at the temple. Her paternal uncle was ordained as a monk in Bangkok, and she regularly visited him at his *wat* with her father to offer alms.

Despite spending her childhood visiting temples and making merit with her parents, Nara was not very interested in Buddhism until she came back to Thailand from New Zealand during school breaks. Her parents had started attending Phra Dhammakaya Monastery regularly, and her mother took her to the temple to offer food to the monks and meditate every Sunday. Nara began to volunteer at the temple and helped organize the ceremonies on Sundays and Buddhist holy days. She also attended a three-week course that provided basic teaching about Buddhism, Buddhist culture, and intensive training in Dhammakaya meditation.

Her experiences at the temple and the Buddhist club she started when she was a university student encouraged her: "I realized how good the Buddhist teachings were, and that they could be adapted for my daily living. Taking the five Buddhist precepts is a good way for normal people to lead their life in the modern world. If everybody kept the five precepts, then human beings would be able to live together peacefully in this world. . . . Today because people don't follow the five precepts, the world has become chaotic, and there is war and trouble everywhere. . . . The laws of karma and of cause and effect are also important Buddhist principles for modern Buddhists. When you do something wrong to others and you already know it is wrong, then you will be affected immediately and in the long run. . . . Even if you later regret your bad deeds and try to make up for them, it will be too late to avoid the result of wrongdoing in this life." Nara comments that Buddhist teachings about heaven, hell, and rebirth are complicated and difficult to prove to nonbelievers, but it is easier for her to explain how keeping the precepts, making merit, and meditating will create a better world for everyone.

In addition to following the precepts and observing the law of cause and effect in her daily life, meditation is also an important part of Nara's Buddhist practice. She remembers meditating with her grandmother when she was a child, but today she practices the Dhammakaya meditation technique taught at the temple. Meditation helps her focus on her work. "It is very helpful for my study," she said. "I did very well in my exams even though I did not spend much time reading." In addition, meditation has helped change her behavior. "In the past I was a very impatient person. I could not wait for anything, and this often made me a fussy person. Since I have been practicing meditation regularly, my personality has changed and I am now a much calmer person."

Because of her background in computer science, Nara is interested in the role that technology plays in modern Buddhism. In the past people had to read books or go to the temple to learn about the dharma. Nowadays her temple broadcasts the dharma by satellite 24/7. There is also an official Web site online that contains doctrinal media such as pdf files of books, songs, animations of the *Jatakas* and the life of the Buddha, audio files of *dharmadesana* (preaching), and instructions for meditation practice. The ready availability of dharma media is essential for busy people who have no time to go to the temple or study texts. Nara notes that the dharma media produced by her temple is essential to modern Buddhism, which must compete with the secular entertainment available online. In her grandparents' time, when people lived in rural communities, they could go to the temple on Buddhist holy days (*wan phra*). Today, people who study or work can only go to the temple on the weekend or during public holidays. However, they can still keep *wan phra* in their minds. Examples of how busy Buddhists can do this include making offerings to monks passing by the house, doing extra chanting or long meditations, listening to sermons on Buddhist TV, or observing the Eight Precepts. People also use Facebook as a tool to share merit-making activities with friends.

Nara is representative of a modern Thai Buddhist laywoman. During the week she helps her parents run their business. After work she watches TV, chats with her friends on the phone or on Facebook, goes to concerts, and travels to different places. However, she never forgets that she is a Buddhist. She offers food to the monks, meditates, goes to the temple on Sundays, and observes *wan phra* at the temple or in her mind. She uses social media and satellite television to make merit and support her friends in keeping the precepts. Dhammakaya is also representative of many new Buddhist movements in Asia that embrace technology and focus on founding university Buddhist clubs and aiming their teachings at children and young adults. Some criticize movements like this for creating "future customers"; others, like Nara, see it as allowing her to be both modern and Buddhist.

A DAUGHTER OF LAMAS, YOGIS, AND SHAMANS
Chözang
AMY HOLMES-TAGCHUNGDARPA

Buddhism in Sikkim has been historically associated with the Vajrayana of Tibet, but Sikkim's experiences with colonialism and globalization have led to considerable changes in its functions for local practitioners, especially those who have left the state to seek their futures elsewhere or to gain skills now sought after in a capitalist economy. Chözang (1989–present) represents two categories often absent from studies of Buddhism: young laywomen and northeastern Indians. Her attempts to reconcile her ancestral traditions with her immediate needs to secure her livelihood and realize her aspirations outside of the familiar space of her home state demonstrate the way that young Himalayan Buddhists are engaging with their traditions and remaking them for use in a complex world.

Vijay Nagar is, at first glance, a typical middle-class neighborhood in northern Delhi. Home to private doctors' surgeries, snack food joints, vegetable carts, and a number of Old Delhi's ubiquitous wandering cows, the neighborhood thrives in the commerce and energy brought by its proximity to the University of Delhi, one of India's premier educational institutions. The most obvious sign of the student friendliness of the neighborhood is its diversity. Students from all corners of India stay in student housing, and Christians, Hindus, Buddhists, animists, and Muslims come together to share their festivals and food far from home. Significantly, such shared space has also led the neighborhood to be seen as a safe haven for those marginalized by the very real threats of racism and sexual violence elsewhere in the city.

Vijay Nagar resident Chözang is a twenty-five-year-old graduate student from Sikkim, a small state in northeast India historically associated with Vajrayana Buddhism. She has lived in Delhi for six years, completing during that time a bachelor's degree, a master's degree in political science, and a teaching degree. She calls herself a Buddhist, an identity that has become endowed with a new significance for her since arriving in Delhi and finding herself an ethnic and cultural minority. She says that identifying as a Buddhist has provided her with a sense of community in a large, overwhelming, and, at times, hostile metropolis. She has found cultural connections with other Himalayan Buddhists, who all gather together to celebrate Tibetan and Himalayan New Year (*Lo gsar*) and other important Buddhist holidays. Identifying as a Buddhist has become important for her as a way to communicate with other religious groups as well. Chözang recalls how, early in her undergraduate degree, a professor asked her to talk about her religious tradition, which led to a feeling of awkwardness when she realized she could not respond with the philosophically informed answers that her Hindu and Muslim peers provided. In order to respond to such situations, Chözang has become self-educated, reading works by the Dalai Lama, Géshé Kelzang Gyatso, Sogyal Rinpoché, and other modern English-language Buddhist writers so that she can now feel confident to engage in discussions with her friends from elsewhere in India about her tradition.

Chözang is aware, however, that these philosophical explanations of Buddhism are only one possible construction of it, as, for her, Buddhism is primarily representative of her cultural heritage as a Sikkimese and a member of the Bhutia ethnic community. Chözang grew up steeped in these traditions due to her family's participation in Sikkimese ritual life. Every year, at the monastery during Losar, they attended ritual monastic dances (*cham*) to ward off obstacles for the coming year and invited ritual specialists to recite sutras to bring blessings to their home. Her parents' active patronage of the monastery is somewhat typical of Bhutia Buddhist participation in the ritual calendar; however, their motives are less ordinary. Both of Chözang's parents are dedicated religious practitioners. She describes them as "tradition junkies," as her father is a *ngakpa* (*sngags pa*), or non-celibate lama, who is actively involved in the local monastery that her grandfather, a renowned yogi and ritual specialist, leads, and her mother spends hours in prayer daily. Much of Chözang's own identification with Buddhism is through these rituals and prayers, though she sees these events more as opportunities for family gatherings than as expressions of personal faith. Chözang has an expansive view of Sikkimese tradition aside from Buddhism as well, as her maternal grandfather is a well-known local healer and herbalist. She recalls growing up between two quite different forms of practice, as she would visit her paternal grandfather, a yogi, at the monastery for large ceremonies propitiating the mountain deities of Sikkim, and then would return home to find her maternal grandfather chanting mantras and sucking poisonous snake venom out of the feet of local villagers.

Chözang's expansive notions of Buddhism are also influenced by her earlier education at Christian missionary schools. Her parents sent their children to these schools to learn English well and thus gain better career opportunities, ideally in government service. Though Chözang is thankful for the education she received, she is also aware of some of the damage that missionary education did to her sense of cultural identity, as earlier in her life she says she was more Christian than Buddhist. She also feels that her knowledge of her mother tongue, Bhutia, suffered, as she had to speak only English or Nepali at the school hostel.

This concern for the preservation of tradition is central to Chözang's out-look, and she credits it to her parents' explanations of Buddhism. She sees Buddhism as a tradition that emphasizes compassion and respect for all beings and hopes that she can learn more in order to continue the traditions of her ancestors. Recently, some of her cousins have become interested in Buddhist practice as well and have participated in the Nyungné (*Smyung gnas*) fasting ritual practices that are held throughout Sikkim. I ask Chözang whether she intends to take part, and she jokes that she loves Kentucky Fried Chicken too much to make the commitment to the intermittent vegetarianism that the tradition requires. More seriously, she questions the relevance of the practice to her personal life at this point. Noticing the bumper stickers of Tibetan Buddhist deities on her apartment wall alongside pages torn from Indian and Western fashion and design magazines, I ask about their relevance for her. Chözang replies that her parents gave them to her as gifts, and that her parents' faith inspires her own. Whenever a challenge emerges in her life—whether it be an illness or an exam—she knows her mother and father will go to the monastery and offer butter lamps and prayers for her. She says that the comfort of knowing that others are praying for her is enough, providing her with the love and confidence that she needs to negotiate the wider world beyond the lanes of Vijay Nagar, far away from home and the world of the yogis, shamans, and local spirits of her birthplace.

TAIWAN'S NEW AGE BUDDHIST
Terry Hu
PAUL J. FARRELLY

The New Age has grown to be a visible and dynamic part of Taiwan's religious land-scape. Terry Hu (Hu Yinmeng; 1953–present), a former movie star, was one of the most important authors and translators and propelled the New Age's growth in the late 1980s and early 1990s. One of Hu's favorite figures to translate and promote at that time was the Indian-born philosopher and former Theosophist Jiddu Krishnamurti, whom she helped re-create in Taiwan as a Buddhist figure.

On a damp evening in January 2013, over 250 people gathered in the hall of the Tien Educational Center, part of the Jesuit campus in central Taipei. Yet it was not the Catholic faith that had drawn this flock. Rather, the Psygarden Publishing Company had rented the hall for a "sharing session" to celebrate the launch of Terry Hu's Chinese translation of the spiritual teacher A. H. Almaas' *Luminous Night's Journey: An Autobiographical Fragment* (1995). Lisa Gerrard and Pieter Bourke's funereal and droning minimalist track "The Unfolding" played twice as the audience found their seats. Editor-in-Chief Doris Wang then welcomed the audience, affirming "your heart knows why you are here." Accompanying Hu in discussing the book and answering questions from the audience were the physics professor/tai chi exponent Chen Kuo-gen and cosmetics entrepreneur Chiang Jung-yuan. This assemblage of science, spirituality, and glamour appears throughout Hu's long career as a pioneering translator, author, and, as she was described on the cover of *Luminous Night's Journey,* "teacher of body, mind and spirit healing."

Born in Taichung, central Taiwan, to parents who fled China before the end of the Chinese civil war, Hu was an only child. Her father was a politician in the Nationalist government who spent much of his time away in Taipei. Hu's relationship with her mother was fractious and she moved to Taipei for high school. After graduating, she studied for a short time at Fu Jen Catholic University and mingled in Taiwan's nascent campus folk music scene before spending a year in New York City, where she trained as a model. Upon returning to Taiwan, Hu's entertainment career blossomed and she starred in a number of popular movies and television serials. In 1979 Hu met the prominent writer and public intellectual Li Ao, whom she quickly married and divorced.

Hu returned to New York City in 1988 as a retired actor. She immersed herself in popular New Age literature, reading books such as Lee Sannella's *Kundalini Experience,* Marilyn Ferguson's *The Aquarian Conspiracy,* Ken Wilber's *The Spectrum of Consciousness,* and Fritjof Capra's *The Tao of Physics.* These books are emblematic of the New Age, the name given to a long-evolving form of spirituality that became popular in the West in the 1970s. Typified by organizational decentralization, theological perennialism, and an often contradictory embrace of alternative religious systems and scientific methods, the New Age remains as disparate and incoherent as it is popular and, in certain cases, mainstream. The repudiation of religious and social authority is common in New Age thought.

Hu would later often write of how she struggled to navigate tradition and modernity, particularly with regard to spiritual matters. In one of her earliest pieces extolling the New Age, she predicted that "the fossilised cage between all religions will be broken open." In her 1989 guide to the New Age, *Ancient Future* (*Gulaodeweilai*), she critiqued the authoritarian tendencies of Chinese culture in Taiwan, particularly with regard to male chauvinism and childhood education. While Hu ultimately rejected the title "New Age" for being too shallow, she continues to publish and teach in a realm closely related to it. She devotes much energy to translating the works of A. H. Almaas and astrology texts, and in lectures she will still refer to the teachings of Jiddu Krishnamurti (1895–1986).

Krishnamurti's writing had a profound effect on Hu, and she decided to translate his books for the benefit of readers in Taiwan. As a boy, Krishnamurti was recognized by the Theosophical Society as Maitreya, the future Buddha. He was taken from India and raised as a Theosophist but left the group in 1929 to teach independently. Living in the United States for much of his life, his books, lectures, and dialogues reached a broad audience and he has long been associated with New Age thought.

Despite Krishnamurti's avowed secularism, Hu represented his teachings using Buddhist language and imagery in her translations and explanatory articles. Hu described his teachings as having elements of philosophy, Zen, the middle way, and the original teachings of Buddhism. She once wrote how Indian Buddhists consider him to be the twentieth-century reincarnation of the major Buddhist figure, Nagarjuna. Hu's tendency to render Krishnamurti's work in Buddhist terms is evident in her 1991 translation of *Exploration into Insight* (1979; *Borezhilü*, lit. *Prajñic Journey*). In the preface to her translation, Hu wrote that his later teachings, in which *Exploration* belongs, vividly displayed the essence of Zen (*Chan*), despite the term not appearing in his original text.

Hu adopted an explicitly Buddhist tone for *Exploration*, as she wanted her translation to appeal to the vast number of Taiwanese Buddhists. It was reprinted twice within twelve months and later published in simplified Chinese characters for readers in Mainland China. Hu recalled that after reading *Exploration into Insight* she thought it held the same views as Buddhism and was impressed by how it explained *prajñā* (wisdom) in a way that no other teachers or scriptures had been able to. While Hu used Buddhist language to translate the works of Krishnamurti, she also framed her understanding of him in an antiauthoritarian manner resonant of the New Age, and in other publications drew parallels between his rejection of the Western schooling imposed on him by the Theosophical Society and her own resistance to formal education.

Hu's introduction of Krishnamurti into late twentieth-century Taiwan is grounded in the cultural context of the time. Coming from a privileged family, her education and foreign experiences coupled with her own profile as a popular entertainer equipped her to re-create her identity in Taiwan as a New Age authority. In depicting Krishnamurti as a modern figure attractive to Taiwanese Buddhists, Hu drew on the creativity encouraged by New Age culture to promote a contemporary and globalized form of Buddhism.

A MODERNIST MONK WITH CHINESE CHARACTERISTICS
Farong
BRIAN J. NICHOLS

In 1981 a new generation of monks began to be ordained in Mainland China, the first since ordinations were interrupted in the 1950s. This generation has had to focus much of its time and energy on rebuilding institutions, training novice monks, and establishing sources of income. Among hundreds of monks of low education and low ambitions, there is an increase in the number of ambitious, thoughtful, and energetic monks eager to build invigorated forms of Buddhism. Farong (1970–present) is a monk who is critical of Chinese folk customs as he seeks a return to "original Buddhism."

I first met Farong in the courtyard of a large monastery in southern China where he resides. The abbot had arranged for him to give me a tour of the monastery as I was a scholar, and Farong, as the most educated monk at the monastery, was most able to provide an informed introduction to the site. It was a hot and humid summer day and Farong seemed preoccupied and annoyed at having to play tour guide. He nonetheless provided a helpful introduction to the distinctive features of the monastery, such as its Ming dynasty hall and Song dynasty artifacts. As we stood in front of one of the halls, several individuals came forward to place smoldering bundles of incense into the censer, which already held dozens of smoking sticks. Rather than regarding this as an act of piety, Farong wore a look of incredulity as he remarked: "If Buddhas and Bodhisattvas could really receive this incense they would all choke to death. I don't know why they burn so much; it's meaningless and wasteful." This would be the first of many such critical comments I would hear Farong direct at popular forms of Buddhism over the course of my research from 2005 to 2012.

Farong was born around 1970. After graduating from college he became a teacher of Chinese history at a middle school in his home province. He felt, however, that as an introvert he was not cut out to be a teacher. His real pleasure was to travel independently during holidays. These travels took him to tourist sites, which, in China, inevitably include Buddhist temples. It was through such travels that Farong was first exposed to the Buddhist tradition. He decided to become a monk somewhat abruptly while traveling during the Chinese New Year at the age of twenty-seven. At the time he was not happy with his job, and he never liked the noise and crowds of Chinese New Year celebrations. He was staying at a hostel in the mountains when his roommate announced that he wanted to become a monk. The promise of a contemplative life free from worries like food, money, or clothes drew

Farong to the monastic vocation. He now holds a post at a large monastery in southern China and has become the head monk of a small temple. He is respected by monks and laypersons alike for his knowledge, demeanor, and sincerity.

Farong is not only a critic of folk customs that have become a part of Chinese Buddhism such as burning paper offerings to the dead, but also of standard beliefs and practices like those associated with Pure Land Buddhism, which he considers a degenerate form of Buddhism. He is instead interested in what he refers to as "original Buddhism" (*yuanshi fojiao*). Yet his openly critical stances are juxtaposed with his own mastery of Buddhist ritual; his reverent and sonorous chanting and his careful attention to ritual detail intriguingly temper his otherwise caustic critiques of ritual. It seems that his mastery of Buddhist ceremonial culture has enabled him to both see through these forms and be disgusted at the crass performance of ritual by monks interested in the income such performances can generate. He characterizes monks specializing in income-generating ritual services as the least-respected types of monks, motivated by material benefits rather than the thought of helping others.

The language of critique he uses is a combination of terms derived from an educated lexicon associated with official discourse mixed with Buddhist terminology. From the official (state-approved) lexicon come terms and their conceptual frameworks, such as folk customs (*minjian fengsu*) and folk religion (*minjian zongjiao*). These terms are used in the discourse of public figures and the educated to distinguish the "high" cultural forms of the five officially recognized religions (Buddhism, Daoism, Protestantism, Catholicism, Islam) from practices that are variously considered "backward" or marked by "superstition," such as divination and ritual interactions with the spirit world. The modern education received by Farong has facilitated his critical distance from ritual practices and encouraged his search for an original Buddhism, centered on ethical behavior and the cultivation of wisdom. His vision of Buddhism shares features with what has been termed "Protestant Buddhism" or "Buddhist Modernism." Farong is not the leader of a large movement, but he is an outspoken advocate of a more rational form of Buddhism marked by less ritual excess, more ethical behavior, and more rational insight. He shares his vision with visitors to his monastery and through a variety of online social media sites.

An example of Farong's online propagation is a post about the celebration of the "Pure-Bright" (*qingming*) or "Tomb-Sweeping" Festival, recognized as a national holiday in 2008. In this post he first traces the history of this Chinese festival from the seventh century before launching into a critique of burning "gold paper" as an offering to ancestors during the festival. He explains that it is not proper for Buddhists to make such offerings with the thought that it will benefit one's ancestors, arguing that the Buddhist mechanics of karmic retribution render such offerings ineffectual. Nevertheless, he advises Buddhists to carry on with traditions of making offerings to ancestors, but specifically not to do so under the delusion of assisting ghosts, but as a skillful means (*upāya*) to express one's filial respect and prevent non-Buddhists from slandering Buddhists as non-filial. Farong's critiques, in the end, are not as iconoclastic as they first appeared to me. It turns out that he embraces the symbolic value of ritual as a sign of respect to Buddhas, bodhisattvas, and ancestors and as an expedient means to attract those of lower understanding and motivation. Farong, like other modern Buddhists, has developed a vision of Buddhism marked by rationalism and a critique of supernatural beliefs, yet differing in that he maintains a faith in traditional conceptions of karmic retribution. It is too early to tell how widespread such a vision may become in China and whether it will generate a modern Buddhism with Chinese characteristics.

AN ANTICOMMUNIST MONK AND VIOLENCE
Achan Chanh Ly
IAN G. BAIRD

Buddhist monks and Buddhism more generally are often imagined, especially in Western countries, to be inherently nonviolent. While the Buddha certainly never advocated violence, many Buddhists, including Buddhist monks, have variously advocated for violence and participated in violent acts. Achan Chanh Ly (1941–2004) was a Lao-born Theravada monk in Thailand whose life and death became dominated by Cold War politics, counterinsurgency and insurgency, and associated violence.

On the morning of October 18, 2004, two young men arrived by motorcycle at Wat Sammachanyawat (also known as Wat Mai Khlong Song) on the outskirts of Bangkok in Minburi Province, seemingly intending to make merit by providing food offerings to the Theravada Buddhist monks there. First, one of the men casually went to a pond on the temple grounds to feed the fish. He then proceeded to enter the residence of the abbot of temple, Phra Khru Uthai Thammasophit (better known as Achan Chanh Ly), with what appeared to be offerings. But instead of making merit, he proceeded to shoot the sixty-three-year-old abbot three times at point-blank range with a .38 revolver, killing him instantly. The assailant then fled the monk's residence and jumped on the back of the awaiting motorcycle of his partner, who rapidly drove out of the temple grounds and away. The targeted assassination was carried out exactly as planned.

Later, a picture of the supreme patriarch of Buddhism in Thailand, together with Achan Chanh Ly, was found at the crime scene. The photograph was apparently used to identify the victim, whose face had been crossed out with an X on the photo. Phra Rat Sara Vethi, the abbot of Wat Phrasi Maha That in Bang Khen, oversaw the funeral ceremony, and Vichan Meenchaiyanan, the local member of Parliament for the ruling Thai Rak Thai Party, attended the funeral. The Thai-language *Daily News* reported the murder, though without identifying anything particularly unusual about the victim other than that he had been a respected monk.

As it turns out, however, Achan Chanh Ly was far from an average monk. Indeed, he was one of the most radically militant monks in Thailand, someone who many believe had violated the Buddhist *vinaya,* or rules of conduct for monks, by supporting anticommunist insurgents fighting against the Lao PDR government and their Vietnamese supporters.

There are two versions of the early life of Achan Chanh Ly. Both acknowledge that he was born in 1941 in a rural village in Khong District (present-day Champasak Province), southern Laos, but then they dramatically diverge. Achan Chanh Ly claimed in the first version, which I obtained from one of his speeches recorded in the late 1970s or early 1980s, that he joined the communist Pathet Lao movement at the end of the French colonial period, eventually gaining the rank of captain before traveling to Thailand as a Pathet Lao spy. According to Achan Chanh Ly, once in Thailand he became aware of the evils of communism and ordained as a Buddhist monk. This story, however, is apparently a complete fabrication. According to another Buddhist monk from the same area as Achan Chanh Ly who is now the abbot of a Buddhist temple in France, both ordained as novices in 1955, and later both became monks in Bangkok in 1963. Achan Chanh Ly later returned to Laos, but was never a communist, let alone a Pathet Lao soldier. Instead, he fled the communists in Laos as a monk and traveled back to Thailand in 1977. There he met with members of Thailand's Internal Security Operations Command (ISOC), who recruited him to help spread anticommunist propaganda in Thailand.

After the brutal massacre of students at Thammasat University on October 6, 1976, large numbers of students had fled to the forest to join the militant Communist Party of Thailand (CPT), which was fighting a guerilla war against Royal Thai Army. Many Thais were suspicious of the Thai military and were not easily convinced by anticommunist government propaganda.

Achan Chanh Ly thus became a perfect propaganda tool, willing to fabricate his life story for the anticommunist cause. As another monk explained, "People did not believe what officials told them, so they needed a monk who would lie for them, as people believed monks more." Achan Chanh Ly traveled around Thailand making anticommunist speeches from 1977 to 1982, until an amnesty was given to CPT members, at which time the antipropaganda effort declined, along with the monk's role in it.

In 1978, in appreciation of Achan Chanh Ly's anticommunist efforts, the supreme patriarch of Thailand provided the monk with land, where Achan Chanh Ly subsequently established Wat Sammachanyawat with considerable support from his far-right supporters in the security services.

Achan Chanh Ly not only actively supported anticommunist efforts in Thailand; he also played a major role in assisting insurgents fighting against the Lao PDR communist government. According to various sources, Achan Chanh Ly raised considerable funds for insurgents, and even went so far as to provide advice regarding military strategy. This led many Lao Buddhist monks to conclude that he had "crossed the line" by supporting military activities, even if he did not directly engage in battle. Freeing the Lao nation from communism was apparently his highest priority, even if it meant violating the Buddhist code of conduct.

Achan Chanh Ly continued to support various anti–Lao PDR insurgent groups in the 1990s and early 2000s, right up until the time he was assassinated. According to various former insurgents, he would give money to any anti–Lao PDR insurgent who sought support from him. Furthermore, due to his close connections with Thai military figures, he was able to raise considerable funds, much of which he channeled to insurgents. Thus, Achan Chanh Ly became a serious threat to the Lao PDR government, and this is almost certainly the reason he was eventually murdered. Although the best-known anticommunist monk in Thailand was Kittiwutto, who infamously stated that it was not a sin to kill a communist, others such as Achan Chanh Ly also played important roles in supporting anticommunist efforts in both Thailand and Laos. Unlike Kittiwutto, however, Achan Chanh Ly's radical militant politics eventually cost him his life.

LOOKING INWARD

New Asceticism in Modern Buddhism

For Buddhism, a tradition long associated with meditation and inner contemplation, looking inward would seem to be the most straightforward of our four themes. What we soon found, however, was that envisioning "looking inward" as encompassing meditation alone excludes some central Buddhist contemplative and cognitive activities. It also leaves out some fascinating characters. As with all of our themes, we wanted something broad enough to offer intriguing new comparative possibilities while still maintaining meaningful distinctions. Our first step was to consider looking inward under the broader theme of Buddhist mental purification, which allowed us to include a whole host of activities, such as making merit, creating art, serving the sangha, performing divinations, and translating. We believe that including these activities in this section complicates the concept of Buddhist mental purification, as well as bifurcations that are often taken for granted (such as monastic/lay and socially engaged/introspective). While looking outward and forward evokes the visionary, looking inward introduces us to visions, ruminations, self-mortifications, and socially disengaged practices. But looking inward is not simply retreating from the world. It should also be approached as an equally engaged response to the pressures of everyday social, familial, and economic life—one that is just as active, innovative, and progressive as looking outward and forward.

Looking inward frequently interacts with the invisible. Spirits, past and future lives, hidden texts, secret teachings, and karmic bonds are all under its purview. This inner vision, though often born of meditative practices removed from society, can take profoundly political forms in its outward expression. Sometimes precariously close to madness, looking inward questions and transgresses many cultural, institutional, and political limits.

Several of our figures in this section retreat from society in some way, like the cave-dwelling *yoginī* Khandro Rinpoché, who was devoted to Buddhism as a child despite having little access to its symbols or institutions. Or consider the unnamed, "schizophrenic" Laotian translator of the *I Ching* and part-time monk whose forms of inward turning run from imbibing backyard whiskey to meditation in a cremation pit.

Like many of the figures described here, Sri Lankan "son of Buddha" Maniyo turned inward after a traumatic experience, in this case the assassination of her boss. Over time, this trauma led her to reach out and help others, a common pattern among some of the figures in this section. Her scathing criticism of "nuns who try to find their self-worth and security by joining an order that marginalizes them," her advice that nuns "find their own religious path," and her conviction of a "direct connection" to future and past Buddhas make her an exemplary example of a Buddhist figure who looks inward. In the case of Jiang Xiuqin, her spiritual insights came from daily sutra recitation in response to the death of her husband. Jiang's ability to see the postmortem fates and past lives of others led her to preach outwardly in the courtyards of Beijing's temples, though even her outreach involved preaching inner forms of purification centered on merit making. Sometimes figures who look inward end up leading lamentable existences. Take Ay Phit, the young Shan Buddhist novice whose early training in meditation and ritual did not lead to a life of peace but to a stint in army intelligence, failed relationships, and an early death; or Sum, a devout Buddhist living in the Kantu ethnic region of Laos, whose independence and visions have partly led her to be seen as a wanton and untrustworthy woman.

Burmese monk/layman Bodaw Aungteza also turned to meditation in response to trauma: the anguishing loss of his teenage son at age seventeen. He moved in and out of madness just as he moved in and out of his Buddhist robes. Like many of our figures in this section, his inner visions provide him with much power and respect in both the lay and monastic communities. And like others whose vision turned inward, he provides an ongoing critique of established divisions: colonial/postcolonial, religion/politics, and magic/meditation.

Meditation as a cure is also a theme, as it is in the case of Lok Bo and his mother. Although meditation does not appear to have helped Bo with his "peculiarities," it did transform his illiterate mother in seemingly profound ways, though one wonders if Bo did not find his mental purification in planting flowers rather than in the formal meditation setting.

The South Korean nun Hŭisang exemplifies one of our goals in this section, which is to expand the concept of looking inward to include more than simply meditation. This expectation, demonstrated by South Korea's largest Buddhist organization's rebranding of its preaching halls as "meditation centers," also explains why Hŭisang must downplay her artistic accomplishments, despite her conviction that they are an ideal "medium through which one can objectify and subsequently transform the sufferings of daily life." Hŭisang's enrollment in a psychotherapy certificate program also demonstrates a focus on inner forms of development that might otherwise be left out of models of mental purification found in traditional Buddhist studies research.

For several of the figures in this section, looking inward involves divinatory practices. The Tibetan female diviner Palchen Lhamo "sees" hidden treasures of Buddhist scripture. Like figures such as Jiang Xiuqin and Bodaw Aungteza, these inward visions also spur outward action and can thus be profoundly political. Inversely, looking inward also reminds us of a key element of tantric Buddhism—secrecy. In the case of the Tibetan tantrist "Mr. D," the secrecy takes on a deeply political tone as Mr. D's dual identity as both retired official and religious specialist prevents him from overtly displaying his tantric colors. Of course, alongside divination and observations of past lives, looking inward also reveals karmic visions and considerations of merit. Sri Lankan Rev. Ratanasara's story demonstrates the ongoing significance of "karmic realism" in the face of modernist attempts to categorize Buddhism as not religious.

In the case of the young nun who drowned in the village of Lo Monthang, Nepal, a reading of her *kyekar,* or "birth star," what one might call her horoscope, revealed that it was her karma to have a short, selfless life. Here, then, is a fascinating parallel to other stories of looking inward that also emerge from a need to respond to the trauma of a sudden death. In this case, however, it is a community, rather than an individual, that must turn to invisible explanations to make sense of death. The young nun's story demonstrates how looking inward allows us to connect common, accepted Buddhist practices and explanations to those inner visions of other figures who seem insane or disturbed. Whether individual or communal, looking inward is a fundamental element of Buddhist culture and practice.

ART, SERVICE, AND A HIGH-RISE TEMPLE
Hŭisang

HWANSOO ILMEE KIM

Almost half of the monastics of the largest Buddhist denomination of Korean Buddhism, the Chogyejong, are nuns. However, because monks control the monastic institution of the denomination, and because lay Buddhists still tend to believe that there is less merit in supporting female monastics, the system prevents highly educated and motivated nuns from thriving in Buddhist circles. Hŭisang (1963–present) represents one of these nuns who, despite these odds, is actively shaping the face of contemporary Korean Mahayana Buddhism.

Korea's "Manhattan" is Haeundae, a booming, skyscraper-filled district located in Pusan, the second-largest city in South Korea. The Yuyŏn Sŏnwŏn (Yes Buddhist Meditation Center) stands among these high-rises in an unlikely place: a commercial and residential apartment complex. It was founded in 2012 by a nun named Hŭisang who converted her apartment into a temple. Comprising about 1,400 square feet, this temple apartment is one of hundreds of such centers around the country. When I saw her last summer, prior to the temple's opening, Hŭisang was standing on a ladder, decorating the walls with Buddhist artifacts that she made by hand. Although she had inherited a village temple in Cheju Island from her teacher, Hŭisang, instead of settling in the rural temple, opted to bring Buddhism to city people.

Despite her productive life as an artist-nun, Hŭisang has faced two professional hurdles. First is the fact that monastics in Korea tend to prioritize Zen practice and experience and thus consider monastics' engagement in anything other than meditation to be irrelevant (at best) and disruptive (at worst). Even though she is an accomplished artist, as attested by people who praise her exhibitions, Hŭisang maintains a low profile. Second, there are few professional opportunities for nuns like her: though half the Chogyejong is made up of female monastics, it remains male-dominated. Despite these impediments, Hŭisang remains convinced that the arts are a great medium through which one can objectify and subsequently transform the sufferings of daily life. She has offered courses in what she calls Zen drawing (Sŏnhwa) at numerous temples in cities across Korea. The opening of her own temple was the natural next step in bringing formal art programs to the public in a more stable environment.

Ordained at twenty-two, Hŭisang graduated from the nuns' monastic college at Unmunsa Temple, where more than 90 percent of the Chogye order's five thousand nuns take residence for at least four years as part of their monastic training. After finishing two three-month retreats, she attended Dongguk University where, in 1996, she earned a BA in modern arts. She then spent eight years at the University of Bremen, receiving a master's degree and also exhibiting her work in Germany and France. Upon returning to Korea in 2004, she taught art courses at her alma mater while she continued to exhibit her work.

Art courses alone cannot support the operation of a temple so, like other monastics who run apartment temples, Hŭisang offers a variety of Buddhist services, including a one-thousand-day prayer and a lecture and discussion session on different Buddhist texts every hundred days. Every Saturday, she gives a dharma talk to her forty to fifty members. Preaching is characteristic of the monastics who run apartment temples like hers. In fact, temples with a regular preaching program hark back to the early twentieth century.

Inspired by Christianity, Japanese Buddhism, colonialism, and other modern forces, Korean Buddhist reformers, spearheaded by Paek Yongsŏng (1864–1940), Han Yong'un (1879–1944), and Kim T'aehŭp (1899–1989), encouraged monks to return to cities from the mountains and establish preaching halls (*p'ogyodang*) to disseminate Buddha's teachings. The reformers claimed that the physical return to central Seoul and other cities would be imperative to attempts to overcome the collective trauma that Korean monastics had undergone during the neo-Confucian hegemony of the Chosŏn dynasty (1392–1910). For example, the neo-Confucian government confiscated vast numbers of temple lands, and over time Buddhist monastics were often thought of as social outcasts. Propagation in cities suddenly became a pressing discourse for modern Korean Buddhism, and the reformers believed that the future of Korean Buddhism depended on these halls. Throughout the colonial period (1910–1945), over four hundred preaching halls, supported by the major temples, were established around the country. However, preaching halls (or temples) founded by individual monks did not appear until the 1980s, and nuns were not part of this development until much later. Thus, this hundred-year history renders Hŭisang's apartment temple unique: without financial support from major temples, and despite her lack of institutional clout, she diligently offers as many rituals and teaching programs as possible.

Two trends in contemporary Korean Buddhism and society have prompted Hŭisang to add two more programs: meditation and mind healing. The recent revival of Sŏn (Zen) meditation, driven by the popularity of meditation in general society, and the Chogye Order's recently enforced retreat-centered curriculum led monastics not to use the term "preaching halls" for their new city temples. Instead, a fashionable new title for the city temples is "meditation centers" (*sŏnwŏn*), although they are not very different from the traditional preaching halls. Sŏn meditation has become the defining feature of contemporary Korean Buddhism.

Another trend is the widespread desire among Koreans for relief from stress. Korean nuns, more so than monks, have taken advantage of this opportunity to earn certificates to practice psychotherapy. Hŭisang has followed both trends. She calls her temple a "meditation center," has incorporated meditation as part of the temple programming, and is also enrolled in the psychotherapy certificate program. She is fully aware that, given the male-dominated nature of Korean Buddhism and the fact that she has limited resources, she must make an extra effort to run her temple. She accepts the subsequent challenges and difficulties as part of her practice.

Hŭisang is typical of many Korean nuns: highly educated, motivated, and conscious of the marginal status of women in Buddhist institutions and Korean society. And so, instead of competing for the administrative positions available to monks, nuns often devote their attention to developing skills for excelling in academic studies, teaching children, and administering social welfare programs. It is no wonder that there is increasing sentiment among Buddhists, including some monks, that the future of Korean Buddhism depends on the leadership of nuns. Hŭisang now has two women as her disciples, and she hopes to help them confront the challenges that they will face as nuns. In the meantime, Hŭisang, like many other nuns, will continue to strive to make a meaningful contribution to Korean Buddhism, one high-rise temple at a time.

STATE SECULARISM AND THE TIBETAN NON-MONASTIC TRADITION
Mr. D

NICOLAS SIHLÉ

Tibetan Buddhism, unlike other Buddhist traditions, has the particularity of comprising a dual clergy: monastic and non-monastic. The practitioners of the non-monastic path, most often called "tantrists" in Western languages and *ngakpa* in Tibetan, have received comparatively much less attention than their monastic counterparts. Mr. D's (1943–present) example shows us how being a tantrist impacts the ways in which contemporary Tibetan practitioners within the PRC negotiate the regulations of a state marked by its relatively inimical brand of secularism.

I keep with fondness a photo of a group of Tibetan Buddhist religious specialists on my desk. These religious specialists are tantrists (Tib. *ngakpa*):

non-monastic specialists of tantric rituals who generally belong to family lineages, with the son typically following in the steps of the father. The men in the picture are the contemporary inheritors of a distinctively Tibetan tradition of Buddhist religious specialization, which, though not devoid of its own religious and historical reasons for pride, has existed in a somewhat subaltern position with regard to the demographically and politically dominant monastic model.

The picture captures a particular moment in early twenty-first-century trends among Amdo (northeast Tibet) tantrists. Encouraged by certain religious masters, tantrists are increasingly beginning to wear the "white [and red] shawl" (*zenkar*) that until recently was mainly a hallmark of elite practitioners among them. When I took the picture in 2011, the twenty or so tantrists who were posing in front of their village temple, almost all wearing the *zenkar*, were still a rare sight. When I inquired why one of the senior tantrists, Mr. D (whom I know well), was among the few not wearing a shawl, Mr. D himself repeatedly avoided answering my question. Other informants were not helpful either, all suggesting vague and unconvincing reasons.

Ultimately I was able to get to the bottom of the mystery, thanks to one of the tantrists in the photo (who knew and trusted me sufficiently to be open about the matter): it had to do with the fact that Mr. D was a retired official, still receiving a state pension, and that as such he was barred from participating—particularly as a specialist—in public religious activity. In the recent past, as Mr. D was taking part in a large regional ritual gathering of tantrists, he had received a warning that this would not do. That day, Mr. D had preferred to interrupt his participation and quickly returned home. He had then become more cautious, at the very least by shedding conspicuous signs of religious identity, such as the *zenkar* shawl.

Mr. D, although an official in the later part of his life, was in fact profoundly involved with the tantrist tradition of his village. Born in 1943 as the grandson of a tantrist, he had embarked on that path, following his grandfather's advice, and had learned in his early teens all the major ritual texts that were practiced in his community. In 1958, all religious activity had then been banned by the Chinese state, a situation that on the whole was maintained for close to two decades. Turning to secular topics, Mr. D had pursued his studies in high school and beyond, and eventually worked as a translator and a teacher. When he finally retired, remembering the words of his grandfather, he returned to the path of the tantrist. Through his encouragement, and sometimes even his financial help, Mr. D played a significant role in the reemergence of a very committed younger generation of tantrists in his village.

But with the warning he received on the day of that large ritual gathering, Mr. D was reminded of a red line that one should not cross within Tibetan areas under Chinese Communist Party rule. And thus the picture has acquired for me another layer of meaning. In the ethnographic thickness of the event captured in the photo, a number of threads are intertwined. Why this particular gathering of tantrists? What are the meanings associated with this current spread of the white and red shawl? And, important for us, what can we learn from the situation of Mr. D.?

There are two key elements of historical and socioreligious context here. The first is that we are dealing with a Buddhist tradition, Tibetan Buddhism, that attempts to live and develop under conditions of strong state secularism—and a rather inimical version of that, to say the least. This particular brand of secularism, inspired by Maoist ideology, has undergone some significant variations since the mid-twentieth century, including an attempt at complete eradication of religion during the Cultural Revolution, but also a policy of liberalization of religious practices starting in the early 1980s. This was subsequently followed, however, by a return—at the end of that decade—to more restrictive regulations, in particular in Tibetan and Uyghur areas, and to brutal suppression when the hegemony of the party-state has been challenged.

The second key element is that Chinese state surveillance of religious affairs cannot work in the same way among tantrists as it does in the monastic sector of Tibetan Buddhism. Tantrists are primarily individual householders who only occasionally congregate for collective rituals. They are not as readily recognizable as monks, as they are marked at the most by a distinctive hairstyle (albeit with regional, generational, and individual variations). Tantrists, if at all present, constitute only a small portion of any given village population. Thus they constitute a very diffuse, noncentralized, and lesser-known form of Buddhist clergy, which, to a large extent, has been able to elude close state surveillance and control since the 1980s. (As many Tibetans are aware, this situation mirrors somewhat the famed resilience of the tantrist tradition at the moment of a breakdown of Buddhist monasticism in the early history of Tibet.) Concretely, parties of local state officials may visit larger ritual gatherings of tantrists; they are welcomed politely, treated to good food, and typically they leave after a while, without really having observed or controlled anything.

It was probably on one of those visits that Mr. D was spotted and given a warning. He himself, however, had no intention of putting an end to his participation in such events, which are key moments at the heart of the tantrist tradition in Amdo. He thus chose simply to adopt a more discreet, cautious presence in later collective ritual gatherings, confident that his tradition afforded a reasonable measure of invisibility to modern Chinese state scrutiny—and shedding the still rather conspicuous white shawl.

A BUDDHIST SPIRIT MEDIUM
Mae Sim OK
VISISYA PINTHONGVIJAYAKUL

In Chaiyaphum, a province of northeast Thailand, spirit mediums contribute a great deal to local Theravada Buddhist culture. They attend meditation, play a key role in monastic activities, and donate a considerable amount of money to temples. Mae Sim OK (1938–present) is a spirit medium who cultivates her magical power in a monastic setting. She exemplifies the idea that Buddhism and local spirit cults are mutually constituted.

Mae Sim OK (b. 1938) is a spirit medium in Chaiyaphum Province of northeast Thailand who lives in a small wooden house, which she enters by cutting through a neighbor's yard. When she was young, her family moved from Chaiyaphum city to a small village in Kaengkhror District. Her father sold his property but left no land for her. She feeds her pigs in the local school grounds and sells them to make a living. Along with other poor spirit mediums in the region, Mae Sim OK understands her life hardships to have brought the visitation and aid of spirits. The stories she tells about her poverty and asceticism reveal the source of her power and charisma.

The "OK" in Mae Sim's name comes from her ability to make people's wishes come true. Men who do not want to be called up for military service, women who want white husbands, villagers whose animals are ill, and those who wish to win lotteries all come to see her. A former minister also relies on her spirit shrine. People know that whatever they bring to her will be "OK." Mae Sim OK's slogan, "I chew and eat chili and salt," connotes that her words are powerful and can bring both auspicious and ominous consequences. Villagers are afraid of making her angry and being cursed. Male villagers do not want her to pass by while they are fishing because they will not catch any fish. Why is this poor old lady so potent and celebrated? From where does she draw her power?

Mae Sim OK obtains power and prestige from her mediumistic and Buddhist practices. She has been a master of her network of mediums for forty years. She said spirits from three master mediums came to stay at her shrine after they passed away, which gave her a shortcut to power and prestige. There is one important rule among practitioners: if the master of a mediumistic network falls ill and is about to die, the disciples have to resign and move to a new network. Otherwise, their health will deteriorate and they will probably die after the master does. The master's shrine functions as a spiritual engine producing and distributing vitality (and potentially death) to the members.

Buddhism and monasteries are crucial domains where Mae Sim OK cultivates her religious virtue and spiritual potency. Even though she is very poor, she donates any items and money that come her way to charity and temples. At seasonal pilgrimages and festivals, she raises a lot of money from her disciples. They can count on Mae Sim Ok to secure their merit (*bun*) and power (*barami*) in the same way lay Buddhists rely on monks as "fields of merit" (*nuea-nabun*). Mae Sim OK follows ethical guidelines similar to those of other spirit mediums: she does not ask for money when she conducts healing rituals or communicates with deities to help her customer-devotees. However, they usually put some money in envelopes and give it to her later.

Spirit mediums divide money from customer-devotees into two parts: for donation and for personal expenses. I know one medium who opened a bank account under the provincial celebrated deity's name, "Phaya Lae." All money from her jobs is put into the account for donation to monasteries. In intimate mediumistic circles, the master's reputation is manifest in the way she deals with money. Mae Sim OK contributes a great deal of money to monasteries. Monks in the village temple asked her to donate and buy items such as a television, a satellite dish, an air conditioner, and construction materials. The concept of well-being to her is not about how much money she has but how many disciples participate in her network and how much faith they have in her. They are the indicator of her "power" (*barami*). At her house, she was proud to show me some items that her disciples gave to her: pillows, blouses, mats, mosquito nets, and so on.

Mae Sim OK lives an ascetic life and intensively engages in monastic activities. On Buddhist holidays, she will stay overnight and practice moral precepts in the temple. At home, she meditates and speaks to her deities in front of the spirit shrine. She had a husband when she was young, but marital life was not for her. Mae Sim OK said that the deities did not allow her to have a husband. They gave her power to help mankind but required that she live a life of celibacy. She shared her story with me about her body being resistant to the pleasures of sexual intercourse. Whenever her husband was about to sleep with her, she became sick and her genitals became swollen and inflamed. However, her disciples and spirit mediums in other networks know that she only lived a nonheterosexual life; she had a same-sex partner.

When visiting temples and local shrines, Mae Sim OK collects offerings and brings them back to her own shrine. They are colorful cloths, plastic garlands, and small human and animal figures that people give to Buddha images and spirits to complete their vows. The concept is to re-enchant and recycle these offerings. She puts them on her private shrine to enhance her power and transforms them into amulets before giving them away to her disciples. One afternoon at Phaya Lae's shrine, Mae Sim OK led me to a big tamarind, which was believed to be the spot where the deity had been killed in the past. She took off some bark, saying that it was the flesh of the deity, and gave some to me. Since we met, many items she gave me cluttered the car I borrowed from my brother for fieldwork.

I remember the first day I visited Mae Sim OK. She took green, pink, and orange cloths from her shrine, plucked some leaves from a street plant, and asked me to open the car door. She confidently wrapped the cloths around the wheel, stuck the leaves in, chanted a mantra, and honked the horn three times. In Chaiyaphum, it is not unusual to see spirit mediums perform rituals, like this one, that are normally conducted by Buddhist monks. Oddly enough, I survived a car accident a few months later. And my brother, who had previously complained about his car being full of strange items, has yet to remove Mae Sim OK's cloths.

AN ACT OF MERIT
Rev. Ratanasara
JONATHAN S. WALTERS

Prior to the opening of its economy in 1977, most of Sri Lanka's rural Buddhists had little direct connection with the modernizing forces by then already at work in the country's more cosmopolitan centers. Modern medicine, machinery, roads, vehicles, homes, sanitation, agricultural practices, banks, higher education, electricity, and English have only recently, and still very unevenly, transformed rural life. Theravada Buddhist monks like Rev. Ratanasara (1972–present) help villagers navigate this transition, mobilizing them to maintain and expand their temple and the Buddhism it serves in the face of a rapidly changing world. His modern affirmation of traditional merit making proves compelling to a broad spectrum of contemporary Sri Lankan Buddhists, urban as well as rural.

It is 10:00 a.m. on November 13, 2012. Distinguished guests cluster around the shrine, newly renovated in artifact-studded concrete. The rest of the crowd extends across this highest plateau and spills down into the court-yard of Magnificent Stone Hermitage. The plateau and the wall encircling it, like the shrine, are strewn with two-thousand-year-old granite pillars and slabs. Cheers of "Excellent! Excellent!" and movement—now clearing a path, now closing in to touch—commence outside the monastic residence and follow Rev. Ratanasara as he processes a Buddha image through the crowd and maneuvers up the new staircase. He places the statue in an unoccu-pied, glass-windowed niche, the last one empty among the twenty-eight that newly surround the hoary Awakening (Bodhi) tree, growing in this an-cient raised bed atop solid rock and fully leafing out again after decades of neglect. Then he descends and joins the crowd. The primary donors, middle-class families visiting this north central Sri Lankan village from the suburbs of Colombo, 200 kilometers distant, unveil the memorial stone on which the details of this moment already have been inscribed. At precisely 10:32 a.m., a monk accompanying them declares the restoration officially complete.

Most of those assembled were here a year earlier for the project's cere-monial inauguration, and without their support the shrine would still consist of propped-up ruins. Rev. Ratanasara, in particular, worked tirelessly—especially during his three-month monastic "retreat"—to meet the self-imposed deadline. He hauled rock and mixed concrete, managed funding, and met production schedules by pouring pillars and fashioning Buddha images himself. Even with generous donations of materials and labor, the project cost SLR500,000 (about US$5000), too rich for overextended local donors who already had restored the ancient stupa (2003–2005), likewise neglected until Rev. Ratanasara arrived in 2000. Fortunately, members of the Sri Jayawardhanapura Joyful Worship Foundation, including a village native, undertook the "primary donor" responsibility. Busloads came from Colombo to join the distinguished guests, prepare the alms meal to follow, or accompany the monk's procession. The urban, rural, poor, rich, male, female, young, old, monks, laypeople, uneducated, and university gradu-ates all earned a proportionate share of the good karma, including that generated by future worshippers. The merit-conducive conviviality was in-tensified by reflections on shared effort, previous Buddhas, and the likeli-hood of future-life, merit-making reunions.

Such karmic realism counters some modernist (and colonialist) claims that Buddhism is not "religious" or that karma and rebirth (and gods, de-mons, heavens, hells, astrology, tree worship) are merely metaphorical, cultural accretions, pious wastes, and/or profit-driven manipulations. Yet these "popular" forms have tenaciously persevered since long before colonialism, modernism, and now post-colonialism and post-modernism. This cross section of contemporary Sri Lankan Buddhists made real sacrifices to preserve a sacred tree and facilitate its worship in the expectation that such meritorious acts result in eventual nirvana.

This is the kind of contemporary Buddhism Rev. Ratanasara practices, even typifies. His previous-life "familiarity" produced a childhood attraction to the orange robes; he knew all the requisite liturgies without ever attending monastic schools. At sixteen he was extrajudicially abducted and detained "on suspicion" by police (1988–1990), traumatically rendering school impossible and life unsatisfying. Even then his overly attached mother refused him permission to renounce, so he farmed the family fields until he was twenty-eight, when she finally relented. Four days after his ordination he was sent to Magnificent Stone Hermitage, where he and everyone believes he had been a monk during previous lives. He quickly attained higher ordination (2002), which, like many subsequent benchmarks, also produced much merit. He built a library, planted gardens, and started a Sunday school and associations for village youth and women. Along with the tree, he brought the whole languishing temple back to life. He promised his left kidney to a beloved village schoolteacher in 2007. When she died while he was being prepped for surgery, he nonchalantly gave it to the next stranger in line. One is born Buddhist, he believes, as a result of previous-life merit. Such a life is best lived by producing more merit in order to progress even further towards nirvana in subsequent lives.

Rev. Ratanasara, like the crowd, affirms this "popular" Buddhism fully aware of other modern "monks who flap their arms for TV cameras . . . so busy being for this or that candidate . . . that they forget what 'monk' means." In his definition, monkhood is an especially effective way to earn merit, which, pursued diligently and sincerely, simultaneously enables many people to do the same thing. This belief informs his understanding of the verse monks chant at their first ordination ("removing every sorrow, experiencing nirvana") and this is how he lives his life.

It pleases this crowd, especially today, which happens also to mark the annual Robe Merit Festival. This ancient, particularly meritorious ceremony is typically one of the year's largest. It marks the end of the monastic "retreat" to reaffirm ties between monks and their supporters, who give the former gifts, beginning with a new robe. Today Rev. Ratanasara has completed his tenth retreat since higher ordination, inching everyone, starting with himself, closer to nirvana. But he is not thinking about gifts. He has combined the ceremonies so the villagers only have to shoulder that burden once. For now. Still, this occasion requires at least the new robe, so Rev. Ratanasara has conceded to that much, doubling everyone's merit. The temple's hangers-on—older men, off track, who find refuge there—have been up since dawn cutting white cloth, dying it orange, stitching it together. Everyone touches the robe as the Temple Committee president carries it up to Rev. Ratanasara, seated in the preaching hall after eating a meal prepared and served by the primary donors.

A BUDDHIST LAY LEADER
Jiang Xiuqin
GARETH FISHER

Buddhism in China has survived many persecutions, not least of which have occurred from campaigns against religion during its recent communist period. Yet it has managed to survive, regrow, and adapt, largely through the creative abilities of both laypeople and monastics, to spread its teachings to new generations. One such layperson in contemporary Beijing is Jiang Xiuqin (1935–present), a one-time Red Guard leader turned active preacher and distributor of Buddhist-themed literature.

I first met Jiang Xiuqin in the outer courtyard of the Temple of Universal Rescue in Beijing on a snowy, windswept day in 2002. She was surrounded by a small crowd who were asking her questions about the role of sutra recitation in healing illness, the significance of certain dates in the ritual calendar, and, in the case of one practitioner, how to determine whether a potential marriage partner was suitable for her daughter. The courtyard is a common place for laypeople to gather and exchange their ideas and experiences as (mostly new) practitioners of Buddhism. Out of these laypeople emerge certain preachers who are particularly knowledgeable about Buddhist teachings. While some of these preachers actively seek out their roles, others enter into them reluctantly. Jiang is one of these reluctant preachers: she told me many times that she despised the atmosphere of the courtyard, where all manner of heterodox views were spread. She claimed that she often just wandered through and, hearing these false views being taught by other preachers, felt compelled to stay and offer her corrections. After she had patiently corrected one or two preachers, other laypeople would crowd around her to ask questions, so that she in effect became a preacher herself.

While Jiang does not actively seek out this "preacher" role, she is a very active leader in the regrowth of Beijing-area Buddhism following its devastation during the Maoist era. Born in 1935, she was fourteen when the People's Republic of China was founded. While in her twenties, she worked at an important guesthouse and once shook the hand of China's former premier Zhou Enlai. During the Cultural Revolution, she functioned as a mentor to younger Red Guards, leading groups of teenagers on marches over and through the Beijing-area mountains. Deeply influenced by Maoist-era critiques of religion, Jiang did not take the refuges as a layperson until the 1990s, after her husband had died. After some years of reciting sutras daily, she claimed to have developed spiritual insights into the fate of her husband and other members of her family: she could see that he had been reborn as a boy in a neighboring county and that her mother-in-law had been reborn in a hell. She also claimed to be able to determine the past lives of others simply by looking at them. She told me that she often kept her head down on buses because it was alarming to look at all of the animal forms around her representing the past lives of the passengers.

By the time I first met her, Jiang was putting the skills she had developed as a Red Guard leader to work in spreading Buddhism. With the same slow, patient, but firm tone of voice with which I had first heard her preach at the Temple of Universal Rescue, she promoted Buddhist teachings to whoever would listen. Even to the ears of a largely atheist public, Jiang's patient explanations of the workings of karmic consequence, sudden manifestations of famous bodhisattvas, and use of sutra recitation to exorcise wayward spirits sounded cogent and persuasive. On my visits to her home, Jiang would often take me to meet her recent converts: a pair of migrant vegetable sellers struggling to make ends meet in a ramshackle store; a young, unemployed man in his forties who had never married and whom she kept trying to persuade to become a monk; and a taxi driver and his girlfriend, whom she educated in Buddhist compassion by taking them on a trip to release fish from the market into a local reservoir. Jiang was also highly active in mobilizing her fellow practitioners to donate their time and money to reprint important Buddhist texts that she thought were insufficiently available, such as sutras like the *Huayan Jing;* hagiographies of well-known monastics; or moral lessons from contemporary Buddhist masters. She also once wrote her own booklet on lessons she had learned from Buddhist teachings that she made into poetry. After collecting money from her impressive network of laypeople and monastics, she would copy the texts she wanted to distribute and then have them handed out at temples. In this way, Jiang engaged in good works that she hoped would improve her own merit while at the same time interesting others in the teachings that had become so meaningful to her.

A widow who turned to Buddhism in earnest after her husband's death was a common figure at many times in Chinese history, as was the practice of printing and distributing religious-themed literature at temples—Buddhist or otherwise—for the purposes of gaining merit. It is certainly noteworthy that, despite modern efforts to repress religion in China, a contemporary laywoman like Jiang Xiuqin, who had once been heavily involved in Communist Party activities, has still gone on to take a leading role in the rapid revival of Chinese Buddhism in the latter part of her life. I would suggest that what distinguishes Jiang Xiuqin most from lay Buddhists in earlier times can be measured as a difference in degree rather than as a difference in kind: as a result of the PRC's aggressive efforts, literacy is much more widespread today than it was in earlier periods. Also, because of modern printing technology, it costs relatively little for Jiang and her fellow practitioners to fund regular projects to print and bind hundreds of Buddhist texts. Jiang has average economic means and only an elementary school level of education. Had she lived in earlier times, she would probably not have been taught to read at all, and could not have afforded even a portion of the funds it would have taken to reproduce hundreds of Buddhist texts on a regular basis. The story of Jiang shows how, in the modern period, it is possible for practitioners with a wide variety of economic means to influence the direction of popular Buddhist discourse with little more at their disposal than a minimum of funds and a large amount of charisma.

A MODERN-DAY BURMESE *WEIKZA*
Bodaw Aungteza
HIROKO KAWANAMI

There is something unique about the *weikza* phenomenon that continues to inspire people's imaginations at the periphery of conventional Theravada Buddhism in Burma. A *weikza* is a charismatic master of esoteric arts who is endowed with extraordinary powers as he waits for the Buddha to come and restore the world order. However, few *weikza* have modern relevance and appeal to contemporary followers as does Bodaw Aungteza (1919–2005).

Bodaw Aungteza was an unusual Burmese Buddhist monk who represented both the traditional features of a saintly monk and the modern characteristics of a layman who appealed to the contemporary sensibilities of Burmese people. He became a monk relatively late in life and settled in the wilderness of Sagaing Hill after an experience of possession, but spent the last decade of his life in the United Kingdom, and then in the United States. I had the good fortune of getting to know Bodaw Aungteza before he passed away in San Francisco on July 17, 2005. He was charismatic and knowledgeable, and enjoyed conversation over a range of topics, from international politics to boxing, his favorite sport. He was followed by urban Burmese devotees as well as political dissidents in the Western diaspora, who flocked to meet him and receive his blessings.

Bodaw Aungteza was born U Ba Win in 1919 in the Ayeyarwady division in the lower delta region. His early life coincided with the country's struggle for independence and the period of postindependence nation building. He was one of those aspiring youths from the countryside who was deeply affected by modern awareness and optimism; he read English newspapers, drank stout (as he could not afford whisky), and looked to the West for inspiration for the country's future. He joined the Union of Burma Boy Scouts, which became an important part of the modern school training in Burma. His experience as scoutmaster led him to a job at Myoma boys' high school in Yangon, one of the first state schools to introduce a Burmese curriculum (as opposed to an Anglocentric one). He was there when the school played an important role in the national educational campaign to imbue young students with patriotism and national pride. The country was in turmoil after the general elections in 1960, with an escalation of ethnic dissent, political instability, and high inflation. As domestic politics degenerated into intraparty squabbles, U Ba Win became an active member of the labor movement. In early 1961, he was invited to attend a labor conference in Kuala Lumpur as a member of the trade union, but the government would not grant him a passport, so as a last resort he applied for a job on a large ship to make it out of the country. The ship, *Aungteza*, was bound for Singapore, but due to heavy seas it capsized on June 7, 1961, eighty miles south of the Mawlamyaing coast, and sixty-nine passengers were reported to have drowned. After several days of rescue efforts, U Ba Win was the only one to be found by a passing boat as he clung on to a floating plank. Later he described this experience as being "reborn" and came to be called "Aungteza."

Within a year, in March 1962, there was a military takeover by General Ne Win and U Ba Win was arrested for taking part in labor strikes. By then he was married to a Japanese woman and had one son, but due to frequent and long intervals spent in jail, the marriage did not last. To add to his grief, his son was killed in a motorbike accident when he was only seventeen years old. Although he had been brought up in a Buddhist family, U Ba Win was not religious; it was only when emotional turmoil and anguish engulfed him that he started to meditate seriously. He practiced calming meditation night and day, and began to see a vision of a higher spiritual being, who frequently commanded him and caused him confusion. For a while he roamed around like a madman, but eventually settled in Theragirí Gyaùng monastery in Sagaing Hill and became a monk. Whenever commanded by the "higher being," he left the monkhood, and during this period his appearance is said to have resembled a *bodaw*, as he wore a turban around his head and a white ceremonial shirt. This was when people started to call him Bodaw Aungteza.

Aungteza eventually settled back into monastic life and meditated in his bamboo hut in front of the pagoda, which he referred to as *dat-khan* or "power room." Burmese Buddhists believe that these power spots are conducive to the cultivation of mind power, and whenever he meditated in his *dat-khan*, there was a residual vibration that made it possible for him to plug into the mysterious current as source of his special powers.

In Burma, *weikza* are known as ascetic practitioners (normally male) who have attained esoteric knowledge, acquired special powers, and can expect to live extraordinarily long lives. According to local beliefs, there are various types of them, and some are known as masters in medicine, alchemy, astrology, or the use of magical inscriptions. Bodaw Aungteza, however, did not fit any of these traditional *weikza* prototypes and did not delve into any of the higher arts or profess to have them. Some saw in him the image of Bo Min Gaung, who was neither a monk nor a *weikza* but was known as a great lay meditator of his generation and had a reputation as a fully realized saint. Bodaw Aungteza never spoke about having any special powers, nor did he show any desire for them. He never solicited cash for giving predictions or received donations for worldly gain. Interestingly, although he had not received any conventional monastic training, he was often summoned by senior monks in the sangha to give them advice and bestow power upon them. His unique ability to communicate with the spirits as well as his understanding of political woes in the secular world came to be endorsed by conventional monks, who appreciated his special ability. The life of Bodaw Aungteza was characterized by bridging the colonial and postcolonial periods, the practices of magic and meditation, religion and politics, lay and monastic life, and East and West.

NEGOTIATING RELIGION AND THE STATE
Khandro Rinpoché

SARAH H. JACOBY

Religion and the state often appear as oppositional forces in studies on Tibetan Buddhism in the People's Republic of China. However, the reforms launched by Deng Xiaoping catalyzed the revitalization of religion in Tibet beginning in the 1980s. Some Tibetans such as Khandro Rinpoché (1954–present) have successfully secured state sanction for projects involving rebuilding religious sites through personal connections, ingenuity, and persistence.

I met Khandro Rinpoché by accident on a public bus heading westward from the city of Barkham in the deep gorges of Gyalrong in far eastern Tibet, part of Sichuan Province. About an hour after setting out, the bus halted on the side of the road by the riverbank. The Tibetan driver gestured to me to follow the procession of passengers walking up a dirt path on the densely forested hillside. Our destination proved to be a famous cave that once housed the eighth-century Tibetan translator Vairotsana. Inside the cave, we met a middle-aged Tibetan woman with long black hair braided into two plaits and wearing a long maroon-colored cloak typical of Eastern Tibet. She sat cross-legged on a low bed, offering blessings and sacred substances to the line of bus passengers and devotees filing up to see her. I wanted to know more about her, who she was and what she was doing in that cave, but the bus driver was already herding his passengers back towards the bus.

I got my chance to learn more about this cave-dwelling female practitioner or *yoginī* the following year, when I encountered her again in downtown Serta, part of Kandzé Tibetan Autonomous Prefecture in Sichuan. There I learned that her name was Khandro Rinpoché, and that she had been born in 1954 in Darlak County, Golok, a Tibetan region comprising the southeastern corner of Qinghai Province. I spent many hours talking with her over several visits, and in her strong Golok dialect—inflected Tibetan, she told me her life story.

Out of everything Khandro Rinpoché told me about herself, she was most eager that I record the story of how she helped her main religious teacher, Khenpo Munsel (1916–1993), rebuild Pönkor Monastery in Darlak after the traumatic years of the Cultural Revolution (1966–1976). Khenpo Munsel was a monastic hierarch of great learning educated at Katok Monastery in eastern Tibet who was particularly renowned for his mastery of the Great Perfection, the pinnacle contemplative teaching of the Nyingma School of Tibetan Buddhism. During the Cultural Revolution, his status as a religious master led to his conviction as a political prisoner. After serving a twenty-year prison sentence, Khenpo Munsel returned to his homeland in Darlak County, where Khandro Rinpoché helped him reestablish himself. In her own words:

> This is important history: since the lama [Khenpo Munsel] had no monastery or summer retreat place, he wasn't pleased to stay in the region and prepared to go to another area. I said don't go. Let's find an opportunity here. We'll go ask the Chinese; they'll listen to us. My husband Püntsok was one of the highest officials in the [local] Chinese government. . . . I went back to Püntsok and Chinese officials and begged them. I appealed to Püntsok on account of our relationship. I also gave other Chinese officials presents of my jewelry and they accepted my request to give the lama the land for his monastery.
>
> . . . Without me the lama would have wandered around. At that time, since he was a prisoner of the Chinese, he didn't have any wealth and had to wear a hat [indicating he was a counterrevolutionary]. At that time he only had three disciples. For six years he had prepared to build the monastery. Various Chinese officials arrived, and not only did they not give him permission to build, they blew smoke into his face and displayed many forms of disrespect. Then, I arrived there. Since my husband was a high-ranking Chinese government official, he went around and made connections here and there and finally obtained the building permit and the lama built the monastery.

Much attention gets paid to the oppositional relationship between Tibetan religion and Chinese state control in Tibet since its incorporation into the People's Republic of China (PRC) in the 1950s. However, the narrative of Chinese state regulation and restriction of religion pitted against Tibetan resistance and religious revitalization does not adequately describe Khandro Rinpoché's situation. Rather, Khandro Rinpoché is an example of someone who has been able to successfully leverage state authority to reinforce her own agenda of rebuilding Tibetan Buddhist institutions and encouraging religious practice. Khandro Rinpoché's life closely mirrors the phases of religious repression and liberalization that mark the past several decades of Tibetan history.

She was born to Golok pastoralist parents in 1954, the year that the PRC officially established its governance of Golok, transforming what had previously been a largely independent confederation of nomadic groups into the "Golok Tibetan Autonomous Prefecture" in Qinghai. By the late 1960s, when

Khandro Rinpoché was in her early teens, the Cultural Revolution was in full swing, entailing the collectivization of Golok's pastoralists into communes and the destruction of all of Golok's fifty-plus monasteries. This resulted in a childhood devoid of external religious symbols and institutions. Nevertheless, Khandro Rinpoché explains that inwardly she felt great devotion to and faith in the Buddhist teachings. In the early 1970s, when she was nineteen, Khandro's parents arranged a marriage for her to a Tibetan man she had never met, Püntsok, who held a position as an official in the local Darlak County Chinese government. Five children followed, making her home life extremely busy, not to mention her responsibilities milking and tending their large herd of yak/cow crossbreeds, as well as entertaining the Chinese officials Püntsok regularly brought home. All this led Khandro Rinpoché to a spiritual crisis that manifested itself in an illness that left her unable to talk. Meeting Khenpo Munsel for the first time in the late 1970s during his brief parole from prison cured her symptoms and turned her mind towards religious practice.

As Khandro Rinpoché's devotion to Khenpo Munsel deepened, Deng Xiaoping initiated a new era of "reforms and opening" (Ch. *gaige kaifang*) that led to the softening of PRC policy against the practice of religion and the rehabilitation of Tibetan lamas who had formerly been imprisoned as enemies of the state. During the 1980s, as these liberalization policies supported the rebuilding of Tibet's destroyed network of monastic institutions, Khandro Rinpoché dedicated herself to this revitalization effort wholeheartedly, one example of which is this account of helping Khenpo Munsel resume his leadership in 1981. Her story underscores both the power of various levels of the PRC state to control religious affairs in Tibet and the complex ways in which religious and state authorities in contemporary Tibet coexist and interrelate.

MOTHER AND SON AND MEDITATION
Lok Bo
JOHN MARSTON

Cambodian Theravada Buddhist practices are deeply rooted at the village level, although this is not to say that profound changes do not continue to take place that relate to increasing mobility and the emergence of a new Buddhist movement of a national character. Lok Bo (1986–present) and his mother, Yiey Lon, illustrate some of the ironies of change and personal practice in the story of how they went to reside at a large meditation center.

In 2001 I arranged to stay for a week in a temple (*wat*) in rural Kampong Cham, Cambodia. When I had no other commitments I hung out in a rough-hewn pavilion on the edge of the *wat* that served as a shelter for people from one particular village during festivals. There, a middle-aged woman I will call Yiey Lon prepared my meals. A farmer with no formal education, she was good-hearted and friendly and devoted to the temple and its monks in an unpretentious way. I also got to know her husband and children, who were open and generous rice farmers and craftsmen. Her youngest son, about fifteen then, did my laundry and was enthusiastic about the small amount of money I paid him. I will call him Bo or "Lok" Bo, using the title he assumed when he became a monk.

In subsequent years, after Bo ordained as a novice, I began to realize that his family and other members of the community regarded him as a bit "off." He was just slightly more in his own world than other people, often in rather charming, childlike ways, such as in the great, excessive enthusiasm he showed for my photographs. When I visited the *wat*, I would typically find him off doing something totally unrelated to what the rest of the monks were doing, such as planting flowers along the roadway leading to the *wat*. Somehow everyone assumed that he would always be a bit different.

It was maybe three or four years after Lok Bo ordained that I heard he had taken up residence at the Cambodia Vipassana Dhura Buddhist Center. The large *wat* was famous as the well-funded meditation school originally created by Ven. Sam Bunthoeurn, who was assassinated under mysterious circumstances. While some feared that the center would fall apart after Sam Bunthoeurn's death, it continued to flourish under the direction of a strong board of directors, with the important participation of several prominent laywomen. Not only had Lok Bo gone there, his mother had also gone with him, apparently because she felt the need to keep an eye on him. She took up residence in the nun's quarters there and began studying *vipassana* (insight) meditation herself.

I visited the meditation center a couple of times after they began living there. I always wondered whether the intensive practice of meditation would in some way bring about a transformation in Lok Bo's character, "curing" him of his peculiarities. Lok Bo seemed to adapt well to the temple's routine but did not appear in any fundamental way transformed. The twist in the story comes with his mother's steady progression in her meditation training, despite the fact that she could not read or write. I eventually heard that she had become a meditation instructor herself. That is to say, *she* was the one who was transformed.

The story illustrates how, at the local and national level, Buddhist temples provide a niche for people like Lok Bo who might otherwise have difficulty fitting in. Further, Yiey Lon's progression from her role as mother and faithful laywoman to that of lay ascetic pursuing the higher goals of meditation reveals the way in which the categories of lay and ordained do not always make sense in Cambodia. It is not unheard of for Cambodian women (and to a lesser extent men) to pursue *vipassana* meditation as they approach old age. Here it seemed to begin almost accidentally, combined with Lon's desire to protect her son. One tends to think of nuns who serve monks as in a different category from those who pursue meditation, and both types of nun as contrasting with women who devote themselves to their families. The story of Yiey Lon suggests the degree to which these categories may be less rigid than we suppose, and how one impulse may feed the other.

Finally, the story is interesting as an illustration of how new institutions, such as the Cambodia Vipassana Dhura Buddhist Center, with a more national orientation, are transforming the nature of Buddhism in Cambodia. Unlike other major Theravada Buddhist countries, Cambodia does not have a significant meditation tradition outside of local *wats* and remote, primitive ashrams. The Cambodia Vipassana Dhura Buddhist Center, which has small offshoot centers scattered around the country, is innovative for clearly having a national vision and for providing a solid institutional framework for meditation. The story offers a glimpse of how mobile Cambodians can be in pursuing religious vocation in a new context; it also suggests how new possibilities are opening up for Buddhist women in the country.

The last time I saw Yiey Lon was a couple of years ago, when she returned to her home village for a religious event to set up boundary stones for a small temple. Her head was now shaved and she was dressed completely in white in the style of a *doun chi* (nun).

RECONNECTING WITH THE LAND (AND THE GODS)
Palchen Lhamo
ANTONIO TERRONE

Vajrayana in Tibet is a form of Buddhism that understands the land of Tibet as inhabited by numerous deities that can interact with realized beings. Benefiting from the recent boom in religious practice in the People's Republic of China, forms of Buddhist divination and visionary revelation continue to be significant activities at the heart of popular Tibetan Buddhism. Palchen Lhamo (1963–present) is a Buddhist diviner who operates in eastern Tibet, where she puts her visionary talent at the service of the local community.

"Hail to the three jewels, the Buddha, the dharma, and the sangha . . . Tseringma is here!" Palchen Lhamo begins to read what she "sees" on the mirror as letters, phrases, and images. Her husband, Tashi Gyaltsen, himself a Buddhist master, assists her in the mirror-divination as a scribe, writing down what she says on a sheet of paper.

Next to the couple, knees and elbows on the floor in a posture of reverence, the customers wait patiently. Spellbound, their eyes open wide in awe and their lips quiver in pious continuous repetition of sacred mantras. Their questions are being answered by the goddess Tseringma, one of the most revered divinities in the Tibetan Buddhist pantheon. Soon their worries will be relieved and their hopes fuelled.

Palchen Lhamo is a female diviner, a profession widely accepted in traditional Tibet. Female oracles, spirit-mediums, and diviners act as a counterbalance to the predominantly male and monastic institutions that have monopolized sacred power, often with substantial political influence. Through Palchen Lhamo's meditation, Tseringma, who is a mountain goddess and Buddhist protector, gives advice regarding weather forecasts, journey-related concerns, health alarms, financial dilemmas, and family difficulties. Her prophetic answers are often convoluted and require her husband's explanation and clarification. They also always require the patron to perform some type of spiritual practice such as make a pilgrimage journey to a sacred site and/or a donation to Buddhist institutions. In addition, the patron leaves a discretionary donation to the couple for their service, as Palchen Lhamo, in the pure spirit of Buddhist practice, does not require fees for her divinations.

Today, as a Buddhist tantric specialist couple, she and Tashi Gyaltsen live a life dedicated to Buddhist practice, focusing on achieving spiritual experience and building their own community of followers. For more than thirty years they have followed their root teacher, Dechen Osel Dorjé (1921–2010), one of the most popular tantrist masters in Nangchen in the Yushu Tibetan Autonomous Prefecture in Qinghai Province, in order to cultivate their spiritual achievements. While Palchen Lhamo has developed her divinatory skills and put her prophetic talent in the service of her devotees, her husband is known as a visionary who retrieves Buddhist scriptures. Emphasizing tantric over sutric sources, and favoring meditative and contemplative techniques over the scholastic and philosophical aspects of Buddhism, noncelibate tantrist Buddhists such as Palchen Lhamo and Tashi Gyaltsen represent several religious traditions emblematic of Tibetan Buddhist history and culture. One such tradition is that of the "treasures," or *terma* in Tibetan, which refer to both objects and scriptures that the eighth-century Indian saint Padmasambhava allegedly concealed in the Tibetan soil and sky for the welfare of future generations. He pledged that his closest disciples would reincarnate repeatedly to help disclose those hidden treasures and assist in their dissemination.

Over the past three decades, many Tibetans have strived to revive their religious and cultural traditions and to identify with their past. Due to decades of suppression and control, revelation and divination are two of the ways in which Tibetan Buddhist leaders and other religious professionals have reconnected with their cultural heritage. Since Deng Xiaoping's reforms and campaign to embrace the market economy and tolerate certain civil liberties, religion has been allowed to become part of people's lives again. However, although the Chinese constitution guarantees "freedom of religious belief," this does not mean the Tibetans have complete freedom as religious believers. The publication of regulations on religious policy and political education, as well as the frequent launching of patriotic education campaigns in Tibetan areas, enforce restrictions on religion.

Since the founding of the People's Republic of China in 1949, religion has received various degrees of attention, ranging from condemnation under the ideological concerns of Marxist-Leninist theories, to tolerance in the early Deng Xiaoping era, to acceptance within limits in the recent years under Hu Jintao and currently Xi Jinping. During the iconoclastic decade of the Cultural Revolution (1966–1976) launched by Mao Zedong, religious professionals like Tashi Gyaltsen and Palchen Lhamo were physically and verbally abused and sent to labor camps for reeducation under charges of engaging in counterrevolutionary activities, encouraging superstitious beliefs, and supporting what was seen as a feudalistic society. Since the 1980s, although religion is tolerated, control has been imposed on expressions of religious fervor and on every religious group and institution that does not conform to Chinese laws on religious practice. Despite this political agenda, however, many Tibetan traditions have managed to survive, including religious professions such as treasure revelation and divination.

Nowadays, Tashi Gyaltsen and Palchen Lhamo's activities are tolerated as part of a policy to preserve Tibetan (and all ethnic minorities') cultural heritage. When not performing divination for a living to support their family, the couple travels across Tibet to visit sacred places on pilgrimage, receive blessings from various Buddhist masters, perform meditation retreats in caves and hermitages connected with Tibet's ancient history, and occasionally erect Buddhist reliquary stupas and other monuments. Until Tibetans' sense of loss in a rapidly modernizing world with the prospect of an uncertain future dissipates, Buddhist professionals like Tashi Gyaltsen and Palchen Lhamo will thrive in their attempt to revive traditions and reconnect their fellow devotees to the Tibetan sacred land and its divine lords.

A BUDDHA IN THE MAKING
Maniyo
SANDYA HEWAMANNE

Sri Lanka is undergoing massive social, economic, and cultural changes, and religious practices are consequently adjusting, accommodating, and changing with the times. It is in such conflicted times that charismatic religious figures such as Maniyo (1967–present) emerge with creative new combinations of varied religious discourses and practices. Maniyo fills a lacuna wherein village women who have migrated to work in global factories are looking for new forms of social, political, and spiritual leadership that are more in line with their changing senses of self.

Maniyo's ashram was about a kilometer east of the holy city of Anuradhapura. Although the city's infrastructure has developed significantly in the last few years, these narrow byroads were rutted and weedy, and the newly whitewashed splendor of the ashram seemed incongruous. A young man asked us to wait until Maniyo ("Respected Mother," a common term for female ascetics or shamans/astrologers) could receive us after her morning rituals. Soon she came to the parlor and beckoned us to sit on some cushions at her feet. Wearing a long brown skirt and white blouse, she looked the same as other Sri Lankan women her age.

According to her sister-in-law, Maniyo was very educated and beautiful. Many men wanted to marry her, but she refused. She was private secretary to a senior cabinet minister, later a presidential candidate, and when he was assassinated at a political rally, she was devastated. She lost interest in worldly things and spent a few years at home. At the urging of her sister-in-law, Maniyo started teaching Katunayake Free Trade Zone workers computer literacy for a nominal fee. She took to it with enthusiasm and spent extra hours helping weak students. Although the family home was not far from Katunayake, she moved to a boardinghouse to spend more time with her students and gradually developed a reputation as a person to approach when in trouble. She helped not only with wise counsel but by networking with NGOs. The workers affectionately called her "elder sister" and spent time with her whether they had troubles or not.

At some point, a rumor circulated that Maniyo was having an affair with the nineteen-year-old son of the house where she boarded. She was in her early forties, and the relationship was considered highly inappropriate. Verbal battles broke out in the home, and one turned into an ugly public scene. Maniyo responded by marrying the young man the next day. Within weeks, they bought land in Anuradhapura and built a hut. Maniyo's sister-in-law thinks the young man is more of her personal assistant than her husband. Maniyo started meditating at the ancient Buddhist site of Ruwanwalisaya, where she also recited Buddhist protection verses to the crowds. Word of her piety spread, and people came from the neighborhood, other towns, and finally Colombo. Unsolicited donations from rich followers built her new ashram.

I visited her in October 2010, three years later. She called herself a "son of a Buddha," a term normally used only for monks. She also said that she was ready to become a Buddha and was waiting to receive final permission when the future Buddha, Maitreya, appears. We talked about her time in the Free Trade Zone and her current connection to the workers. Most of her original followers are now married, and although they visited at first, they were soon caught up in their own lives and could no longer come as often as they wished. "I have advised these young women repeatedly not to get married and lose their independence, but they did not listen. They are regretting their choice. I am just trying to save at least some of the younger crowd."

Maniyo disapprovingly mentioned a ceremony in which Free Trade Zone workers entered the Buddhist nuns' order. She said they began their religious journey at her ashram but were later influenced by one of the nuns. Maniyo offered an astute critique of the nuns' order by noting how nuns are treated as second-class citizens by monks and laypeople. She was especially upset about women not having the right to be initiated as full members of the order and having to remain novices all their lives, kneeling in front of "little boys who put on robes because of poverty." She also felt that many laypeople revile nuns and think they all have sad histories with men or that their own moral wrongs forced them into the order. "I myself don't have much respect for nuns who try to find their self-worth and security by joining an order that marginalizes them," she noted.

Maniyo's Buddhism, a mixture of textual understanding and folk practices, evinces a woman stretching the boundaries of normative religious roles and creating a path that women can follow. Maniyo is not the only Sri Lankan woman to become a lay ascetic. Many have gone into trances and become healers or soothsayers, but their fame is local and short-lived; they fail to attract the urban elite or educated middle classes. Maniyo's education, fluency in English, knowledge of textual Buddhism, and "refined" manners set her apart from trance-related female asceticism. She started her ascetic life only after creating a group of followers and did not have to perform miracles or be possessed by a god. She took pride in her "direct connection" to the future Buddha and the twenty-eight past Buddhas, which made her more appealing to urban, middle-class, and educated clientele, who are skeptical of folk beliefs in gods and miracles. Maniyo's mixture of textual Buddhism and modern, cosmopolitan thinking appeals to both their spiritual needs and the requirements of their modern lives.

Maniyo's success has depended on personal charisma, economic independence, and cultural capital that enabled her to network in both Colombo and Katunayake. She has presented urban middle classes with a new model that combines the conventional and the new in a creative way. Chanting verses from old texts and conducting prayer rituals per her clients' instructions (the purest form of prayer, according to Maniyo) while remaining an independent woman ascetic is one example of Maniyo's inward-looking practice. She also presented Free Trade Zone workers with a different type of female ascetic. Further, offering a religious model derived from the Buddhist monastic establishment as a solution to the social class and gendered problems with which Free Trade Zone workers struggle would seem to prevent workers from reflecting on their exploitative working conditions. In other words, charismatic religious leadership may be detrimental to workers' collective resistance. Maniyo represents a new kind of partial renunciate, an independent woman who moves fluidly between the middle-class, urban clientele who sustain her ashram and a gender specific group of industrial workers who remain her faithful followers.

Although it was purely by chance that an educated, middle-class woman ended up helping a group of female Free Trade Zone workers, the manner in which she embarked on a mutually beneficial spiritual relationship with them speaks volumes about the particular moment in history when village women who have migrated to work in global factories develop new senses of selves and look for new forms of social, political, and spiritual leadership. The difficult question, however, remains: Is Maniyo another barrier to workers' empowerment? The answer is not clear. After all, she ended her diatribe against the current status of the *bhikkhuni* order with: "Girls try to find solace in belonging to the order, just like they did with families, factories, and boyfriends. I tell them to find their own religious path and live virtuous lives as they see fit and not follow blindly."

THE SINGING NUN
Ani Choying Drolma
CARINA PICHLER

Ani Choying Drolma (1971–present) is known as "the singing nun." Her extraordinary story started with family struggles as a young girl in Nepal. It was the main reason for starting a new life in the monastery as a Vajrayana Buddhist nun. Now she tours the world and shares her spiritual songs through which she spreads the teachings of the Buddha.

Ani Choying Drolma, "the singing nun," lives in Nepal and travels around the world to share her spiritual songs with people. The lyrics in Nepalese and Tibetan language carry the messages of the dharma: *May my heart always be pure. May my speech always be enlightened. May the soles of my feet never kill an insect.*

When she is singing on stage, she is sincerely devoted to the moment and seems to be in a kind of meditative state. Her voice is soft, the music melodious. It feels like a personal, intimate sharing, and when the sound of her voice fills the room, the atmosphere becomes warm and calm. She appears almost vulnerable, but at the same time full of inner strength and confidence.

Ani Choying feels great gratitude for being blessed with the ability to sing and having the opportunity to share her songs with so many people, especially as a nun, which is very unconventional. She describes it as her offering to people. Some may gain a deeper understanding of the dharma through her music and others may just enjoy the soft melodies. Both are fine, according to her, as everything that makes people feel comfortable through listening to her songs is valuable. Rather than aiming to inspire people and trying to make them change, she sees greater value and effectiveness in inner changes of oneself for creating real change. She also applies this approach to social injustices such as gender inequality and domestic violence.

However, even though she is most concerned with the "inner life," she acts in the world. The income generated from her shows, CDs, and books is used to support educational opportunities for women in Nepal. One year after producing her first CD, Ani Choying founded the Nuns' Welfare Foundation in 1998. Her main project is the Arya Tara School, which was established in 2000 and provides education for young girls living as nuns in Kathmandu. She now wishes to provide these girls with the safe and secure environment that she herself was unable to experience in her childhood.

Currently seventy-five girls whom she lovingly calls her "daughters" are living at the nunnery school. She wishes to support them in realizing their own potential so they can be comfortable and confident. Considering the suppression many women in Nepal have to face, such inner change would not only benefit the girls themselves but also pave the way for greater respect and social recognition.

Ani Choying describes social inequalities as being mainly rooted in ignorance—not only that of the suppressors but also of women who suppress themselves by ignoring their own value and potential and blindly believing in their inferior status. "Reacting with anger to injustices in society requires a lot of effort and creates disharmony," says Ani Choying. "Whereas confidence and kindness naturally attracts social acceptance and respect." Since she had faced violence from her father as a child and had not been able to protect her mother from his assaults, Ani Choying longed for her own adult life to be different from that of her mother and of so many other women she knew.

She decided to avoid getting married and living a family life. A way to escape such a future was to enter the nunnery, which she did at the age of thirteen. At that time she was driven by anger towards society for the injustices that she had experienced herself and that she had observed around her. She describes how she managed to transform negative emotions into more positive ones by changing her perceptions with the help of the dharma. Today she is able to use the energy that once was anger to help others. "However bad a situation might seem, in the end it is about how we decide to look at it," Ani Choying says. During our interview and follow-up discussions in Bangkok, she stressed the role of perceptions for forming our realities, a message that is also expressed in the lyrics of her songs:

In the eyes of flower, the world appears as flowers.
In the eyes of thorn, the world appears as thorns.

The two people whom she describes as having inspired her most in her life are her father and her teacher: her father showed her both strong hate and love, and her teacher applied the Buddha's teachings in his life and supported her with loving-kindness. To her, the dharma helped her transform her mind from destructive tendencies to more helpful ones and supported her in analyzing and confronting her feelings.

Ani Choying's life seems to be marked by contrasts: having experienced a polarity of emotions from her father as a child, today she receives both high praise and highly critical responses to her unconventional ways as a nun. How does she deal with criticism? "I don't care," she answers straightaway. "Instead of letting ourselves be destroyed by critical voices, we should keep walking our own way with confidence," she says.

Despite her success, Ani Choying does not allow herself to be impressed by the celebrity status that people accord her. She feels gratitude for being treated well but is also aware of the potential traps for the ego. She describes herself as having a long way to go to achieve enlightenment and says that she still has to deal with emotions like anger and irritation. Though carrying the roles of a woman, a nun, a singer, and so on, she does not seem to be attached to these labels but describes herself simply as a human being.

THE ONLY BUDDHIST IN THE VILLAGE
Sum
HOLLY HIGH

The dominant ethnic group in Laos practices Theravada Buddhism. As a result, Buddhism is a key cultural marker of mainstream modernity in that nation. Members of ethnic minorities in Laos are often non-Buddhist, although some will adopt Buddhism as a part of a project of self-refashioning, as the example of Sum (1980–present), the Kantu trader, shows.

Sum arrived and sat inside the party leader's house: she clearly had business with him, but when she addressed him he ignored her. I asked her why she had come. She did not answer, but looked at the party leader with a frown. He did not return the eye contact. He eventually asked me if a decade-old newsletter in the dusty pile of papers he was suddenly absorbed in was written in English. It was. I crawled under my mosquito net. The two of them were still sitting in silence as I drifted off to sleep. The next day I visited Sum in her little house and store. It was just the two of us, so I asked her about the incident. She said she thought he was jealous that I had given her some soap the day before, even though I had conspicuously given him a larger gift. Another time, she told me, he had threatened to cut off her electricity when guests came to eat in her store. "I never do anything out of line. I never say anything wrong. When there is a crowd, I keep silent. But people in this village hate me. . . . People from elsewhere like me. I speak a lot with strangers, but I do not speak at all with people in my own village. . . . The Party leader is angry with anyone here who is my friend."

In fact, the chatty, giggly Sum does have local friends, but it is also true that she stands out. Unlike most other ethnic Kantu, she regularly attended

Buddhist festivals in a neighboring town to make merit for her deceased relatives. Usual Kantuic ideas of the supernatural are focused on an array of spirits, most notably those of deceased ancestors, the forest, villages, and houses. Diviners and mediums can communicate with spirits, but most ritual activity is direct, with supplicants sacrificing animals without the mediation of permanent religious specialists. Although beliefs in spirits form an important undercurrent of Lao Buddhism, its temples and monkhood censure the slaughter of animals and thus present a strong counterpoint to Kantu supernaturalism. This was a contrast that Sum embraced, along with other markers of difference. While social interaction among Kantu men, women, and children centers on sharing a sweet tobacco pipe, Sum did not smoke. The handwoven textiles produced and worn by women in her village are ethnically distinct, but Sum wore jeans. She was the only person in the village who lived entirely on her own, a situation unthinkable for most Kantu because ancestral spirits indicate their displeasure at nonreproduction by imposing illness on the living. This morality, often glossed as "listening to the mothers and the fathers," keeps families close, sometimes claustrophobically so. Embracing Buddhism was, for Sum, part of a project to escape from familial expectations and other aspects of her past.

Sum's parents had died when she was still a child and the entire village was living in a remote, mountainous part of eastern Laos. All village residents are obligated to remain within the village for a period when a new house is built, but her father had broken this prohibition. The village spirit took its retribution and no one could cure him. Sum's mother struggled to feed the family, but she eventually died of hunger when Sum was six. She, her brother, and two sisters then went to live with her mother's brother. One sister died then. Growing up, Sum remembers that her uncle gave her little food, beat her about the head with a stick, and made her work very hard. She explained that in the old village violence was common and no one would intervene. Always hungry, she developed a reputation as a thief but claims she was only stealing to eat. Once, when her uncle caught her stealing food, he nailed her hand to the floor.

The entire village was relocated to a more accessible area in 1996. She remembers that some foreigners were so moved by the sight of her walking out of the mountains in tattered rags, shoeless, and carrying a heavy load that they gave her a hat and shoes. Two years later, Sum ran away to a shoe factory in Vientiane, while her brother went to Thailand. Troubled by a dream of her sister bleeding from the mouth, she set out for home after only five months away. She arrived to learn that her sister was dead. The uncle had arranged a marriage. Unhappy with the match and unable to escape it once the bride-price had been paid, the sister drank rat poison fifteen days after the wedding. Deep in mourning and determined to forge an independent path, Sum found work and began to build a small house and store.

In her store Sum accepts a bowl of rice in exchange for tiny packets of merchandise (MSG, salt, sweets). She sells the rice to traders, making sure she turns a profit even though she never did learn how to read or write. She also lends money within the village at 30 percent per month. According to village gossip, she does not have a husband but sleeps with visiting men (civil servants, workmen, and traders) and then asks them for whatever assistance they can offer, a bold behavior well nigh unthinkable under Kantu supernaturalism. The party leader and Sum are similar in that way, spending a great deal of time talking to newcomers and exploring the possibility of the connectivity and flows they might offer. But while the party leader is feared and grudgingly admired for his ability to negotiate skillfully with the inundation of outsiders that now visit the Kantu, Sum is often ignored or disparaged. When Sum asked me how she could attract more foreigners to her store, I suggested that she convert it to a more traditional Kantu-style thatched structure. She replied that doing that would require an animal sacrifice and the assistance of many people to collect and bundle the thatch. Though most houses in the village today are built with such reciprocal, spiritually sanctioned labor, she explained that such activities were now barred to her.

While Sum was hurt by this marginalization, she was not defeated by it. Rather, she keeps her Buddhist offering bowl on top of her color TV, which is next to her fridge—luxuries few others in the village can afford. Her Buddhism is part of this larger effort to establish connections and possibilities beyond the small, poor, and sometimes violent world in which she grew up. It offered her an alternative way to respect and honor her dead relatives, and to claim respect and honor for herself.

STARS FOR THE DROWNING
A Young Nun
SIENNA R. CRAIG

The principal figure in this vignette is not a famous scholar or practitioner but an unnamed young nun (dates unknown) from a village on the northern Nepali border with Tibet. In the story of her untimely death, we learn about how Tibetan Buddhism informs the principles and practices of everyday lives in Himalayan communities.

Tashi arrived in the village of Lo Monthang harried, his face pale. "There has been an accident," he said. This young man from the Kingdom of Lo, a culturally Tibetan enclave of Nepal's Mustang District, flung himself down on the bench outside his uncle's hotel and explained. "Some nuns were playing beside the river while the abbot was managing construction on the new nunnery, out between Thinkar and Kimaling villages," he began. "They were washing their robes, having fun." I could imagine the scene: sweet young girls, heads newly shaven, bathed in the warm light of summer. I'd seen them the previous afternoon, laughing near a glacial stream, lounging on tussocks of summer grass, eating Chinese army biscuits, and sucking on hard candy. It was clear that they were still growing accustomed to this new life as religious women.

Tashi's next words shattered this bucolic image. "Several of the nuns decided to play in a pool villagers had dug for irrigation. The mud on the bottom was thick, sticky. Two of the girls got sucked under and started to drown. None of them can swim." In many Tibetan communities, swimming is not a skill most people learn. Rivers and streams remain lifelines—pulsing like veins through this high, dry landscape—but also harbingers of misfortune and unpredictability. The element of water (*chu*) is fickle here.

"They began to shout. Others came to help," Tashi continued. "They unwound their robes and threw them out to these girls. One was pulled out first. She was freezing and in shock. Her friend, the second one, was near death once they got her out. We tried to revive them, but it may already be too late for the second girl."

Tashi's words spilled forth. "I've returned to get Lhundrup," he said, referring to a local man with minimal biomedical training who staffed a health post and, in a land still dominated by foot traffic and horses, had a motorcycle. Quickly, we gathered thermal blankets and hand warmers my colleagues and I had been using for our research project that summer, hoping that these might help revive the nuns. Tashi and Lhundrup took the supplies and flew away on the medic's Honda Hero—an unlikely ambulance, stirring up dust, carrying some hope.

By early evening, Tashi called to say that despite Lhundrup's efforts to perform CPR and warm both girls, the second nun had died. The abbot and the parents of this lost child were distraught. Over the coming days, explanations of this event began to course through the lives of this community. Even as people whispered in empathetic tones, they also spoke about how such an inauspicious event negatively marked the building of this nunnery. Perhaps it would be a year filled with obstacles. Perhaps a local serpent spirit who lived in this pond had been disturbed by the girls' antics. Perhaps an autochthonous deity of earth had not been properly propitiated during the groundbreaking ceremony for the new nunnery and was now seeking revenge. The abbot was kind and a skilled Buddhist practitioner, but local cosmic balance might have come unhinged, villagers speculated, for such an unfortunate event to have occurred. Here, as in other Tibetan Buddhist communities across highland Nepal, scriptural renderings of the dharma lived alongside strong senses of sacred geography and the need to honor distinct forms of local power.

Soon after the young nun's death, an even more specific narrative emerged around this incident. The story not only continued to emphasize cosmological probabilities of the sort described above, but also became connected to Tibetan Buddhist astrology: concrete signs, as in stars, to be deciphered. Specifically, it rested on conceptions of karma as they surfaced through the abbot's consultation of the dead nun's natal horoscope.

The girl had had a reputation for being generous. She had apparently insisted that the girl drowning beside her be rescued first. Despite her youth and her "lower" birth as a woman, people ascribed to her—now, in death—the qualities of *bodhicitta,* a mind that strives towards the awakening of others. I wondered if it made a difference that this lost child was a nun not a monk, a girl not a boy, a daughter not a son. Rumors circulated that when she was pulled from the murky pond, before she lost consciousness, she whispered, "Tell my parents not to worry. I will be okay. It is my karma to die now."

Upon hearing this, the abbot asked the girl's parents if he could examine her *kyekar,* the encoded reckoning of her "birth star" that would have been prepared shortly after her birth. Here in Mustang, the preparer of the horoscope was likely a tantric householder priest, and may have also been a practitioner of Tibetan medicine. Now, before throwing the horoscope into the hearth fire—an act to help this girl's consciousness find rebirth—the abbot reviewed the document. It confirmed that her life span was foretold to be short.

Clifford Geertz argues that we human animals are suspended in webs of significance, or webs of culture, that we ourselves have spun. With respect to Tibetans, Geoff Childs (2004) writes that their "life course is sketched out in rough form at birth, and can be ascertained in part through astrological reckonings. One's path through life's trials and tribulations is greatly influenced by the accumulated actions of previous lives. The key to understanding one's life course is in the stars." In this way, what was a horrible accident also became understandable in distinctly cultural terms, through an analysis of the victim's horoscope.

The young nun was given a sky burial. The household would grieve for the forty-nine-day period of the *bardo,* the liminal realm between death and rebirth in Tibetan tradition. Villagers would remember this event as part of the history of this nunnery. Even so, despite the failure of local efforts to save the lives of both girls, this young nun's death was made cosmically comprehensible. Far from being simply "fatalistic," this reckoning of the purpose, duration, and scope of one human life was contextualized within a broader understanding of core Buddhist concepts—karma, *bodhicitta,* and reincarnation—in a particular cultural milieu. We can also view this story as an example of the more broadly human struggle to accept death, particularly of a young, vibrant person who had also decided (or whose parents had decided) that her life should be devoted to Buddhist practice.

The circumstances surrounding this event were inherently modern: a foreign patron was supporting the restoration of this Himalayan nunnery; a worldly abbot with his iPhone in one hand and his prayer beads in the other was overseeing this work; a health worker rushed off on a motorcycle to intervene. Yet the explanation of misfortune resonated with centuries of Buddhist sense-making.

ALIEN BEHAVIOR
One Man
GRANT EVANS

With government restrictions, economic conditions, and the slow recovery of monasteries after the war and subsequent Marxist crackdowns of the 1970s and 1980s, the path to becoming a Theravada Buddhist monk in Laos is very difficult. Moreover, mental health care in Laos is rare and often of poor quality. These conditions make the life and work of "One Man" (1950–present) even more remarkable.

Either in defiance or ignorance of notions of patient confidentiality, the entrance to the psychiatric unit at the main hospital in Vientiane had a list of its patients written on a whiteboard on the wall, including the reason for their admission: "Schizo, . . . Schizo," and so it went down the list until patient number 8, who reportedly had trouble sleeping. In a country where little psychiatry is practiced, wider disputes about the very category "schizophrenic" remain unknown, let alone elaborations like "bipolar disorder" and so on, beloved of psychiatric establishments. In Laos "schizophrenic" simply means *baa,* crazy. My friend was listed as "schizophrenic," though he insists that what he had (and has) is a "genetic" disease. Scientists who are on the trail of the genetic basis of schizophrenia and all other mental disorders would love to agree with him. However, his characterization of his disorder was in fact a typical somatization of it in Laos (as in many other places in Asia) where "genetic" is simply the new code word.

My friend is an alcoholic who spurns modern hard liquor favored by the new rich (Johnnie Walker Blue, etc.) and drinks only *lao khao* or *lao lao,* a backyard pure white whisky distilled from rice. As he would insist, a physical disease requires strong physical treatment, and *lao lao* always does the trick!

I had known for a long time that my friend was not normal, and so when I saw an English copy of the *I Ching* in a secondhand bookshop I knew it was the perfect gift for him while he was in the hospital doped up on Valium and other drug cocktails in place of the *lao lao.* The hexagrams, I thought, should keep him focused for weeks. I did not expect him to begin to translate it into Lao, however.

My friend had been a monk for three months before I went to visit him in the psychiatric ward. He had entered the monkhood in early 2000 as a result of his mother's death. Many Lao do this, if even only for half a day, as a way of earning merit for the deceased. His family and I tried to convince my friend that perhaps the temple was the best place for him. It was quiet, he could meditate, and he would not have to worry about where his next meal was coming from. It almost worked. But his propensity to pose unorthodox philosophical questions to the monks—that is, a mixture of Buddhist, Hegelian, and Marxist-Leninist queries—soon exhausted them and him, and so he left. He swears he never drank alcohol while a monk, but his desire for a drink was a good reason to leave too. Soon after that he was in the psychiatric unit.

After he was discharged, he retreated to a cave in Vang Vieng, 106 kilometers north of Vientiane, where he lived for eight months and worked on the translation. His father, who runs a resort close by, kept an eye on him. But the father had rather hastily taken a new wife (as Lao men are wont to do after the death of their wives), and so my friend was keeping his distance—not, however, from the local villagers, for whom he used the *I Ching* for fortune-telling.

He began the translation of the *I Ching* as an act of memory for his mother, whose father was Chinese—a kind of retrospective acknowledgment of Chinese descent. The *I Ching* also offered him another avenue of philosophical exploration and speculation beyond Buddhism.

He retranslated the whole of the Wilhelm version during mid-2008 to 2009, this time doing a digital version. It was subsequently "improved" by his looking at other English versions on the Internet, and by consulting *I Ching* Web sites all over the world. He joined *I Ching* Reader Groups in the United States and entered into e-mail exchanges with them. He was their Lao outpost. The aim was to publish the *I Ching* in Lao, and I tried to advise him on how to raise money from the Chinese community.

During this period he became monk again at Phatang temple in Vang Vieng as a way of avoiding a brewing family dispute over inheritance (all too common these days when land prices have gone through the roof). However, it was only for ten days, after which his "disease" once again "invaded his body."

In 2012 he became a monk at the Lao National Moral Vipassana Meditation Training Centre just outside Vientiane to try to overcome his alcoholism. He became an assistant trainer for Lao, and a junior guru for thirteen foreigners because he could speak English. He began meditation in what he called the "cremation hole," that is, where monks reflect on the transience of life by contemplating death. At first he could meditate for twenty-four hours, then six, but finally he collapsed. He resigned after five and a half months because, he explained, "my disease erupted again." It did not help that there were differences between the monks about correct meditation procedures, and for someone whose mind is never in equilibrium anyway, being pulled this way and that by temple factions was intolerable. To compound his struggles, his computer died and the *I Ching* ascended into digital heaven, leaving only the prerevision, handwritten original that he had made in the cave. If my friend's translation ever appears in Lao, it will not be seen as Buddhist or non-Buddhist by most people. They will just add its hexagrams to their ever-widening religious repertoire.

The ability to move frequently, obtain a semblance of secular hospital care, and have access to the Internet and multiple sources of non-Buddhist philosophies and religions are certainly things that are particularly modern about my friend's life in Laos. However, all of these modern options had no effect on his struggle with alcoholism, which, as in many places, has neither been caused nor fixed by our modern condition.

THE LIFE AND TIMES OF A SHAN BUDDHIST
Ay Phit
NICOLA TANNENBAUM

Somsak Maniipratom (Ay Phit) was a young man from the Shan community in Maehongson Province, northwestern Thailand. He lived his life during a transitional period when Maehongson was becoming incorporated into the larger Thai political, economic, and social worlds. While Ay Phit's (1969–2003) life is not typical of most village boys, the ways in which he engaged with the local Buddhist context provides some insight into these changing times.

Somsak Maniipratom, or Ay Phit as I knew him, was a young man from the Shan community of Thongmakhsan in Maehongson Province, northwestern Thailand. He was born on September 18, 1969, and died on September 1, 2003. His life is important, not because he was an ideal or particularly dedicated Buddhist practitioner, nor was he a famous teacher or even particularly devout. However, this short snapshot of his life reveals the way Buddhist activities pervade every part of normal village life in Maehongson.

I first met Ay Phit in the summer of 1977 when I was in Thongmakhsan exploring dissertation research possibilities. I returned to the community in 1979–1981 and stayed with Ay Phit and his grandmother. Ay Phit's parents are alive and well but he chose to live with his grandmother when his parents moved to their own house. At ten, Ay Phit was a bright, funny boy. I liked him a lot. At the time he was in second or third grade.

When I finished my dissertation research, I left money to help sponsor Ay Phit's and the son of my best friend, Ay Phan's, ordination as Buddhist novices, which would be held when they were eleven or twelve. Shan in the area are Theravada Buddhists and typically ordain boys as novices who keep ten precepts rather than the 227 precepts of fully ordained monks. These ordinations are not lifetime commitments but rather act as rites of passage for the boys and for the parents who sponsor them. These sponsorships were a way of thanking the people I knew, but also of maintaining the relationships we had forged.

Ay Phit's childhood was a privileged one; grandmother doted on him. She ran one of the two small sundry shops in the community, and Ay Phit could take candy and other treats from the store. Ay Phit's life was going well. He had opportunities not available to every child in Thongmakhsan and the intellect and ambition to pursue them. At the time, he was the only student from Thongmakhsan who finished high school. Except for his access to education, his childhood was typical of most boys. And his interactions with local Buddhist practices were also typical: as a little boy he went to the temple with his grandmother; he spent two weeks as a novice monk in the Thongmakhsan temple; and he helped sponsor his cousin's ordination as a novice. Like most young adult men, he didn't go to the temple services.

Once he graduated, however, things started going badly. He could not find a job that suited him and he didn't want to farm because he had been in school and had not learned to farm like his peers who quit school at fourth grade. Besides, he did not want to do that kind of labor. The first girl he wanted to marry chose someone else.

Sometime in the early 1990s, Ay Phit enlisted in the Thai Special Forces. The army recruited two men from each subdistrict along Thailand's border to train as intelligence agents. One summer when we were both in

Thongmakhsan, Ay Phit told me that he traveled along the Burmese border area disguised as a trader collecting information and that the work made his stomach hurt. He worried about what would happen to him if people discovered he was an army intelligence agent. During that time, his second plan for marriage fell through. The second girl he wanted to marry was a Muslim, and if it had worked out, he would have had to convert and promise not to ordain as a monk to earn merit for his grandmother when she died. This would have seriously alienated Ay Phit from his relatives, friends, and coreligionists. This was not the life he had envisioned for himself when he was a young Buddhist novice. However, he never had the opportunity to see where his choices would have led him in the long term, for he died on September 1, 2003, from complications from a fall. He would have graduated and received his commission in a few weeks.

If he had been born ten years earlier, Ay Phit would have had a much easier time of it. He would not have had access to education and, by default, would have become a farmer or perhaps a trader like his father. If he had been able to get a high school education, he could have taught elementary school and become a civil servant. But by the time he had graduated from high school, teachers needed at least a two-year degree from a teacher's college, and by the 1990s teachers had to have a BA degree. Graduates of the high school in Maehongson could not compete with students whose high schools better prepared them for college admissions tests.

If he had lived ten years later, Ay Phit would also have had a wider range of opportunities for education or other career possibilities. Now there is a technical high school, a community college, and a branch of Chiang Mai's Rachaphat University. Maehongson is more integrated into the national economy, infrastructure, and culture.

In 2005, his friend and age mate, Ay Phan, dreamed that Ay Phit asked to stay with Ay Phan. When Ay Phan's son was born, people said he was Ay Phit reborn. Ay Phit's father would visit at Ay Phan's house, saying he was coming to see his son. And, so far, he remains a Buddhist in his next life.

LOOKING OUTWARD

Local Buddhists Becoming
Global Citizens

Buddhists have always looked outward, so what exactly has changed? Why turn to processes and motivations of looking outward in the modern era rather than static traits such as sect, country, or ethnicity? We would argue that what has changed is both the looking, which has grown immeasurably easier, and the outward, which has become increasingly global. Though Buddhist figures have been looking outward since Prince Siddhartha left the warm confines of his palace, new technologies such as television, radio, CDs, smart phones, and the Internet have made reaching out a radically new proposition. And the world to which these figures are reaching out is broader, more accessible, and far more complex than ever before. International travel, global education, and priestly networks have expanded the "outward" in fundamental ways. Buddhist figures have interacted with those in other traditions and locales in the past, but never on the scale and with the level of access that we see today. Scholarships and bursaries, intellectual exchanges, fellowships and postdocs, global networks of temples and lineages all make more of the Buddhist world open to more Buddhist figures. And even for those who cannot travel, the digitization of texts, the recording of sermons, the automation of translation, and the YouTubing of rituals make other traditions and teachings immediately accessible in a way barely imaginable only thirty years ago.

Looking outward in its most general sense can be as simple as engaging with the world. The Chinese monk Dingkong promotes his English-language blog with bilingual business cards and a fake iPhone. Like Houguan in Taiwan, Dingkong is a representative of Buddhism for the Human Realm, which promotes socially engaged and politically active Buddhism alongside innovative forms of outreach. More provocatively, looking outward can mean challenging tradition, transgressing boundaries, and subverting norms. Many of our figures cross national boundaries; for example, the Vietnamese nun Lieu Phap who, though initially trained in Mahayana nunneries at home, later switched to Theravada, was ordained in Sri Lanka, and then completed her graduate studies in India. Some, like Dutch monk Olande in Sri Lanka, leave their homes to become Buddhist monks in other countries; in the process, they become representatives of the local tradition and then carry it abroad. This mode can also include looking past one's own school or tradition, like the Theravadan precept nuns of Sri Lankan who went to Sarnath, India, to receive higher ordination with the help of Mahayana nuns from Korea.

Like those from before the Common Era who used classical Greek imagery to create the first representations of the Buddha in human form, our figures also look outward to different artistic forms. Korean artist Park Chan-Soo blends native wooden sculpture techniques with European classicism and modernism in order to create works that range from the solemn to playful. In the case of the Tibetan artist Gade, we see a figure looking outward to different religious (Tibetan thangka) and cultural (Mickey Mouse) icons, not only to create provocative works that make people laugh and think, but also "to reclaim Tibet from others' appropriations." While most of our examples here involve progressive moves, looking outward can also represent a conservative turn. Gade's example shows us that looking to outside influences and forms can be a move towards protection. Looking outward may not merely be to mimic, but also to appropriate, to protest, to upset, or to undermine. In the case of Park we see a figure looking outward in order to reinvigorate and reinforce his own culture and tradition.

Looking outward is also a key element of propagation. Australian-born, Singaporean monk Dhammika, whose 1987 book answering basic questions about Buddhism has been translated into more than thirty languages, uses a dedicated Web site to disseminate his books around the world and post "Dhamma Musings" on topics like "pole dancing Buddhist style." Here, too, looking outward can include missionizing strategies that are more conservative than progressive. Consider the examples of Korean nun Che-Un, who, like Dhammika, propagates in English to combat the success of Christianity in her home country.

Art and proselytization also remind us that Buddhist propagation operates in the financial as well as a spiritual marketplace. The story of U Paragu reminds us that looking outward has also involved "triangular trade in Buddhist people and things, including relics [that] emerged between Calcutta, Colombo, and Rangoon."

In some cases, looking outward means expanding beyond sectarian organizations and national boundaries to create networks of particular Buddhists, such as Ranjani de Silva's establishment of Sakyadhita Sri Lanka, an international organization for Buddhist women. Looking outward can also include leaving the priesthood, as we see in the post-monk activities of Samnang, who gave up being an abbot in Cambodia and migrated to New Zealand. Samnang, who exists "somewhere between a monk and a poultry worker," represents figures who blur the lines between monk and layman and force us to look beyond narrow definitions in understanding the lives and shifting identities of Buddhists. Woon Wee Teng, the Singaporean lawyer who has perhaps the largest collection of Burmese and Thai amulets in the world, also challenges us to look beyond monks to private collectors as curators and disseminators of the Buddhist heritage.

In contextualizing Olande in the present moment, David McMahan characterizes Buddhism in the modern world as "increasingly transnational and protean, incorporating elements from various cultures and forming unique hybrids that then circulate around the globe by means of literature and traveling teachers." We would certainly agree, but we would also emphasize that looking outward offers a potential to connect frameworks for approaching Buddhists that cross the premodern/modern divide. Because looking outward has always been integral to the spread and continuity of Buddhism, the category is ideally suited to frame Buddhist figures, teachings, activities, and artistic representations across time.

TEACHING BUDDHISM AS A SECOND LANGUAGE
Che-Un
FLORENCE GALMICHE

Buddhism in Korea has been shaped by a monastic culture of community, meditation, and study, based mostly in classical Chinese. Lay practitioners play a growing role in temples, but Buddhism remains largely perceived as rather distant or difficult to access. As a nun leading her own temple and trying to respond to the needs of urban life through the dharma, Che-Un Sǔnim (1955–present) echoes current concerns in the Korean Buddhist world over bridging the gap between monastics and laity.

An expatriate living in Seoul might visit Che-Un's temple out of curiosity after having read about the meditation classes in one of the Korean English-language dailies, while a mother might walk up the stairs of this unremarkable building to take her child to an English class. People also gather here to participate in the regular ceremonies of the Buddhist calendar, in sutra study courses, and in a memorial services. Apart from ceremonies and classes, anyone who wants to visit this temple can call Che-Un for an appointment.

Although she runs her own temple and consciously tailors her activities to the needs of her public, Che-Un is not one of the many individual ritual specialists who are to be found in the Korean religious landscape. She is actually part of the Chogye Order, the largest Buddhist organization in Korea, and her religious project, which mixes together doctrinal teaching, English training, and meditation, echoes the attempts made by Buddhist institutions during the twentieth and twenty-first centuries to increase their influence within the population and to counter the rise of Christianity.

Che-Un entered the monastery when she was in her late twenties. For most of her first five years, she trained as a novice, studying formal and informal monastic rules, as well as sutras and commentaries. After being fully ordained, she joined a Korean Buddhist community in Southeast Asia and continued to study Buddhism for the next few years, while also incorporating English into her curriculum. Back in Korea, after having furthered her training in various monasteries, Che-Un decided to immerse herself in the busy life of Seoul. On the basis of her international experience, she decided to specialize in teaching Buddhism in English, joining her organization's new effort with the so-called international propagation of Buddhism. With the support of a few devotees and some members of her family, she rented a small apartment in a popular district of Seoul and installed a

Buddhist shrine in one of its rooms. She officially registered this place with the Chogye Order and began to advertise.

Advertising is a sensitive matter for Korean Buddhists. For five hundred years, until the very end of the nineteenth century, monks were prohibited from entering the capital. Then, in the twentieth century, fast-growing and effusive Christian churches eclipsed the presence and visibility of Buddhism in Korea. Among Buddhist organizations, marginalization has become a key concern and "propagation" a major and explicitly formulated priority. However, like many of her coreligionists, Che-Un has mixed feelings about the proactive forms of proselytism that mark Korean Protestantism. She gladly contrasts them with the quietness of Buddhism, which, she emphasizes, does not "push people into conversion." Nonetheless, she does not hesitate to consciously draw some inspiration from neighboring churches. Since she opened her temple in 2007, she has resolutely made use of the newest means of communication and advertisement. She has spread information about her center's activities by way of her acquaintances, launched a blog, published articles in various newspapers, and presented her project through interviews on the Buddhist radio station.

Having dedicated herself to the propagation of Korean Buddhism, Che-Un consciously aims to reach new sections of the public. She has decided to focus her activities on two groups: children and foreigners. Reaching a younger public was one of Che-Un's major goals when she decided to open her center. Her knowledge of English and her connections to several native English speakers allowed her to set up courses that closely associate Buddhism with language training. She started with introductory meditation courses. Assisted by English-speaking volunteers, she teaches children about the basis of meditation, such as posture and breathing, and progressively leads them to reflect on existential questions, such as their interdependency with other beings. The young participants train themselves to memorize English expressions related to Buddhism and try to express some of their ideas in this new language. Since the program has met with success— partially because of its links to the centrality of English in the Korean education and evaluation system—Che-Un decided to take it one step further by organizing "English dharma camps" for middle and high school students. During the summer break, she takes between twenty and thirty teenagers to a mountain monastery. With the help of a few other nuns, she schedules these four- to six-day retreats with Buddhist teachings in English and recreational activities for the campers. Like other summer camps now popular in Korea, this program emphasizes the educational, moral, and psychological benefits of a collective experience in a natural environment far from the urban life of Seoul.

The second part of Che-Un's program had a more unexpected outcome. She scheduled a weekly dharma talk and meditation class in English, which she advertised in international circles. Every week, her program attracted a few foreign visitors—expatriate professionals or students—but they were quickly outnumbered by Koreans with a dual interest in the religious and the linguistic aspects of the program. This situation is far from exceptional; most temples offering Buddhist classes in English attract a predominantly Korean audience. This phenomenon relies not only on the ubiquitous importance given to the mastery of English in contemporary Korea, but is also emblematic of the dynamic but still fragile position of lay Buddhism in the country. In spite of recent efforts to translate sutras and commentaries into vernacular Korean, Buddhist teachings have a reputation of great difficulty among the public, particularly as they entail a large number of specialized expressions originating from classical Chinese. By contrast, as the teachings in English organized in Korea generally involve more common vocabulary, they are frequently regarded by lay Buddhists as, paradoxically, more accessible. Mixing Buddhism and English gives Che-Un's project a conspicuously "modern" flavor. Her adaptation of knowledge and practices commonly associated with monasticism to connect with a larger audience clearly reflects the current state of Buddhism in Korea.

THE EMPOWERMENT OF BUDDHIST WOMEN
Ranjani de Silva
ELIZABETH HARRIS

Buddhism in Sri Lanka is Theravada. Sri Lankan Buddhism in the modern period has experienced revival, in response to British imperialism and a bitter internal ethnic war. The work of Ranjani de Silva (1937–present) was carried out against the background of civil war and an energetic national women's movement, as well as a nascent international Buddhist women's movement.

"Now, did you notice my letterhead? I am purposely using it so that you know what we are doing. We started the Institution with four young nuns on the eighth of this month and I was so busy running around to find all the facilities to make them comfortable." So wrote Ranjani de Silva in a personal letter dated August 1997. The letterhead read "Institute for International Buddhist Women," situated in Mount Lavinia, Sri Lanka. Ranjani was then president of the Buddhist women's organization, Sakyadhita International (SI; lit. Daughters of the Buddha), a post she held until 2000. Addressing the Fifth International SI Conference in Cambodia in December 1997, she declared: "Sakyadhita has been working not only to help Buddhist women, but all Buddhists and all women seeking a spiritual path. It has fostered an international Buddhist sisterhood that has united women of the various Buddhist traditions."

SI was founded in 1987 in Bodh Gaya, at a conference on Buddhist nuns that brought together 150 Buddhist women from twenty-six countries. Its principal aim was to support and network Buddhist women globally. Implicit in this goal was facilitating the possibility of higher ordination (*upasampadā*) for all Buddhist women, which the historical Buddha had permitted. In the centuries following his death, orders of nuns (Pali: *bhikkhunis*), following a monastic discipline of over three hundred rules, were established in Sri Lanka, possibly Myanmar, and many Mahayana countries. By the 1980s, however, only a handful of Mahayana countries offered women higher ordination. Sri Lanka possessed an order of ten-precept contemporary nuns (*dasa sil mātās*), having lost its *bhikkhuni* order in about the eleventh century. When Ranjani wrote to me, few people believed that higher ordination for women could be brought back to countries such as Sri Lanka. After all, ten Theravada nuns with higher ordination were needed for the ceremony to take place, and the majority view was that that quorum could not be replaced by the still extant Mahayana nuns. Prominent Buddhist monks had even stated that the ten-precept nuns were little more than laypeople and should not wear orange robes.

Women such as Ranjani, working with the support of Sakyadhita International, helped to change this mind-set. Her work was practical, illustrating not only the agency of laywomen as drivers of change in contemporary Buddhism but also the importance of social engagement in Buddhist women's practice. Her work complemented that of women academics such as Chatsumarn Kabilsingh (now Ven. Dhammananda), who argued that the Mahayana monastic discipline for women was so similar to the Theravada monastic rule that Mahayana nuns could ordain Theravada nuns.

Ranjani took early retirement after twenty years as a manager of human resources and administration in a Sri Lankan state corporation. In 1984, she attended a ten-day meditation course conducted by Ayya Khema, a German-born Buddhist nun who spent many years in Sri Lanka. This experience led her to attend the Bodh Gaya conference in 1987. Inspired by the Mahayana nuns who were present and aware of the needs of Sri Lanka's contemporary nuns, Ranjani joined the Social Service Training section of its Development

Committee. Once back home, she helped to establish Sakyadhita Sri Lanka (SSI), but she met with opposition, even from women. The annual general meeting of SSI could not be held in 1988 because there was not a quorum. She and her colleagues persisted. Their first aims were to help the contemporary nuns of Sri Lanka and to bring the dharma to families at the village level. Ranjani herself was particularly committed to training the nuns for social service so that they would be more visible and valued in society. She attended the next SI conference, held in 1991 in Bangkok, and suggested Colombo as the next venue for 1993. She later told a national Sri Lankan newspaper, "I had no idea how we were going to have it, as we were not well off with resources. But some unseen power was directing me, and I had the courage to work on it." The conference, in fact, was a resounding success, organized with precision and creativity. Ranjani became vice president of Sakyadhita International and, in 1995, president.

For political reasons, the Colombo conference did not prioritize the reestablishment of *bhikkhuni* orders in Theravada Buddhist countries. However, the presence of robed *bhikkhunis* from Taiwan, America, and Europe, and references to higher ordination in some presentations, meant that it was not ignored. It was to the task of enabling Sri Lanka's *dasa sil mātās* to gain higher ordination if they wished (and not all did) that Ranjani turned next, with the help of SI. She also sought the support of key members of the *bhikkhusangha* (the community of monks). In 1996, ten *dasa sil mātās* received higher ordination in Sarnath with the help of Korean nuns. In 1998, twenty were ordained in Bodh Gaya, with the help of Fo Guang Shan, a Taiwanese international Buddhist organization. In 2000, another twenty-one were ordained in Taiwan itself. By this time, some of those who had gained ordination were ordaining others on Sri Lankan soil with the help of sympathetic monks. Ranjani worked behind the scenes to help with the facilitation of these events, receiving little media recognition. Most important for her was that, after a lapse of almost a thousand years, Sri Lankan *bhikkhunis* existed, although they were not officially recognized by the government. There were still many who believed that the ordinations were invalid because they had been carried out by Mahayana nuns.

Ranjani continued to work, particularly at training nuns to visit prisons, schools, and homes for the terminally ill. In 2002, for instance, a Sakyadhita Centre for Training and Meditation was established with support from the Heinrich Böll Foundation. In addition to meditation and dharma study, nuns were schooled in social development work, leadership, and counseling.

In 2004, Ranjani was among fifteen Buddhist women honored by the United Nations for their contribution to Buddhism. She has never defined herself as leader. She has written no academic articles. In 1997, she expressed doubt to me about whether she was important enough to be mentioned in a book I was writing. Yet, her contribution to reclaiming the feminine within Buddhism in the twentieth and twenty-first centuries has been and remains considerable.

A BUDDHIST MICKEY MOUSE
Gade
LEIGH MILLER

The novel cultural phenomenon of contemporary Tibetan art emerged in Lhasa in the 1980s and gained international visibility in the first decade of the twenty-first century. Whereas traditional Tibetan art is exclusively Buddhist, contemporary art evinces radical and rapid social changes, including complex relationships to Buddhism and difficult pasts. Some artists, such as Gade (1971–present) find in Buddhist imagery a visual language that speaks beyond traditional religious interpretations, to query processes of globalization, secularization, and cultural identity formation and transmission in post-Mao Lhasa.

Gade (*dga' bde, "Gah Deh"*) was working in his small, sunlit painting studio, the living room of a modern apartment on the campus of Tibet University, one spring afternoon in 2007. An artwork in progress lay on the large, waist-high table, surrounded by small ceramic bowls for mixing traditional Tibetan stone-ground pigments or preparing gold powder. Gade was not a painter of Buddhist divinities, however. The founding leader of the Gedun Choephel Artists Guild, the first independent artists' association and gallery in Lhasa, had invited me to see a recently completed contemporary Tibetan painting.

From across the room, the long, vertical painting in gold and uneven muted hues on thin cloth created the effect of a fading mural, damaged from age and exposure to water seeps and streaks. The painting recalled the familiar Himalayan Buddhist composition of a central enlightened being surrounded by rows of identical figures, each on his own lotus petal throne. The color palette was darker towards the bottom, while the top rows faded into pale gold. I was focused on the center of the painting, where the throne and halo were vacated of its Buddha, seeming to bear witness to former grandeur and to the legacies of violent loss and haunting absences. As I neared the painting, I was startled to discover the surrounding rows of niches were filled with Mickey Mouses seated in meditation posture and wearing the monastic robes of the Buddha! I laughed aloud, and Gade beamed; his more than five hundred Mickey Mouse figures had elicited just the response he had intended.

Gade was born in the middle of the Cultural Revolution, in 1971, and has childhood memories of the visual spectacle of parades and rallies. He studied traditional Chinese art at the Central Academy of Fine Art in Beijing, but never the highly codified painting of Tibetan Buddhist divinities, nor religious concepts and practices banned before his birth. The post–Cultural Revolution revival of tradition thus complicated his sense of Tibetanness.

Gade reflected, "Initially I was very focused in my works on the aesthetic properties of color schemes, nice lines, compositions, and so on, and into these I tried to fit some ideas from Tibetan Buddhism, or apply that approach to art about Buddhist ideas. But I came to feel it was too superficial, because my knowledge of Tibetan Buddhism was not very deep." Though aesthetically acclaimed by others, this approach to cultural responsibility became burdensome and stifled expression of the breadth of his own experiences. In the early 2000s, Gade found a playfulness in art making by turning to rapidly modernizing Lhasa and discovering strategies for art creation to function as deeply connected to the past on the one hand, such as through use of traditional materials and iconographic conventions, without sacrificing individual experience of the "actual situation of this sad culture" on the other.

When we sat down to drink tea, Gade commented that *Mickey Mural* borrows from the Buddhist art historical tradition in its compositional genre, materials, and style to "show the growing distance between myself and previous generations' religious traditions." Mimicry of aged and damaged murals refers both to Tibet's more than a millennium of Buddhist scholarship, practice, and art, and to the mid-twentieth-century end of traditional Buddhist Tibet. In the wake of the communist takeover of Tibet, Gade is among contemporary artists concerned about what has survived and what has been lost.

Since this work, Gade has continued to employ the figure of Mickey Mouse, as well as Ronald McDonald, the Incredible Hulk, Spiderman, and Chairman Mao, in works that play with Tibetan Buddhist genres, materials, and aesthetics to locate Tibetan art in a contemporary context, even detached from religion. *Mickey Mural* highlights the complicated tensions about the place of religion in this changing society by making the blasphemous substitution of a cartoon for a Buddha alongside depiction of actual iconoclasm in the vacated halo. Gade knows that to do so will cause offense to some Buddhists, but he is "bored with the Shangri-la others want to see." He imports global icons to image; these are, after all, images just as familiar to Tibetans in Lhasa today as the Tibetan Buddhist art historical tradition. Gade deploys traditional and global icons not for religious edification but to affirm his twenty-first-century Tibetanness and to reclaim Tibet from others' appropriations.

Mickey Mural was first exhibited in a show I co-curated at Red Gate/798 in Beijing. On the opening night, Gade stood in a second-floor loft from which he could unobtrusively observe Tibetan, Chinese, and Western visitors approach *Mickey Mural* hanging below. He watched, gratified, as from a distance they became captivated and then delighted when recognizing Mickey Mouse in robes as they got closer. Gade's humor skillfully draws them to the space between the Mickey of today and the ruins of the past, showing Tibetan despair, hopefulness, resistance, and determined presence.

Gade's whimsical take on the melding of Tibetan and global cultures deploys traditional Buddhist elements to render paintings that "look Tibetan." They also ask viewers to consider the implications of rapid and radical social change and the role of creativity in cultural sustainability. Reflecting on the future of contemporary Tibetan art in his studio, Gade told me that "without traditions, there is no soil or ground upon which to build a new path. In this transient time, when memories are disappearing, all we can do is pick up the fragments."

A TWENTY-FIRST CENTURY CUSTODIAN
Jamyang Phuntsok
JANE CAPLE

At the end of the 1970s, when restrictions on religious practice in China were relaxed, there were no functioning Tibetan Buddhist monasteries. Within a decade, thousands had reopened, resuming important religious, social, and economic activities in many Tibetan communities. The monk Jamyang Phuntsok (1980–present) belongs to the first generation to enter monastic life in the 1980s—a generation now responsible for maintaining and developing Tibetan monastic Buddhism in the twenty-first century.

Jamyang's quarters are a hive of activity with preparations under way for his departure that morning to a monastery some two hundred kilometers away where he is to give teachings. A senior monk at a widely respected scholastic monastery in northeastern Tibet, Jamyang has mentioned more than once that he has little time these days because he has so many students. The previous evening, as we sat talking over tea, he had shown me the fruits of his latest self-funded publication project—a volume of the collected teachings of an eleventh-century Tibetan *yoginī* that he was freely distributing to teachers. However, the main reason for my visit was not to discuss Jamyang's efforts (as he sees them) to disseminate Tibetan Buddhist knowledge at a time when much knowledge is flowing in from the outside. I was there to talk business.

The first time we met, Jamyang had taken me on a whistle-stop tour of projects he had been involved in as one of the monastery's leaders. These included a shop, a restaurant, and a medical clinic—part of his efforts to make the monastery economically self-sufficient. Sitting in his quarters five years later, Jamyang pulls out a small, clear plastic box containing a tiny longevity pill the size of a pinhead, nestling in a bed of cloth. He remarks that the pills cost the monastery little money and effort to make but bring in considerable income (being sold at a high profit margin). Proud to claim the development of these monastic businesses as "my work," he reports that they are doing well: "We are now able to support ourselves."

At first glance, Jamyang may seem to cut a contradictory figure—that of a scholarly monk dedicated to the dissemination of Buddhist teachings who insists that such work should not be remunerated ("If you take money you are not a proper religious teacher"), yet also a founder of economic initiatives that tap into processes of commodification and the growing demand for religious products in China. However, for Jamyang and other monks of his generation, the two kinds of work are in many respects opposite sides of the same coin. Economic development has been integral to their efforts to revive and sustain Tibetan monastic Buddhism—and its reputation—in contemporary times.

Jamyang was one of the first of a new generation to enter monastic life in the post-Mao period. He was born in the late 1960s, during the Cultural Revolution. Even though there were no monasteries at that time, he was socialized into monastic life from a young age, spending his summers living and secretly studying with his uncle, who was a monk before monasteries were forcibly disbanded in 1958. Jamyang was in his early teens when his monastery reopened in 1980—a process that began with the return of a handful of elders who had kept their vows during the radical upheaval of the Maoist period. This included his uncle, who was to become one of the "great teachers" instrumental to the revival of monasticism in contemporary Tibet. Jamyang took the "going forth" (*rab byung*) vows in front of his uncle in 1980 and went with him to the monastery the following year. He studied for eighteen years, completing the Gelukpa scholastic curriculum, and went on to hold various monastic offices, finally serving a three-year term on the monastery's management committee. It was towards the end of this term that we first met.

Jamyang's efforts to develop commercial enterprises during his steward-ship of the monastery reflect a trend that has gained momentum since the turn of the millennium. Having lost most pre-1958 sources of income, mon-asteries had been relying on contributions collected from the laity. Monks of Jamyang's generation, influenced by a transnational flow of ideas among monastic authorities in Tibet and India, questioned the ethics of this mode of support (can people really say no if asked to contribute?) and the economic burden it was placing on local Tibetans. They also wanted to shore up mo-nastic authority in the midst of perceptions of moral decline and widespread rumors of fake or dishonest monks collecting donations under false pre-tenses. As a result, many monasteries collected capital funds to invest in businesses, the profits from which can be used to fund religious activities if no sponsor voluntarily pledges support.

These reforms have occurred during a time of breakneck economic and social change. Monastic engagement in the burgeoning market economy has its critics. Yet, somewhat paradoxically, Jamyang sees it as a way to mitigate risks to the integrity of monastic Buddhism posed by state-led development and its attendant materialism. Thanks to his efforts, the monastery can now provide a modest stipend to its monks, enabling and encouraging them to focus on their studies rather than going out to perform religious services for income—but not enough to enable them to buy cars and other material distractions. Although a champion of monastic business development, Jam-yang is leery of the creation of excessive wealth. He is disparaging of mon-asteries that he feels have gone "too far." He appears nonplussed about the new assembly hall under construction at his own monastery ("It's very big, but the numbers of monks are getting less!") and the proliferation of new monks' quarters ("I don't need this"). For him, it is a question of priorities: the means should support the end of sustaining the transmission of Bud-dhism through monastic education and discipline.

Having served his time as a monastery manager, Jamyang is now able to dedicate himself to teaching. After he departs from the monastery, I follow his travels and snippets of his teachings through his posts on We-Chat, a Chinese social media app. Now in his forties, Jamyang represents a generation that bridges the gap between the generation of his teachers (the elders who survived the Maoist years) and that of his students (who are growing up in a rapidly urbanizing, globally connected consumer soci-ety). His business ideas and projects not only reflect the radical economic and social changes of the new millennium. I see them—much as I do his work as a teacher—as creative efforts to fulfill his role as a twenty-first-century custodian of a scholastic Buddhist tradition, ruptured during the Maoist years, but understood to have its roots in the monastic universities of medieval India.

THE RETURN OF THE DUTCH
Ven. Olande Ananda
DAVID L. MCMAHAN

The Dutch once colonized Sri Lanka (then Ceylon) and supported efforts to convert Buddhists of the island to Christianity. Today, many Europeans go to monasteries in Sri Lanka for instruction in Buddhism. A few, like Netherlands-born Olande Ananda (1948–present), have become monks. Olande ministers to locals from his small Colombo meditation center and teaches meditation and Buddhism to people in lectures and retreats around the world as well as on the Internet.

Thinking of meditation centers in Sri Lanka is likely to conjure images of remote hermitages in dense forests. Getting to the Pagoda Meditation Centre, however, requires a *tuk-tuk* ride through the seemingly endless tangle of Colombo streets, dodging cars, buses, pedestrians, and the occasional cow. Then, suddenly, calm descends as you motor down a quiet lane that ends in a green oasis with a couple of neat, small buildings surrounded by Buddhist banners, luxuriant flora, and dogs and cats wandering around. When I arrived on a rainy evening, I peered inside the meditation room and saw two Sinhalese lay Buddhists prostrating themselves, heads to the floor, before an orange-robed monk—not an uncommon sight in Sri Lanka, except that in this case the monk, Ven. Olande Ananda, was a tall, stocky Dutchman and the resident teacher at the center.

I caught him at a moment of transition between two roles. Olande is very much a local monk, ensconced in the community, attending to the needs of his local disciples much as any monk would. In his other more international role, however, he conducts meditation retreats around the world. The Buddha was an itinerant, but could not have imagined the wanderings of someone like Olande. A member of a new species of globe-trotting monk, he is invited across continents to give retreats in Ladakh, Indonesia, South Africa, the United States, Canada, Australia, and various countries in the EU. The two who were prostrating when I arrived, it turns out, were bidding him a reluctant farewell as he was off the next day by plane to conduct a retreat in Holland.

In some respects Olande is typical of the baby-boom generation of Europe and North America. Born in the Netherlands in 1948, he studied economic sociology at the University of Amsterdam, experimented with drugs, and got involved in leftist politics during the height of the countercultural movement. He eventually became disillusioned that the promises of the 1960s had failed to be fully realized. "The people in charge of the world," he told me, "were politicians, corporations, and arms dealers." Like many, he turned inward and began to explore Asian religion, philosophy, and meditation. Unlike most of his generation, though, he quickly moved past casual interest and developed a deep affinity for Buddhism, ordaining as a monk in 1975.

When I visited him in 2011, he was entering numbers into his new smartphone while getting a Skype call on his computer firming up travel plans. He was up on national and international news, voicing disappointment in President Obama and horror at the newly influential Tea Party. Olande regularly gives talks on Sri Lankan television and maintains an Internet presence with accounts on Facebook, Twitter, and LinkedIn. He provides regular meditation instruction at the Pagoda Meditation Centre and has quite a few devoted students, mostly from the rising Sinhalese middle class.

There is little in Sri Lankan history before the last century that would have predicted someone like Olande. The Dutch, after all, were among several European powers that had colonized the island, and most colonists were by no means enamored of the religion of the island's majority. Letters and essays written by colonists mostly portrayed Buddhism as superstitious, nihilistic nonsense so obviously inferior to Christianity that the case hardly needed to be made for displacing it. Yet today, Buddhism is as strong as ever on the island, and the westerners who trickle in are more likely to take a meditation class than try to convert anyone.

Given Sri Lanka's history, I could not help feeling curious about how Olande's lay followers saw him. No doubt part of Olande's attraction is the prestige he brings to Buddhism merely by being from a wealthier, more powerful part of the world. Yet, he reports, what draws his followers from Sri Lanka's emerging educated middle class is not merely that he implicitly gives their religion a stamp of approval; they see him as having given up easy access to what they themselves aspire to—wealth, career, an affluent life—to dedicate himself to the dharma. Even those who achieve this affluence, he said, find the satisfaction it promised elusive. So they go to a westerner to rediscover their own tradition, which began with a man renouncing his wealth and position. They tend to revere Olande more than monks from their own country. "They're used to Sinhalese monks," he says, who ordain for a variety of reasons—social, cultural, and spiritual: it is an option built into the culture. As an educated European, however, who gave up a comfortable, affluent life, learned Pali and Sinhalese and the complexities of Buddhist doctrine, and dedicates himself to teaching meditation, he is de facto a serious practitioner, motivated by the dharma itself, and thus commands more respect.

At the end of our time together, I give Olande a copy of a book I wrote on modern Buddhism, and he gives me some natural mosquito-repelling oil and Swiss chocolate. He calls me another *tuk-tuk,* and we part, each of us with itineraries, plane tickets, and passports in our pockets. Bumping down the road at dusk, I reflect on Olande Ananda's significance in the contemporary moment. In both his globe-trotting and his ministering to the local population, he represents several important features of Buddhism in the modern world. It is increasingly transnational and protean, incorporating elements from various cultures and forming unique hybrids that then circulate around the globe by means of literature and traveling teachers. It attracts serious adherents from the West, some of whom are having a significant influence on the development of the tradition. Yet it remains local, rooted, and relevant to the everyday concerns of ordinary people in specific places.

THE BLOGGER MONK IN SOUTHERN CHINA
Dingkong
STEFANIA TRAVAGNIN

Social media became a defining feature of the new China after the late 1980s. That is also the time when Han Buddhism was offered a new public visibility and engaged in a modernizing process that has influenced modalities of preaching and practice. Nevertheless, Buddhism is still framed within the official scheme and must "serve the Party." This renewed and yet politically constrained environment is where the monk Dingkong (1976–present) has been educated and is now preaching.

In the last few years I have been attending academic conferences on Chinese religions organized in Mainland China, and it has not been unusual to see Buddhist monks and nuns presenting papers and participating in scholarly discussions. However, at one of these conferences, titled "Spiritual Capitalism and Public Goods," it was a young Buddhist monk—in his late thirties and among the few members of the sangha present at the event—who caught my attention. His dharma name was Dingkong, and he introduced himself as the director of the Yuanying Research Center, which is devoted to the study of the life, works, and practice of Yuanying (1878–1953), a monk contemporary of the famous reformer Taixu (1890–1947). Dingkong delivered a paper that summarized Yuanying's life; his study and practice of the Tiantai, Chan, and Pure Land Schools; and his contribution to the modernization of Buddhism through social activism and intervention in the education sector. The paper concluded by characterizing Yuanying as already a follower of the "love country, love religion" (Ch. *aiguo aijiao*) philosophy that the Chinese Communist Party implemented only in the 1980s, decades after Yuanying's death.

Outside of the formal setting of the conference, Dingkong appeared to be an orthodox Chinese Buddhist monk, who spent much of his lunch break making sure the food served to him was fully vegetarian. He questioned whether the vegetables were cooked in a clean wok and not with the same oil used for meat and fish, and thus acceptable to the strict vegetarian diet all Chinese Buddhist monastics must, theoretically, follow. Dingkong is also abbot of the Jile Temple, located in Gutian, which serves the local Buddhist community by organizing dharma liturgies according to the Buddhist calendar. At the conference I noticed that he was also carrying a smart phone in a protective iPhone sleeve (so as to make people think he actually had an iPhone), and double-sided business cards in both Chinese and English, which included not only the mailing address of his temple and his contact details, but also a Web address for his blog, "Dingkong de BLOG" (Dingkong's blog).

One of the many links on the blog leads to photos of liturgies, Buddha statues, Dingkong in his ceremonial robe giving lectures, processions of believers, and Dingkong with his lay followers as well as in meetings with senior monks. Other links lead to essays on Buddhist parables, explanations of scriptural passages, and citations from eminent Chinese monks of the past. One section of the blog also includes considerations and aphorisms by the same Dingkong, who then proposes himself as a Buddhist leader with an authoritative voice. There are also pages on past and future dharma activities, the various activities organized at the temple, and collections of photos of natural phenomena and poems that Dingkong himself wrote. The only page not yet completed is the autobiographical one. So far, hundreds of thousands of people have visited the site, making it one of the most popular religion-related blogs in the country.

The way Dingkong translates and disseminates the dharma makes him a representative of the so-called Buddhism for the Human Realm (Ch. *renjian fojiao*). *Renjian fojiao* was formulated as a new systematization and practice of Buddhism, which thus became socially engaged and politically involved. Most important, *renjian* Buddhism is not concerned with the afterlife but with turning this world into a Pure Land. This Buddhism is rooted in both Taixu's and Yuanying's plans and new interpretation of doctrine and practice. Similarly to Taixu, Yuanying engaged in improving monastic education, was abbot of several temples and seminaries, traveled extensively in South and Southeast Asia, and held important positions like chairman of the Chinese Buddhist Association (1928–1937). Unlike Taixu, Yuanying advocated moderate revision and reorganization of Buddhism in China. He did not agree with Taixu's reform plans for the reorganizational, educational, and social role of the sangha; these he considered too drastic. The *renjian* interpretation of Buddhism was later reshaped by a second generation of monks, like Yinshun (1906–2005), who transmitted it to Taiwan. *Renjian fojiao* has been also preserved in Mainland China through the Buddhist Association of China, which adopted its foundational principles and in the 1980s read it as mirroring the "love country, love religion" ideology. The end of the twentieth century and the beginning of the twenty-first saw a third generation of Buddhists, which included Dingkong, who redefined *renjian* Buddhism even further. One of the features of *renjian* Buddhism is adapting modalities of preaching and teaching according to the audience. Dingkong's blog should be read in relation to this principle, and thus as a strategy to address present and potential Buddhists through popular channels of communication.

Dingkong's blog provides an index of the modernization that now permeates different levels of Chinese society, where, in spite of governmental control and censorship, different forms of social media have become the key channels through which politicians, intellectuals, and religious figures speak to the public. Today the officially recognized religious associations and the main temples all have Web sites, TV programs, magazines, and newsletters.

At the same time, an analysis of the followers of the blog and their comments responding to Dingkong's posts helps one to understand to what extent Chinese Buddhists refer to (and rely on) Buddhism today. The followers of the blog include other monastics, lay adults, and teenagers. Dingkong appears able to address Chinese people of different ages, professions, and social classes. Readers' comments range from the very Buddhist greeting "Homage to you, Amitabha Buddha!" to more personal comments on the greatness of Dingkong through expressions usually reserved for celebrities. Emoticons, very often of a nonreligious nature, fill up the comment space as well.

Dingkong's writings reveal a dharma teacher, an artist, a spiritual guide, a friend, and a human being. At the conference in Fuzhou, Dingkong was accompanied by two young men, a teenager and a university student, who were there as his Buddhist disciples and were therefore taking care of all his needs. However, they told me they were there not just in their role of attendants, but also "to have fun." In other words, the usual distance between Buddhist laity and monastics has been replaced by a form of a friendly and secularized reverence that is a feature of the Buddhism for the Human Realm.

Dingkong is part of Yuanying's lineage, a twenty-first-century practitioner of Buddhism for the Human Realm, a representative of the interplay between religion and social media that characterizes these years, and also a face of the modern Chinese modalities of religion.

CARVING PLAYFUL BUDDHAS
Park Chan-Soo
JY LEE

Although Buddhist wooden sculpture has an ancient lineage in South Korea, it has been neglected during past centuries due to state persecution of Buddhism and the turbulent twentieth-century history marked by colonialism and war. Park Chan-Soo (1948–present) has devoted the past half century to reviving this forgotten tradition and has reinvigorated the art with classical and modernist aesthetics. An activist for "Korean cultural independence," Korea's leading wood sculptor has also founded and operates a museum of Buddhist art and relics outside Seoul.

In the hands of South Korea's government-designated "Important Intangible Cultural Heritage" Number 108 Park Chan-Soo, Buddha has reopened his mouth. Internationally acclaimed sculptor Park believes that the world has become too turbulent for Buddha to remain silent, and his wooden Buddhist sculptures express the whole gamut of emotions that lie beyond perennial serenity.

In his work *Buddha Speaks with a New Voice*, Park created a large gilded Buddha in the middle of a sermon. In contrast to this dynamic Buddha with his open mouth, *Silent Child Monk*, which depicts a young monk napping sideways, reveals a subtle smile and calmness that arise from Park's finesse with the texture of wood.

Park's art is also characterized by playfulness. He emphasizes that the message of the Buddha is to "Enjoy yourself. Be happy. Don't be so serious." Hence his work *Joy, Anger, Sorrow, and Pleasure* shows three wooden faces in progressive degrees of intoxication. While some of his works are solemn and monochrome Buddhist figures, others are bright and multicolored secular works. His woodworks blend Korean Buddhist wooden sculpture with the European classicism of Michelangelo and the modernism of Brancusi. The resulting hybrids emanate harmony across time and place.

Although wooden Buddhist sculptures thrived in Korea after Buddhism entered the peninsula in the fourth century CE, the art declined when the Joseon dynasty, Korea's last kingdom, declared neo-Confucianism the official state religion and suppressed Buddhism. After the Japanese colonization and the Korean War in the twentieth century, this millennium-old Korean wood carving known as *mokjogakjang* had become lost.

Park was left on his own to pioneer the resurrection of the forgotten tradition. He visited numerous temples and monks and perused Buddhist texts. Through these endeavors, he re-created *beopsang,* a preaching pulpit used by Goryeo Buddhist monks that remained only in medieval Buddhist texts. It was this opus that launched him to fame with the presidential award in the National Traditional Arts Competition. Coincidentally, the zelkova tree he used, around seven hundred years old, dates back to the Goryeo dynasty itself.

Born in 1948 to poor farming parents, Park Chan-Soo grew up eating tree bark to relieve his hunger in postwar Korea. At the age of twelve, he moved to Seoul and began an apprenticeship in Buddhist painting before switching to woodwork. "I started woodworking to make a living, and it took me about ten years to be any good," he says. His studies took him to Japan, where he encountered the Korean seventh-century *Pensive Bodhisattva* that would inspire him for the rest of his career. "I could sense the blood running through the face, hear Buddha's whisper, and feel the wood breathe," Park recalls.

Since then, his works have taken him to over thirty nations, with invitations ranging from New York City's UN Headquarters to Thailand's royal family. In addition to exhibiting his works, he has also developed a unique woodwork performance, which is an abbreviated form of his woodworking process. Although most of his sculptures take months to make, Park's mastery also allows him to hew a simple yet elegant work within minutes. In his 2009 performance titled *Reconciliation,* he began by playing the Korean drum (*buk*), followed by meditation on an elevated chair. Only then did he start carving the camellia tree that he had cut himself. After making initial cleaves with hammer and nail, the sexagenarian maestro switched to *moktak,* a wooden percussive stick used by Buddhist monks for meditation. The rhythmic echoes of his *moktak* gave birth to a *jangseung,* a Korean traditional totem pole.

When carving sculptures of Buddha, he starts by meditating, sometimes by a waterfall, to purify his mind to produce a true image of Buddha. The roots of the tree become the head because they hold moisture, and the southern part becomes the face because it receives more sunlight. After six months of arduous labor, Buddha is completed and Park holds a ceremony to infuse life into his woodwork. Buddha is veiled for this ritual, and the Buddhist scriptures, seven Buddhist treasures, five incenses, grains, medicines, and clothing are offered, along with chanting and prayers from monks.

When not on tour, Park lives in the quiet town of Yeoju an hour away from Seoul. There, he has set up a sprawling sculpture garden and workshop called "Moka Museum," named after his own epithet, which means "bud of the tree." Founded in 1993, the museum holds over sixty thousand Buddhist relics, including many of Park's own works and rare Korean Buddhist paintings. He designed the buildings to resemble a Buddhist monastery, and although there are no monks in residence, there are pupils. One of Park's pupils is his own son, who says that his father is a stern teacher.

Park has considered closing the museum, which loses about US$300,000 every year. Nevertheless, he keeps it open, as he views the museum as "the Second Independence movement" for cultural independence. Just as the Independence Movement in the early twentieth century struggled for a politically independent Korean state free from the Japanese occupation, Park strives for culturally independent Korean arts, which are often neglected both domestically and internationally between the two cultural superpowers China and Japan. Since the Japanese colonization and rapid industrialization, Park says that tradition has been regarded as retrospective and valueless in Korea. He also deplores the death of *bulmos,* a centuries-old Korean term given to the sculptors of Buddha. While Buddhist sculptors with impeccable techniques have become numerous, they do not convey the Buddhist doctrine through their art. With the advent of installation art and the rise of video culture, Park also writes that traditional sculptural elements such as form, texture, and weight have become rarified. As more and more of the public demand glamorous and splendid Buddhas rather than simple and restrained ones, *bulmos* no longer have a place in the modern world. Even today, some view craftsman like Park Chan-Soo as technicians, overlooking what he says is the fierce inner struggle to reinvigorate the tradition. Through transfiguring trees into Buddhas, Park continues to breathe life into an ancient Korean tradition.

PROLIFIC WRITER, COOL BLOGGER
Shravasti Dhammika
JACK MENG-TAT CHIA

A former British colony, Singapore, despite its Chinese majority population, uses English as its first language. Therefore, there is a constant need for English-speaking monks to fill the needs of English-educated Buddhists in the country. Meet Bhante Shravasti Dhammika (1951–present), an Australian monk who has been teaching Buddhism in Singapore for the last thirty years.

Located on the second and third levels of a three-story shophouse in the rich historic district of Balestier Road, the Buddha Dhamma Mandala Society (BDMS) is far from being a typical Chinese Buddhist temple in Singapore. An Indian-styled Shakyamuni image is enshrined in the main hall. To the left is a reception counter surrounded by several bookshelves containing books for free distribution. When I arrived on a Sunday in the summer of 2012, the weekly service had just ended, and BDMS spiritual adviser Shravasti Dhammika was chatting with a few laymen. I had first met Dhammika for a college project more than a decade before and had already visited BDMS several times for my research. He shook my hand with no formality and, in a heavy Australian accent, asked, "How're you doin'?"

With the presence of a large ethnic Chinese population, Buddhism is the dominant religion in Singapore. It is no surprise that Buddhist organizations in general and Chinese Mahayana Buddhist temples in particular can be found in many parts of this global city-state. However, Dhammika is hardly a typical Singaporean monk. Born in 1951 in Australia into a Christian family, he became a Buddhist at the age of eighteen. In 1973, Dhammika left for Thailand in hope of becoming a monk. Thereafter, he visited Laos, Burma, and eventually India, to learn the dharma. In India, Dhammika was ordained under Matiwella Sangharatna (?–1984), the last disciple of lay Buddhist activist and scholar Anagarika Dharmapala (1864–1933). Dhammika went to Sri Lanka in 1976, where he studied Pali at Sri Lanka Vidyalaya and later became a cofounder and teacher of the Nilambe Meditation Centre in Kandy.

The changing sociopolitical and economic environment in postindependence Singapore has forced Buddhist monastics to cater to the modern needs of Buddhists, society, and the state since the 1980s. With the use of English as the first language in Singapore's education system and the growing presence of Christian proselytizing efforts directed at English-educated Singaporeans, there has been a rising demand for English-speaking monastics to teach Buddhism in Singapore. Dhammika made his way to Singapore in the

1980s and became one of the first *angmo* (Caucasian) monks in this global city-state. Subsequently, he was invited to become the spiritual adviser of BDMS and has remained there ever since. He runs the meditation and dharma discussion on Friday evenings and leads the Sunday service. The activities of BDMS seem to reflect a competition between Buddhist groups and Christian churches for English-educated members in the country. With one-third of Singaporeans claiming Buddhist affiliation, Buddhist organizations are gradually repackaging themselves to appear more attractive to educated and rational Singaporeans who are more interested in Buddhist philosophy and meditation practices than religious rites.

Dhammika proudly shows me the latest French translation of his famous book *Good Question, Good Answer*. First written in 1987 in response to the increasing interest in Buddhism among English-educated Singaporeans, this book provides answers to more than 140 frequently asked questions on basic Buddhist teachings and practices. The most important question in the book is probably "How do I become a Buddhist?" In it, Dhammika explains how one can become a Buddhist in the spirit of *ehipassiko* (come and see): "So do not impulsively rush into Buddhism. Take your time, ask questions, consider carefully and then make your decision. The Buddha was not interested in having large numbers of disciples. He was concerned that people should follow his teachings as a result of a careful investigation and consideration of facts." Dhammika's response is attractive to educated and rational Singaporeans. Translated into more than thirty languages, this book has been widely circulated around the world as a missionary tract to promote Buddhist teachings. *Good Question, Good Answer* has its own dedicated Web site where Internet users can read it online and also download pdfs of it in various different languages. Dhammika has written over twenty other books, which can be found in many Buddhist temples, meditation centers, and even at vegetarian food stalls in the hawker centers. His prolific publication record as a missionary and scholar-monk has given him a positive reputation among the Buddhist community in Singapore and overseas.

Like those in other Buddhist organizations, Dhammika is quick to use the Internet for missionary activities. On his laptop he shows me his blog "Dhamma Musings," which he started in April 2008. It contains essays on Buddhist teachings and meditation practices, pictures and thoughts on his activities and travels, criticisms of misguided "Buddhist" practices, and occasional comments on religious fundamentalism. For instance, in his post "The Prosperity Dhamma," Dhammika criticizes the misunderstood and deliberately distorted practice of merit making in Theravada Buddhist societies, and particularly in Thailand. He chides Thais for treating monks like "vending machines" that dispense blessings and good merit. Dhammika also comments on religious fundamentalism. In his post "Fundamentalism," he suggests that Buddhism rarely produces fundamentalists or fundamentalist movements because of its generally open and explorative nature. Thus, Buddhists are less dogmatic in their religious practices and more tolerant towards other faiths. "Dhamma Musings" is widely read because of Dhammika's candid writing style and sense of humor. His recent posting, "Pole Dancing Buddhist Style," for example, discusses the Buddha's dialogue with a bamboo acrobat on the four foundations of mindfulness. Dhammika's blog receives an average of five hundred to six hundred hits per day and continues to grow in readership.

A study of Dhammika thus reveals a number of key factors confronting Buddhism in contemporary Singapore: competition between Buddhism and Christianity; new missionary strategies in response to changing demographics, education level, and language preference; and the emergence of reformist Buddhist activities. He also represents the new breed of highly educated, IT savvy, and people-oriented monastics who are actively promoting Buddhism in this dynamic and highly literate society. Dhammika will continue to run activities at BDMS, rely on his trusty laptop to write more books, and propagate the dharma via the Internet.

COLLECTOR OF MAGIC, ESQUIRE
Woon Wee Teng
JUSTIN THOMAS MCDANIEL

Buddhism in Singapore cannot be defined as Mahayana or Theravada, Chinese or Southeast Asian. Like the city itself, Buddhism in modern Singapore is characterized by diversity, hybridity, and innovation. Woon Wee Teng (1957–present) represents these qualities as a lay lawyer and art collector who has studied many forms of Buddhist history, ethics, and ritual.

Woon Wee Teng possesses secret and powerful knowledge. First, he knows where there are secret parking spaces in the densest part of Singapore. When pressed for time, which one always is in Singapore, these spaces come in very handy. Second, he owns what is perhaps the most extensive collection of protective magical Burmese and Thai Buddhist amulets in the world. It is so large that the amulets are kept in two four-story, prewar houses near Singapore's Chinatown. Each floor is packed with rare Buddhist statues, manuscripts, and most especially, amulets meticulously well cared for and respected. Woon Wee Teng can provide detailed information and wonderfully evocative stories about where, when, and from whom he acquired these pieces. He is a living encyclopedia of information about magic and ritual implements in Southeast Asia. Whereas his knowledge of parking spaces has come from years of experience living and working in the city, the origin of the latter knowledge is more mysterious, especially as he is neither a monk nor a scholar, but an English- and Chinese-speaking lawyer with no family or professional connections to Burma or Thailand. The type of knowledge he creates is indicative of the crucial role independent and idiosyncratic collectors and curators play in the construction of Buddhist heritage and history today.

Woon Wee Teng was born in 1957 to a family famous for running the oldest coffee shop in Singapore—Killiney Kopitiam—specializing in *kaya* (a type of delicious coconut and egg jam). At age nineteen, he enlisted in the Singapore Army and thereafter he went to Northumbria University to read law. He became a barrister in London in 1983 and was later called to the Singaporean and Australian Bar. He ended up practicing in Singapore in construction, commercial, and banking law. At age fifty he retired from law practice to dedicate his time and passion to collecting art and antiquities (particularly Buddhist and Hindu artworks), promoting art and culture at Nei Xue Tang Buddhist Art Museum and others, writing articles on Buddhist art, and working on his upcoming book on Yunnanese Buddhist artworks from the Nanzhao and Dali kingdoms. He started collecting as a child and student and over time amassed more than forty thousand pieces to establish a "house museum" in Singapore under the name of "Nei Xue Tang." It is the first Buddhist art museum of its kind in Singapore where a collector's home is permitted to display exhibits publicly. Through it, he helps to promote Buddhist art from diverse Buddhist countries (particularly Thailand, Cambodia, Burma, and China).

As a result of serious illness in 2006 and his desire that a larger and more publically accessible museum be built, Woon Wee Teng made the painful decision to transfer his art collection in Nei Xue Tang to Oei Hong Leong, a Singapore tycoon. He continues to serve Nei Xue Tang as art consultant and helps to promote Buddhist and Hindu art. He is also still an avid collector. Besides collecting, his family donates a great deal to preserve the arts and for arts education. For example, they initiated the biggest annual art prize in the United Kingdom (the Woon Foundation Painting and Sculpture Art Prize), amounting to GBP40,000. Woon gave donations to Pho Chang Academy of Fine Art to promote traditional Thai Buddhist art. He also gave generously to temples to make amulets as a special art form.

Unlike other collectors of Buddhist art and builders of museums, Woon concentrates his efforts on Buddhist ritual and protective objects that traditionally have been ignored by curators. He is one of the only internationally and ecumenically minded promoters of this little-known tradition in Southeast Asia. Among the thousands of important ritual and magical objects, it is worth mentioning that he collected many precious protective "Somdet" amulets of Wat Rakang in Bangkok, which are considered some of the rarest and most sought-after in the world. The Thai royal family ranks them in the "Class Of Five" finest amulets in the country. He also has many Luangpu Tuad amulets and personal religious items like *takruts* (rolled-up metal sheets with inscribed *yantra*) and humpback *pidta* amulets personally made by renowned Thai master Tok Raja from Malaysia.

What also makes Woon's collection unique is his equal focus on collecting magical and protective objects as well as the paintings and large statues usually preferred by collectors and scholars. Further, he collected amulets and ritual implements directly from magically powerful monks in Southeast Asia. Moving from monastery to monastery and ritual to ritual, he amassed not only objects but also extensive ethnographic information and wonderful stories. He even witnessed the shooting of amulets to test their efficacy. From Khun Ko Jun in Thailand, he received the hair relic and amulets of Photan Klai, and from Maha Bodhi Tahtaung Sayadaw in Burma, he received special *dhat lone* (i.e., philosopher's stones made from mercury through alchemy, incantation, and meditation). The list goes on and on. He is the only Buddhist I have ever met who knows about both the ritual traditions and the translocal monastic lineages of Malaysia, Singapore, Thailand, Cambodia, China, and Burma (and increasingly Bangladesh). His vision and tireless work reveal a network of Buddhist magicians and teachers unseen by scholars who focus on their own specific, often country-based, field sites and language groups. He also believes in giving back to those who have taught him. He donated funds to build images and stupas in Southeast Asia and is as much a practicing Buddhist as a self-trained historian, anthropologist, and specialist in art. He has learned from lay and ordained masters across sectarian divisions and national boundaries. The personal connections and friends he has made are as valuable as the amulets he has collected.

Woon not only has found me parking spaces but he has forced me to ask new questions and explore new avenues of research. The jam and toast he serves over our meals together also do not hurt!

A SOVEREIGN BODY BEYOND THE NATION-STATE
Galsan Legden

ANYA BERNSTEIN

After Buddhism came to Buryatia from Tibet via Mongolia in the early eighteenth century, Buryats maintained extensive transnational links with their coreligionists across Inner Asia. These ties, severed by the antireligious campaigns in the Soviet Union in the 1920s, were not restored until the late 1980s, when, with the collapse of the Soviet Union, Buryats reestablished ties with the Tibetan diaspora in India. Whereas earlier Buryat monks went to study in Tibet and Mongolia, today some Buryats enroll in Tibetan monasteries in exile in southern India. Buryatia also became the most significant site in the former Soviet Union for the activities of Tibetan lamas in exile, some of whom permanently settled there during the last two decades.

In 1927, Galsan Legden, a young monk from Siberia, left to study in Tibet. His formidable journey, which took more than a year of overland travel, started in the Buryat-Mongol Autonomous Soviet Socialist Republic, went through Mongolian grasslands, the Gobi Desert, and the high mountain passes of the Tibetan plateau. Upon his arrival in Lhasa, Galsan Legden enrolled at Drepung monastery and soon rose to unusual prominence, becoming the first Buryat abbot of Drepung Gomang Monastic College. Having heard of Soviet violence against lamas in Buryatia, he made a decision to stay in Tibet. Nonetheless, as the socialist project migrated from Soviet Russia to China, he was imprisoned by the Communist Chinese and reportedly died in custody in the mid-1970s. Little or nothing was known about his fate in Buryatia until 1989, when the first Buryat lamas, newly mobilized by perestroika, began visiting Drepung again, by then re-created in southern India by Tibetan exiles. To their amazement, the first late socialist Siberian pilgrims discovered Galsan Legden in India, living, as he himself professed, in his *new* body. That is to say, the Galsan Legden who was found in the Indian Drepung in 1989 is believed to be a reincarnation of the former Buryat pilgrim.

It is said that before his death in prison, Legden asked his cellmate, a Tibetan, if he, Galsan Legden, could come and visit his family. Thinking that he was talking about the time when they would get out of prison, his friend cheerfully agreed. The friend's family subsequently became Tibetan refugees in Kathmandu, where Legden was reborn as one of their sons in 1976. He was later identified as an incarnate lama by Drepung monks, and he went to India to study, where he was discovered by post-Soviet Buryat pilgrims. The monk, now known as Kentul Rinpoché (*ken* means "abbot," and *tul* signals *tulku,* or "reincarnated master"), subsequently visited Buryatia, had reunions with his Buryat "relatives," and became an active member of the Buryat Buddhist revival. Crucially, he ushered in a new kind of body particularly revered today in Buryatia: a Tibetan lama with Buryat "roots." Such lamas are believed to blur classically ethnic characteristics, being simultaneously "Buryat" and "Tibetan." What might such corporeal fluidity, resulting from transnational reincarnations, signify? In 2008, while living in the south Indian Drepung monastery, I asked this young man how he himself understood this reincarnation process.

> When I was told I was a reincarnation of Legden, I was glad, but I didn't feel anything special. It was only when they showed me his picture, I felt something . . . unusual. When they told me my predecessor was a Mongol—I did not know about the difference between Mongols and Buryats at the time—I felt a sense of "us" and "ours." A sense of pride for being a Mongol, even a feeling of some kind of patriotism. A Mongol patriotism.

Only in the late 1980s, when Kentul Rinpoché saw the first Buryat monks and pilgrims arriving in Drepung from Russia, did he learn that his predecessor was not a Khalkh Mongol but a Buryat. After that, Rinpoché became a major figure to Buryat Buddhists, both pilgrims to India and those at home.

While Tibetan incarnate lamas are often considered the source of the highest authority in Buryatia, those of "Buryat descent" are allowed to be detached from the usual Tibetan orbits and incorporated into the Buryat body politic. If reincarnation is a reproductive technology whereby fictive kinship is created through all-male lineages (Mills 2002), the ability of key Buryat lamas to "father" descendants beyond the borders of their immediate nation-state reverses the traditional cultural hierarchy, in which Tibetans are regarded as superior for their more developed and ancient Buddhist culture. For some of the proponents of Buryat religious and cultural autonomy, the bodies of Tibetan incarnates with "Buryat roots" present sites of intensified sovereignty not only by virtue of their human-divine nature but also through viewing them as essentially "ours." It is the ability of such lamas to cross boundaries between nation-states, but also between life and death as well as conventionally defined lines of kinship and ethnicity, that makes them crucial to the contested notions of sovereignty in Buryat political imaginaries.

Kentul Rinpoché can be considered a paradigmatic figure of modernity, given the dramatic means by which his life traversed some of the most famous political and religious struggles of the twentieth century, including

Russian and Chinese communist revolutions and their subsequent violent secularization campaigns, Tibetan exile to India, the collapse of the Soviet Union, and postsocialist religious revitalization in Buryatia. Despite being ethnically Tibetan, Kentul Rinpoché, by virtue of being a reincarnation of a Buryat monk, has become a key exemplar for Buryat self-fashioning. Not only was he the only Buryat to preside over the most famous Tibetan monastery, but he mastered the process of death to be incarnated outside of Chinese-occupied Tibet in order to engineer his return to Buryatia, as well as to relink ordinary Buryats with the Buddhist world as part of postsocialist religious revival. Incarnation here emerges as an empowering technology for mobility and border crossing. It also reveals a particular kind of a sovereign body that is able to control the processes of death and rebirth. Such sovereign bodies, however, are not autonomous and self-owning in the sense of being bounded, but instead reveal a corporeal fluidity unusual for Western contexts, as their sovereignty emerges not only from their mobility through time and space but also from their incorporation of important previous lamas.

POST-MONK LIFE IN NEW ZEALAND
Samnang
ELIZABETH GUTHRIE

Samnang was born in a village of rice farmers near the small provincial capital of Takeo Province in southeastern Cambodia. He was born in 1975, the year the Khmer Rouge took over the country. His family was separated during the Khmer Rouge period, some siblings died, and his older brother ended up in refugee camp in Thailand. From there he migrated to New Zealand.

The first time I saw Samnang was in a video that his brother brought back from Cambodia to New Zealand. Samnang was the abbot of a rural monastery in Takeo Province. He was in his late thirties—young for an abbot—but he had achieved the position because he had been an ordained monk for more than ten years and because of his energy and skill at preaching and performing popular Buddhist rituals such as water consecration. The video showed a consecration of a monastery by having boundary stones set around its periphery. *Bancoh sima* is an important and auspicious occasion. High-ranking monks and dignitaries are invited to participate in the ceremonies, and laypeople flock to the temple or *wat* to share in the merit and celebrations. In the video, the short, smiling, rather plump figure of the abbot Samnang was always at the center of events—greeting dignitaries, preaching sermons, and chanting. Samnang's main patron was his older brother, who had come to New Zealand in the 1980s as a refugee. His New Zealand family was proud of Samnang's accomplishments: in addition to being adept at Buddhist rituals and chanting, Samnang had overseen the reconstruction of the old monastery, which had been badly damaged during the civil war and Khmer Rouge period (1975–1978).

A few years later, I heard that Samnang had decided to leave the monkhood, marry, and migrate to New Zealand. I was a little surprised, but short-term ordination is common in Cambodian Buddhism where life as a monk is more of a life-cycle ritual than a lifetime vocation. Time spent as a monk provides educational and career opportunities for clever rural men who have little opportunity to study after they leave primary school. The monkhood is also seen as good preparation for marriage, and for lay life in general. Samnang's wedding was arranged and a contingent of New Zealand Khmers traveled to Cambodia for the wedding.

After Samnang arrived, I learned more about his life and personality. He explained that he had decided to leave the monkhood because he had achieved his goals there and was ready to experience life as a married layman. He trusted his family to arrange his marriage, as he did not want to look for a wife. He found his new life in New Zealand challenging. He struggled to learn English and had difficulty adjusting to the cold climate. No longer the respected leader of a successful monastery, he was instead an older, unemployed man who was embarrassed that his brother had to drive him everywhere. I found that he had a lot in common with his new wife. Like Samnang, Maya was the youngest, unmarried member of a large family. I learned that the main instigator for the marriage had been Maya's mother: she wanted to see her daughter married to a good man before she died.

Soon after Samnang's arrival in New Zealand, the elderly mother-in-law had a stroke. Samnang and his wife were responsible for her twenty-four-hour care. Samnang joked that he and his wife did not need a baby as they already had one! Because he spent so much time feeding, cleaning, and watching Cambodian videos with his mother-in-law, he did not get much exercise, gained weight, and developed leg problems. His doctor advised exercise, so Samnang began to walk everywhere—even in the winter rain—and returned to a monastic diet, refusing to eat after noon. He and his wife cared for her elderly mother until another stroke put her into a rest home. Samnang was deeply distressed by what he saw there. He could not understand why New Zealanders abandoned their parents in institutions, and he was determined not to abandon the old lady he now called "mother." Every day he walked the considerable distance to the rest home and spent hours assisting the staff with her personal care (feeding was a torturous process, as she was no longer able to swallow). Because of his outgoing nature, he made friends with the rest home staff and some of the residents. He decided to study for a caregiver's qualification.

In 2012, Samnang's mother-in-law developed dementia and no longer recognized her family. Someone still visits her every day to provide her with Cambodian food and make sure that she is well cared for. But Samnang has taken a job in a poultry-processing factory to earn the money to return to Cambodia to sponsor a merit-making ceremony for his recently deceased father. He still hopes to be able to train someday as a caregiver but has now left the purely religious path behind to provide for his wife in New Zealand and for his family back in Cambodia.

Despite all the changes that have occurred in his life since disrobing and moving to New Zealand, Samnang still considers himself an active Buddhist contributing to his tradition. For example, he belongs to a lay association that organizes Cambodian Buddhist ceremonies (Cambodian New Year, Bon Pchum Ben, and funerals) and brings a Buddhist monk from New Zealand's main Khmer temple in Wellington to officiate at these ceremonies. Because of his former role as abbot, he acts as a nonordained ritual expert who sits in between the monk and the laypeople and leads the chants. Samnang is the type of Cambodian Buddhist who is often forgotten in descriptions of the religion and its history. He falls somewhere between a monk and a poultry worker. He is neither a scholar of Buddhism nor a complete novice in the religion. He is a Cambodian Buddhist who may never return to Cambodia. However, for the small Cambodian community in New Zealand and those non-Cambodians interested in the practice and teachings of Buddhism, Samnang is an informative, caring, and living example of the ways in which globalization and modernization affect and are affected by itinerant Buddhists.

THE FIRST THERAVADA *BHIKKHUNI* IN VIETNAM
Lieu Phap
CARINA PICHLER

Lieu Phap (1967–present) is the first fully ordained nun in the Theravada tradition in Vietnam. In this way she is doubly marginalized. There are not only very few Theravada *bhikkhunis* (nuns) in Southeast Asia, but also nearly none in the majority Mahayana country of Vietnam. Lieu, though, is a good example of the choice many Buddhist women have had to make, becoming minorities as their choices are only accepted on the margins. She is also an example of the ways in which Theravada nuns have had to reach out to international communities of nuns because they have few domestic resources.

What makes a young woman living in Vietnam decide to live as a nun just after graduating from a teacher training college? Lieu Phap was meant to teach English, but she entered the nunnery only a half year after she graduated in 1991 at the age of twenty-four. She lived as a nun for eleven years in Vietnam and India before ordaining as a fully ordained nun, or *bhikkhuni,* in Sri Lanka in 2002. This made her the first Vietnamese Theravada *bhikkhuni.* After ordination she went back to India and lived there for another ten years, doing her master's and Ph.D. studies at Delhi University. Since returning in 2012 to Vietnam, she has been actively engaged in building up the *bhikkhuni* sangha.

The modern history of Theravada nuns has been highly controversial. In most countries in Asia, women are not permitted to ordain as *bhikkhuni* in the Theravada School and therefore have to take on a less prestigious, ritually insignificant role if they wish to be a professional Buddhist. However, in the modern period, with the rise of the Internet and the ability of women to travel alone and seek educational opportunities in many different places, women like Lieu Phap can ordain. Even though Vietnam has only small communities of Theravada practitioners, it is a place in which the minority, because of the lack of a larger institutional organization preventing women from ordaining, can thrive.

Raised in a traditional Buddhist family in Hué, Lieu Phap had visited the temple every week since she was young. At that time, she could not imagine herself living as a nun due to the limitations imposed by strict monastic rules. During her studies at the teacher training school, however, she realized that her interests were different from those of her colleagues who went to parties and enjoyed various forms of entertainment. She became more and more attracted to learning Buddhist teachings and practicing meditation, especially after she got to know a monk who was teaching her in a way that perfectly matched her view of the world.

Like the majority of Vietnamese temples, the first two nunneries where Lieu stayed followed the Mahayana tradition. She told me that the rules were very strict, there was a lot of work to do, and she could not keep in contact with friends from the "outside world" because the head nun told her that they would bring impurity into the nunnery. She vividly remembers that one of the first pieces of advice she got from the head nun was to imagine herself as a doormat: everyone can step on you, so you need to be patient and humble. When I interviewed Lieu in Bangkok, I was impressed by how reflectively and authentically she described both negative and positive experiences.

She stressed her concern regarding a general educational expectation in Mahayana temples where the nuns are taught to say yes to everything and obey. She linked that phenomenon to the history of the first nuns who came from the royal family. Obeisance and compliance were considered polite behavior at that time. Lieu Phap is sure that agreeing on the outside but not truly agreeing on the inside leads to inner conflicts rather than to true harmony. In 1993, she switched to a Theravada nunnery because she was inspired by a monk who offered counseling via letters. The way he helped people with his words deeply affected her.

Her former teacher warned her about losing benefits when she left the Mahayana tradition. Those consisted of two main things: one was being able to start her own nunnery as woman who could fully ordain in the Mahayana tradition; the second, obtaining vegetarian food. At the Theravada nunnery Lieu started eating meat again, which was challenging after many years of vegetarian diet. When I asked her about her understanding of vegetarianism, she said that what is most important is the state of mind while eating: Can we observe our minds when eating? When we like or dislike food there is greed or hatred. We should observe these feelings and try to see that the food itself only consists of four elements. For herself she prefers not to eat meat, but she sees no reason to judge monks and nuns who eat meat that is offered to them.

In 2000, Lieu Phap attended the Sakyadhita (a highly influential modern Buddhist women's organization) Conference in Nepal where she got to know *bhikkhunis* from Sri Lanka. They informed her about the opportunities accompanying higher ordination. The advantages of ordaining as a *bhikkhuni* included being more independent from monks as well as having a more equal status to them. She went to Sri Lanka and ordained as a *bhikkhuni* in 2002 and then became a member of the management committee of the Mahapajapati nunnery in Vaishali. The nunnery hosts conferences, international ordinations for *bhikkhunis* (following 311 precepts), and *sāmaṇerīs* (following 10 precepts), as well as meditation retreats.

In 2009 Lieu Phap cofounded the first *bhikkhuni* temple in Vietnam, Khemarama, where she organized the first international ordinations and training course for *bhikkhunis* and *sāmaṇerīs* in 2012. Presently she lives in Vien Khong temple in the mountains, which she describes with shining eyes. This is the place where she plans to build up the *bhikkhuni* community. Three times a week she teaches at Vietnam Buddhist University, where she is the deputy head at the Department of Dhamma English. Thinking back to the time when she graduated from college with the desire to teach more than just the language, she now combines teaching English with sharing the dharma.

MONK, WRITER, EDUCATOR, AND INTERNATIONAL BUDDHIST
U Paragu
GITANJALI SURENDRAN

The circulation of Buddhist people, ideas, and things within South Asia in the name of reviving Buddhism in India in the late nineteenth and early twentieth centuries has hardly been studied. In the first half of the twentieth century, as travel became easier, increasing numbers of Buddhist pilgrims began to arrive in India, sometimes to follow the new Buddhist pilgrimage trail and sometimes to participate in the revival of Buddhism in India. U Paragu's (1921–present) time in India as a pilgrim, student, and Buddhist revivalist reflects this little-known history of Buddhist exchange between Burma and India.

One rainy August morning in 2010 I set course for the Paragu Shantiniketan Library, on the outskirts of Yangon, to meet U Paragu, its founder. The complex comprised two buildings. The larger housed the library, which had seen better times having suffered considerable damage during Cyclone Nargis. As I looked around, eighty-nine-year-old U Paragu walked in with the help of his cane.

A man of small stature, his maroon and saffron monk robes entirely enveloped his frail frame. In Yangon, he was a popular writer and translator fluent in several languages, including Hindi and Japanese. We communicated in Hindi and, as he was hard of hearing, I sat near his good ear and spoke as loudly as I could. He had lived in India in the late 1940s and early 1950s and had studied Hindi and Sanskrit at the famous Benares Hindu University. At that time, he said, many Burmese students went to India to study. Indeed, Calcutta had a Burmese temple as well as an association of Burmese Buddhists. Others had settled in holy spots on the Buddhist pilgrimage trail. King Thibaw had ordered repairs of the Mahabodhi temple at Bodh Gaya from his court in Ava in the 1870s. There was even an association of Burmese Buddhists in Varanasi when U Paragu had lived there. Paragu's Indian sojourn was therefore not unusual for the time.

A movement for Buddhist revival led by the Ceylonese monk Anagarika Dharmapala and his Calcutta-based Mahabodhi Society had already set in motion processes by which India came to be seen as a holy land for Buddhists around the world and a new Indian Buddhist pilgrimage route was established. Consequently, a number of Burmese monks had arrived in India to revive Buddhism there, responding to Dharmapala's turn-of-the-century call. U Paragu knew of Dharmapala. He also knew the names of several Burmese monks in India. U Chandramuni was based in Kusinara and in 1956 converted the famous Indian lower-caste leader B. R. Ambedkar to Buddhism; U Kaidima was based in Sarnath, where he had set up the Burmese temple; U Ahsaya lived in Sravasti, where he had learned Hindi to further Buddhism in India's most populous province, Uttar Pradesh. U Paragu had himself traveled to all the holy spots associated with Buddhism in India.

The main financial support that Dharmapala received for his activities came from Ceylon and Burma. Many Burmese took an active interest in Indian Buddhist affairs. One group wrote to the then viceroy of India, Lord Curzon, asking that the Mahabodhi Temple at Bodh Gaya be turned over to Buddhist control. A Burmese member of the Legislative Assembly of India introduced a bill to this effect in 1928. Another Burmese group wrote to the maharajah of the Indian princely state of Kashmir demanding succor for Ladakhi Buddhists who had suffered attacks at the hands of other religious groups. Moreover, a kind of triangular trade in Buddhist people and things, including relics, emerged between Calcutta, Colombo, and Rangoon. Buddhist scholars and monks from India, Ceylon, and Burma traveled around the region on lecture tours. Buddhist relics, too, moved between the three cities, culminating in the journey of the Sanchi relics from London to Calcutta via Colombo and Rangoon from 1948 to 1952.

During U Paragu's time in India he met the North Indian trio of Buddhist revivalists—Bhikku Jagadish Kashyapa, Bhikku Ananda Kausalyayan, and Bhikku Rahula Sankrityayana. He recalled their efforts to translate the Pali canon into Hindi for wider dissemination. After completing his studies, Paragu made a trip to Shantiniketan, the Nobel laureate Rabindranath Tagore's famous experimental educational institution, in Bengal. He was so inspired by the place that he decided to name his own library after it.

Upon returning to Burma in the early 1950s, Paragu remained a monk and became a prolific writer and translator of Indian literature into Burmese. He was involved in the local chapter of the Hindi Sahitya Sammelan (Hindi Heritage Association). He received many awards, culminating in a National Literary Award for lifetime achievement as a writer and translator in 2002. Shortly afterwards, he raised the money required to establish a public library (rare in Burma) with his own collection of more than five thousand books. As I sat talking with him, young people from the neighborhood arrived in a steady stream to use the library.

U Paragu showed me books he had written on Buddhism, including a remarkable text in Hindi on the Buddhist emperor Asoka. Like many Indian Buddhist revivalists, he thought of Asoka as a timeless role model for people everywhere. He pointed to other texts by popular writers on Buddhism, including Edward Conze and Herman Hesse and influential Indian writers like B. R. Ambedkar and P. Lakshmi Narasu, besides copies of the journal of the Mahabodhi Society. Clearly these popular texts enjoyed an extraordinary circulation in the Buddhist world. U Paragu's own life and travels exemplify the tremendous mobility of Burmese Buddhists (and indeed other Asian Buddhists) in his time to the perceived holy land, India. For a brief period in the 1950s, Burma and India enjoyed a close political relationship, during which Burmese prime minister U Nu visited India and took part in official celebrations of the 2,500th year of the Buddha's Enlightenment in 1956. Indian representatives attended the Sixth Buddhist Council that U Nu convened in 1954–1956.

In the secret history of Buddhist revival in India, the efforts of Burmese monks in settling Buddhist pilgrimage sites is significant. Their success lay in transforming newly excavated sites into specifically Buddhist landscapes. But this was not all. Several Burmese contributed funds to further efforts at Buddhist revival, undertook pilgrimages to holy spots, and studied in India to expand their knowledge of Buddhism. U Paragu was a product of precisely this moment of Burmese Buddhist internationalism.

ON BEING A "HUMAN BEING"
Sarunya Chattrapiruk
SUSANNE RYUYIN KEREKES

Thailand is a majority Theravada Buddhist country. Its capital, Bangkok, is home to many Mahayana monasteries, thanks to a long history with Chinese immigrants. These Thai-Chinese communities are increasingly influencing popular religious culture. Institutions like Damnak Jao Mae Kuan Im have already gained recognition, both locally and internationally, for their efforts in educating the community about Mahayana practices, engaged Buddhism, and Guan Yin. Sarunya Chattrapiruk (1978–present) is a woman who has been deeply affected by such institutions.

As any aspiring Buddhist nun (or monk) would have reacted upon meeting the Dalai Lama, Sarunya Chattrapiruk was beaming. A photo souvenir shows Chattrapiruk on the Dalai Lama's left, her abbot on his right, all holding hands. The trio appeared beatific. Indeed, the occasion of their meeting was one of commemoration. Scholars and members of various sanghas were gathered for an international symposium advocating the full restoration of the order of Buddhist nuns. Chattrapiruk's abbot, the Venerable Bhiksuni Shi Kuang Seng, was invited to speak there at the University of Hamburg in July 2007. Earlier that year, the venerable was recognized as the "Greatest Mahayana Bhiksuni of Thailand," and Chattrapiruk had recently started her role as the abbot's foreign affairs secretary. That was a year of firsts for Chattrapiruk; in it she pledged to a vegetarian lifestyle, worked intimately alongside the abbot domestically and internationally, taking on the role of her personal translator, and applied to graduate school to pursue formal academic training in Buddhist studies. The cheerful Chattrapiruk had much to look forward to.

Six years earlier, however, she could not have imagined the development of such events. Symptoms of acute headache and severe swelling to half of her face left Chattrapiruk bedridden for a week and dependent on morphine, a bleak future for a recent magna cum laude college graduate. The cause of Chattrapiruk's sudden illness was unknown. Her doctor, a senior practitioner for over thirty years, had done his best. Her parents continued to insist on a cure for their third and youngest child. For the first time Chattrapiruk was reduced to a deliberate faith.

Chattrapiruk's parents were regular patrons of the abbot's first temple in Bangkok's Ladprao District—a relatively small pavilion featuring an eleven-story pagoda and garden of ten thousand Buddhas, the Damnak Jao Mae Kuan Im (Guan Yin Bodhisattva's Hall). Chattrapiruk confessed that, in those days, unlike her two elder sisters, she hardly paid visits to that (or any other) temple. Religious affairs really held no appeal for her. She and the abbot were merely acquaintances then; so for Chattrapiruk it was a pleasant surprise to see her at her bedside. The abbot—whom she now calls her master—is no medical doctor, did not practice alternative medicine, and did not chant any incantation that evening (though she is renowned in Bangkok among the Sino-Thai community as a medium of Kuan Yin). The abbot simply came to see Chattrapiruk. Nonetheless, all her symptoms and pain had disappeared by the next morning. Both the cause and the ultimate cure of her illness were medically inexplicable. Regardless, Chattrapiruk was then able to return to a normal life.

Putting into good use her training in business and English, Chattrapiruk started off her professional career with Rouse & Co. International (Thailand) Ltd., an intellectual property management firm where she worked as a liaison officer. Eventually, she moved on to another company, TÜV Reinland

Thailand, which provides services for independent testing and inspections. Serving as the project coordinator in the management certification department, Chattrapiruk also returned to school for a master's degree in science in management. She enrolled in the School of Business Administration at Assumption University, her college alma mater. Within two years she had completed the program, receiving the prestigious Srisakdi Charmonman Certificate of Honor for outstanding performance. She had her health, and now wealth. Life was good. But something was amiss. So, she began to pay attention to the religious life.

In December 2006, Chattrapiruk joined a retreat led by her abbot across the Buddhist pilgrim sites of India. It was after this that she would seriously consider a lifestyle change. Chattrapiruk felt that she was successful as a businessperson, but nothing more. It was good in terms of providing for a family, perhaps, but beyond the scope of one's business what further impact could be made on the rest of society? Ultimately, she asked herself, "What about being a human being?" Inspired by the experience of her retreat, by the teachings of her master (and their burgeoning relationship) and those of the Mahayana Buddhist sutras that she would soon grow more and more familiar with, Chattrapiruk realized that a Buddhist path was best.

In the future, Chattrapiruk plans to ordain at Puji Temple on Mount Putuo of China's Zhejiang Province. Her master did in 1991, becoming the first Thai citizen to receive ordination there. The abbot—along with 15 percent of the Thai population—is ethnically Chinese; the majority of these Chinese speak the Teochew (Chaozhou) dialect, including Chattrapiruk's family. Chattrapiruk wishes to learn as much as she can, philosophically and academically, before ordaining in China. Towards such end, she made plans to pursue doctoral work in India, which first required a master's degree in the same or a related field of study. This of course led to her enrollment into the only public Buddhist school that she knew of, Mahachulalongkornrajavidyalaya University. Alongside her studies, Chattrapiruk became privy to the affairs of the abbotship and the affairs of the temple, including their relationship with the surrounding local (and even international) community through their various social welfare and education programs. Gradually becoming further invested in her role as secretary, Chattrapiruk was happy to learn that she need not necessarily study abroad and enrolled in Mahidol University's International Ph.D. Programme in Buddhist Studies. Since June 2009, she has been studying under the mentorship of her adviser, Dr. Mattia Salvini, learning about Mahayana philosophy and working closely on a few key texts. One day she hopes to translate the Heart Sutra, which has not yet been translated directly from Sanskrit into Thai.

Chattrapiruk would like to marry the teachings of her master with those of Mahayana texts, and to share these teachings with the greater public so that they may have a better understanding and thus "practice more wholeheartedly." While she and her master do not discriminate between the various Buddhist traditions and practices (in fact, the temple often promotes ecumenism, as testified by the construction of a temple dedicated to Shiva), Chattrapiruk wishes to dispel certain misconceptions of Mahayana Buddhism in Thailand. Throughout our exchanges, her responses, her musings, and her overall tone and voice were always those of gratitude: filiality towards her parents and her master, and gratitude toward the people. "I feel like I have been given opportunities to contribute my efforts to work for Buddhism, so whatever I can do I will do it." Emphasizing the teachings of her master, Chattrapiruk ultimately wishes for others to feel the compassion of Guan Yin.

THOUSAND HANDS, THOUSAND EYES
Sresthabongs Chongsanguan
ARTHID SHERAVANICHKUL

Chinese Mahayana Buddhist studies have been pioneered in Thailand since the 1950s by Sathian Bodhinanda, one of the most important lay Chinese Thai Buddhist scholars, whose writings and translations on Chinese Mahayana sutras are still referential. Fifty years later in Thai modern society, as Chinese religious practice becomes increasingly popular, Sresthabongs Chongsanguan (1969–present) is following in his footsteps.

"Na Mo Ho La Da Nu Do La Ye Ye. Na Mo O Li Ye. Pu Lu Je Di Sho Bo La Ye . . ." Nowadays if one goes to a Thai temple, it is no longer surprising to hear recordings of the song of the Chinese "Mahakaruna Dharani" Mantra or the Great Compassion Mantra of Avalokiteshvara being played loudly instead of Pali chanting of the Theravada Buddhist tradition. Chinese Mahayana Buddhism has clearly become a part of the Buddhist culture of the Thai people.

Walking into a small street in Phahurat, one of the most crowded commercial areas of Bangkok, past chaotic noisy shops and stalls of food, CDs, electric equipment, and so on, I entered an ancient Chinese temple, Wat Divyavari Vihara, that was established by Chinese communities in Bangkok in the late eighteenth century. Though it is one of the oldest Chinese monasteries in Bangkok, that particular day I did not come to meet with a monk, but a layman—Sresthabongs Chongsanguan. Sresthabongs is an independent scholar and a Mahayana Buddhist practitioner who gave up his profession as a lecturer of architecture and dedicated himself to collecting, studying, and creating academic works on Chinese Mahayana Buddhism.

I first met Sresthabongs in 2004 and was impressed by his humility. I have met him again many times at this temple, and at lectures he gave about Mahayana Buddhism and Chinese religion and culture, which made me realize that beneath his humility is a great knowledge that he has collected with faith and devotion. At present, Sresthabongs is running many academic projects to study and propagate Chinese Mahayana Buddhist scriptures, as well as the Chinese-English-Thai Dictionary of Mahayana Buddhist Terms, which he has been working on for ten years. He even had the opportunity to give a lecture to Her Royal Highness Princess Maha Chakri Sirindhorn on the Gong De funerary ceremony, a traditional Southern Chinese ritual now incorporated into Thai royal funerals. Talking about his practice, Sresthabongs said he had faith in the Madhyamaka School of Mahayana Buddhism and also the Zen Buddhist teaching that emphasizes contemplation on the present moment, living a simple life to benefit others. The Four Teachings of Liao Fan have also inspired him in great deal. His access to multiple teaching from widely different Buddhist schools is certainly a benefit of living as a scholar in the modern period with access to the Internet, large research libraries, and networks of scholars across national and regional boundaries.

What makes a scholar and architect seriously interested in studying and practicing Chinese Mahayana Buddhism? What makes him choose a different way of life—far from the social norms of having a family, working for high income and, instead, staying in a temple, dedicating his whole life to serving the religion? Sresthabongs grew up in a Chinese family in the Talat Phlu area, one of the oldest Chinese communities the Bangkok area. Though the majority of population was Chinese, people in this area had ties with their Thai neighbors through Buddhism. Chinese people did not feel strange going to make merit in the Thai temples and had very few temples of their own. Some Thai temples have Chinese shrines where all people came to worship, and so, over time, Thai Buddhists honored both Chinese and Thai shrines on the grounds of the same temple. Like many ethnic Chinese Buddhists, when Sresthabongs was young he frequently went to Thai temples; he practiced chanting and meditation according to what his uncle, a former monk, taught him. He barely knew about Chinese Mahayana Buddhism. His mother took him to Mangkorn Temple in Chinatown sometimes, but he admitted that he did not learn much from these experiences. The questions he always asked his mother were "Why do the Chinese monks wear pants?" and "Can the Chinese monks speak Thai?"—nothing about the differences in the particular teachings of each sect. His mother later told him that, unlike other boys who commonly liked to play with a plastic gun or a racing car, Sresthabongs loved to play with a little Buddhist alms bowl.

As a teenager, Sresthabongs stayed with his uncle in Chiang Mai, where he met with Master Siw Jae (Thai name: Venerable Luang Chin Khananat Chin Prot), who was revered for his respectful manners and admirable teachings. The master accepted Sresthabongs as his student, gave him teachings, and told him the old stories about the lives of Chinese monks in Thailand. There was a short period when he lived with his grandmother, who was not literate but was able to recite the daily Chinese Buddhist chanting fluently. His grandmother's calmness and serenity inspired him to be more interested in Chinese Mahayana Buddhist teaching and practice. Sresthabongs finally came to assist the Chinese temple managers when they arranged ceremonies. As he knows Chinese, he also can read Chinese scriptures and texts widely.

With both his upbringing in a traditional Chinese family and needing to operate in a larger Thai society, Sresthabongs has struggled between wanting to pursue an academic career and helping to preserve Chinese Buddhism. He fears that the modern period has led to a decline in genuine Buddhist practice. All he feels he can do now is collect, translate, propagate, and pass on knowledge as much as possible with the hope that people will know that, apart from chanting songs, Guan Yin popular worship, rituals to remove misfortune, Gong De funerary ceremony, and the like, there are other dimensions of Chinese Buddhism in Thailand that are worthwhile to study in depth, especially the teachings, scriptures, practices, history, and lineage of the Chinese sangha order in Thailand.

At the end of our meeting, I walked past the Three Golden Buddhas in the Uposatha, the thousand-hand and thousand-eye Guan Yin, the Lord Green Dragon, the protector of the temple, and other Chinese statues, through the smoke of scent-sticks and candles, and through people who came to perform the popular ritual of removing ones' misfortune. After passing through the main gate, back to the chaos and noise of the street market again, one question popped into my mind—"Will Guan Yin really reach out her thousand hands and thousands eyes of great wisdom and compassion to Thai society waiting outside or will Chinese Buddhism be relegated to a few shrines and neighborhoods?"

Further Reading

East Asia

Ashiwa, Y., and D. L. Wank, eds. 2009. *Making Religion, Making the State.* Stanford, CA: Stanford University Press.

Batchelor, M. 2006. *Women in Korean Zen: Lives and Practices.* Syracuse, NY: Syracuse University Press.

Bernard, S. 2011. "A Critical Reflection on the Chogye Order's Campaign for the Worldwide Propagation of Kanhwa Son." *Journal of Korean Religions* 2.1: 75–105.

Blum, M. 2002. *The Origins and Development of Pure Land Buddhism.* Oxford: Oxford University Press.

Buswell, R. E. 1992. *The Zen Monastic Experience: Buddhist Practice in Contemporary Korea.* Princeton, NJ: Princeton University Press.

Chen, Shu-Chuan. 2008. *Contemporary New Age Transformation in Taiwan: A Sociological Study of a New Religious Movement.* New York: The Edwin Mellen Press.

Chen-hua. 1992. *In Search of the Dharma: Memoirs of a Modern Chinese Buddhist Pilgrim.* Edited with an introduction by Chün-fang Yü, translated by Denis C. Mair. Albany: State University of New York Press.

Cho, Eun-Su, ed. 2011. *Korean Buddhist Nuns and Laywomen: Hidden Histories, Enduring Vitality.* Albany: State University of New York Press.

Covell, S. G. 2005. *Japanese Temple Buddhism: Worldliness in a Religion of Renunciation.* Honolulu: University of Hawai'i Press.

Dobbins, J. 1989. *Jodo Shinshu: Shin Buddhism in Medieval Japan.* Bloomington: Indiana University Press.

Fisher, G. 2014. *From Comrades to Bodhisattvas: Moral Dimensions of Lay Buddhist Practice in Contemporary China.* Honolulu: University of Hawai'i Press.

Goossaert, V., and D. Palmer. 2011. *The Religious Question in Modern China.* Chicago: University of Chicago Press.

Jones, C. 1999. *Buddhism in Taiwan: Religion and the State, 1660–1990.* Honolulu: University of Hawai'i Press.

Kawahashi, N. 2003. "Feminist Buddhism as Praxis: Women in Traditional Buddhism." *Japanese Journal of Religious Studies* 30.3–4: 291–313.

Kwong, C. 2002. *The Public Role of Religion in Post-Colonial Hong Kong: An Historical Overview of Confucianism, Taoism, Buddhism and Christianity.* New York: Peter Lang.

McLaughlin, L. 2012. "Did Aum Change Everything? What Sōka Gakkai before, during, and after the Aum Shinrikyō Tells Us about the Persistent Otherness of New Religions in Japan." *Japanese Journal of Religious Studies* 39.1: 51–75.

McMahan, D. L. 2008. *The Making of Buddhist Modernism.* Oxford: Oxford University Press.

Park, Jin Y., ed. 2010. *Makers of Modern Korean Buddhism.* Albany: State University of New York Press.

Pittman, D. A. 2001. *Toward a Modern Chinese Buddhism: Taixu's Reforms.* Honolulu: University of Hawai'i Press.

Prohl, I., and J. Nelson, eds. 2013. *Handbook of Contemporary Japanese Religions.* Leiden: Brill.

Rowe, M. M. 2011. *Bonds of the Dead: Temples, Burial, and the Transformation of Contemporary Japanese Buddhism.* Chicago: University of Chicago Press.

Topley, M., and J. Debernardi. 2011. *Cantonese Society in Hong Kong and Singapore: Gender, Religion, Medicine and Money.* Hong Kong: Hong Kong University Press.

Travagnin, S. 2007. "Master Yinshun and Buddhist Nuns in/for the Human Realm. Shift and Continuity from Theory to Practice of *renjian fojiao* in Contemporary Taiwan." In *The Margins of Becoming: Identity and Culture in Taiwan,* ed. Carsten Storm and Mark Harrison, 83–100. Wiesbaden: Harrassowitz.

Yang, M. ed. 2008. *Chinese Religiosities: Afflictions of Modernity and State Formation.* Berkeley: University of California Press.

Yu, C. 2013. *Passing the Light: The Incense Light Community and Buddhist Nuns in Contemporary Taiwan.* Honolulu: University of Hawai'i Press.

South Asia

Balikci, A. 2008. *Lamas, Shamans and Ancestors: Village Religion in Sikkim.* Leiden: Brill.

Bartholomeusz, T. 1994. *Women under the Bō Tree: Buddhist Nuns in Sri Lanka.* Cambridge: Cambridge University Press.

Berkwitz, S. C. 2003. "Recent Trends in Sri Lankan Buddhism." *Religion* 33.1: 57–71.

Bond, G. D. 1988. *The Buddhist Revival in Sri Lanka: Religious Tradition, Reinterpretation and Response.* Columbia: University of South Carolina Press.

Bubandt, N. O., and M. van Beek, eds. 2012. *Varieties of Secularism in Asia: Anthropological Explorations of Religion, Politics, and the Spiritual.* New York: Routledge.

Chaudhuri, S. 1987. *Contemporary Buddhism in Bangladesh.* Calcutta: Atisha Memorial Publishing Society.

Childs, Geoff. 2004. *Tibetan Diary: From Birth to Death and Beyond in a Himalayan Valley of Nepal.* Berkeley: University of California Press.

Gellner, D. N. 1992. *Monk, Householder, and Tantric Priest: Newar Buddhism and Its Hierarchy of Ritual.* Cambridge: Cambridge University Press.

Gerke, B. 2012. *Long Lives and Untimely Deaths: Life-Span Concepts and Longevity Practices among Tibetans in the Darjeeling Hills, India.* Leiden: Brill.

Goldstein, M., and M. Kapstein, eds. 1998. *Buddhism in Contemporary Tibet: Religious Revival and Cultural Identity.* Berkeley: University of California Press.

Guneratne, A. 2002. *Many Tongues, One People: The Making of the Tharu Identity in Nepal.* Ithaca, NY: Cornell University Press.

Gyatso, J., and H. Havnevik, eds. 2005. *Women in Tibet.* New York: Columbia University Press.

LeVine, S., and D. N. Gellner, 2005. *Rebuilding Buddhism: The Theravada Movement in Twentieth-Century Nepal.* Cambridge, MA: Harvard University Press.

Lopez, D. S., ed. 1997. *Religions of Tibet in Practice.* Princeton, NJ: Princeton University Press.

Makley, C. 2007. *The Violence of Liberation: Gender and Tibetan Buddhist Revival in Post-Mao China.* Berkeley: University of California Press.

McMahan, D. L. 2008. *The Making of Buddhist Modernism.* New York: Oxford University Press.

Mills, M. A. 2002. *Identity, Ritual and State in Tibetan Buddhism: The Foundations of Authority in Gelukpa Monasticism.* London: Routledge.

Salgado, N. 2013. *Buddhist Nuns and Gendered Practice: In Search of the Female Renunciant.* New York: Oxford University Press.

Samuel, G. 1995. *Civilized Shamans: Buddhism in Tibetan Societies.* Washington, DC: Smithsonian Institution.

Samuels, J. 2010. *Attracting the Heart: Social Relations and the Aesthetics of Emotion in Sri Lankan Monastic Culture.* Honolulu: University of Hawai'i Press.

Sasson, V., ed. 2012. *Little Buddhas: Children and Childhoods in Buddhist Texts and Traditions.* Oxford: Oxford University Press.

Seneviratne, H. L. 1999. *The Work of Kings: The New Buddhism in Sri Lanka.* Chicago: University of Chicago Press.

Shakya, M. K. *Beloved Daughter: A Biography of Anagarika Dhammavati.* Kathmandu: n.p., 1990.

Sihlé, N. 2013. *Rituels bouddhiques de pouvoir et de violence: La figure du tantriste tibétain* [Buddhist rituals of power and violence: The figure of the Tibetan Tantrist]. Bibliothèque de l'École des Hautes Études, Sciences Religieuses. Series of the École Pratique des Hautes Études. Turnhout: Brepols.

Skilling, P. et al., eds. 2012. *How Theravāda Is Theravāda?: Exploring Buddhist Identities.* Chiang Mai, Thailand: Silkworm Books.

Tuttle, G. 2005. *Tibetan Buddhists in the Making of Modern China.* New York: Columbia University Press.

Zelliot, E. 1998. *From Untouchable to Dalit: Essays on the Ambedkar Movement.* New Delhi: Manohar.

Southeast Asia

Borchert, T. 2008. "Worry for the Dai Nation: Sipsongpanna, Chinese Modernity and the Problems of Buddhist Modernism." *Journal of Asian Studies* 67.1: 107–142.

Braun, E. 2013. *The Birth of Insight: Meditation, Modern Buddhism, and the Burmese Monk Ledi Sayadaw.* Chicago: University of Chicago Press.

Carbine, J. A. 2011. *Sons of the Buddha: Continuities and Ruptures in a Burmese Monastic Tradition.* New York: Walter de Gruyter.

Cate, S. 2002. *Making Merit, Making Art: A Thai Temple in Wimbledon.* Honolulu: University of Hawai'i Press.

Chia, J. Meng-Tat. 2009. "Teaching Dharma, Grooming Sangha: The Buddhist College of Singapore." *SOJOURN: Journal of Social Issues in Southeast Asia* 24.1: 122–138.

Crosby, K. 2013. *Theravada Buddhism: Continuity, Diversity and Identity.* Hoboken, NJ: Wiley-Blackwell.

Eberhardt, N. 2006. *Imagining the Course of Life: Self-Transformation in a Shan Buddhist Community.* Honolulu: University of Hawai'i Press.

Evans, G., ed. 1999. *Laos: Culture and Society.* Chiang Mai, Thailand: Silkworm.

Forshee, J., C. Fink, and S. Cate. 1999. *Converging Interests: Traders, Travelers, and Tourists in Southeast Asia.* Tokyo: Center for Southeast Asian Studies, Tokyo University.

Goudineau, Y., and M. Lorrillard, eds. 2008. *Recherches nouvelles sur le Laos/New Research on Laos. Études thématiques* 18. Vientiane, Paris: École Française d'Extrême-Orient.

Harris, I. 2005. *Cambodian Buddhism: History and Practice.* Honolulu: University of Hawai'i Press.

Hill, A. M. 1998. *Merchants and Migrants: Ethnicity and Trade among Yunnanese Chinese in Southeast Asia.* New Haven, CT: Yale University Southeast Asia Studies.

Holt, J. 2009. *Spirits of the Place: Buddhism and Lao Religious Culture.* Honolulu: University of Hawai'i Press.

Johnson, I. C. 2012. *The Buddha on Mecca's Verandah: Encounters, Mobilities, and Histories along the Malaysian-Thai Border.* Seattle: University of Washington Press.

Kent, A., and D. Chandler, eds. 2008. *People of Virtue: Reconfiguring Religion, Power and Moral Order in Cambodia Today.* Copenhagen: NIAS Press.

Kitiarsa, P. 2012. *Monks, Mediums, and Amulets: Thai Popular Buddhism Today.* Seattle: University of Washington Press.

Kuah-Pearce, K. E. 2009. *State, Society and Religious Engineering: Towards a Reformist Buddhism in Singapore.* 2nd ed. Singapore: Institute of Southeast Asian Studies.

Marston, J., and E. Guthrie, eds. 2004. *History, Buddhism, and New Religious Movements in Cambodia.* Honolulu: University of Hawai'i Press.

McDaniel, J. 2011. *The Lovelorn Ghost and the Magical Monk: Practicing Buddhism in Modern Thailand.* New York: Columbia University Press.

Nishimoto, F. 2010. "The People Who Live with Spirits of the Dead: The Topology of Death in the Kantu Society of Laos" [Shiryou to tomoni ikiru hitobito: Raosu kantu shakai ni okeru shi no isou]. In M. Nakano and J. Fukada, *The Anthropology of Human Beings [Jinkan no jinruigaku]*, 35–55. Tokyo: Harushobo.

Schober, J. 2010. *Modern Buddhist Conjunctures in Myanmar: Cultural Narratives, Colonial Legacies, and Civil Society.* Honolulu: University of Hawai'i Press.

Scott, R. M. 2009. *Nirvana for Sale? Buddhism, Wealth, and the Dhammakāya Temple in Contemporary Thailand.* New York: State University of New York Press.

Swearer, D. 2012. *The Buddhist World of Southeast Asia.* 2nd ed. Albany: State University of New York Press.

Tambiah, S. J. 1970. *Buddhism and the Spirit Cults in Northeast Thailand.* New York: Cambridge University Press.

Taylor, P., ed. 2007. *Modernity and Re-enchantment: Religion in Post-revolutionary Vietnam.* Singapore: Institute of Southeast Asian Studies.

Tikhonov, V., and T. Brekke, eds. 2012. *Buddhism and Violence: Militarism and Buddhism in Modern Asia.* London: Routledge.

Contributors

IAN G. BAIRD is affiliated with the University of Wisconsin. His more recent publications include "Lao Buddhist Monks and Their Involvement in Political and Militant Resistance to the Lao People's Democratic Republic Government since 1975" (2012) and "The Monks and the Hmong: The Special Relationship between the Chao Fa and the Tham Krabok Buddhist Temple in Saraburi Province, Thailand" (2013).

COREY L. BELL is affiliated with the University of Melbourne. His "Death Note and the Misplaced Agencies of Cosmic Justice" is forthcoming in June 2016.

STEPHEN C. BERKWITZ is affiliated with Missouri State University. His most recent publications are *Buddhist Poetry and Colonialism: Alagiyavanna and the Portuguese in Sri Lanka* and *South Asian Buddhism: A Survey* (2013).

ANYA BERNSTEIN is affiliated with Harvard University. She is author of *Religious Bodies Politic: Rituals of the Sovereignty in Buryat Buddhism* (2013) and "More Alive Than All the Living: Sovereign Bodies and Cosmic Politics in Buddhist Siberia" (2012).

KALZANG DORJEE BHUTIA is affiliated with Grinnell College. He is currently working on a manuscript tentatively titled *Buddhist Modernities in Sikkim: Trajectories of Change, Colonialism, and Reform*.

JANE CAPLE is affiliated with the University of Manchester. She is the author of several journal articles and book chapters on the Tibetan Buddhist revival in post-Mao China.

JACK MENG-TAT CHIA is a graduate student at Cornell University. His most recent English-language publication is "A Recent Quest for Religious Roots: The Revival of the Guangze Zunwang Cult and Its Sino-Southeast Asian Networks, 1978–2009" (2013).

SIENNA R. CRAIG is affiliated with Dartmouth College. Her publications include *Healing Elements: Efficacy and the Social Ecologies of Tibetan Medicine* (2012); she is also a co-editor of *Medicine between Science and Religion: Explorations on Tibetan Grounds* (2010).

WILLIAM ELISON is affiliated with the University of California, Santa Barbara. He is the author of "Amar Akbar Anthony: Secularism and Spectacle in a Bollywood Classic" (2015) and "Sai Baba of Bombay: A Saint, His Icon, and the Urban Geography of *Darsha*" (2014).

CHRISTOPH EMMRICH is affiliated with the University of Toronto. His publications include *Buddhist Rituals for Newar Girls: Mimesis and Memory in the Kathmandu Valley* (forthcoming) and "Ritual Period: A Comparative Study of Three Newar Buddhist Menarche Manuals" (2014).

GRANT EVANS was affiliated with L'Ecole française d'Extrême-Orient in Laos prior to his untimely death in 2014. His publications include *Last Century of Lao Royalty: A Documentary History* (2012) and *The Short History of Laos: The Land In Between* (2003).

PAUL J. FARRELLY is affiliated with the Australian National University. His most recent publication is "The New Testament Church in Taiwan and Mount Zion" (2012).

JANE M. FERGUSON is affiliated with the Australian National University. Her recent publications include "Another Country Is the Past: Western Cowboys, Lanna Nostalgia, and Bluegrass Aesthetics as Performed by Professional Musicians in Northern Thailand" (2010) and "Buddhist Orthodoxy or Ritual Excess in a Shan Novice Ordination" (2009).

GARETH FISHER is affiliated with Syracuse University. His publications include *From Comrades to Bodhisattvas: Moral Dimensions of Lay Buddhist Practice in Contemporary China* (2014) and "The Spiritual Land Rush: Merit and Morality in New Chinese Buddhist Temple Construction" (2008).

DANIEL G. FRIEDRICH is a doctoral student at McMaster University. His most recent publication is "Identity in Difference: Reading the Philosophy of Nishida Kitarō through the Lens of Shin Buddhism" (2006).

FLORENCE GALMICHE is affiliated with Paris Diderot University. Her publications include "A Retreat in a South Korean Buddhist Monastery: Becoming a Lay Devotee through Monastic Life" (2010) and "Refondation et valorisation de la tradition monastique dans le bouddhisme coréen contemporain" (2013).

MICHELE R. GAMBURD is affiliated with Portland State University. Her publications include *Breaking the Ashes: The Culture of Illicit Liquor in Sri Lanka* and *The Golden Wave: Culture and Politics after Sri Lanka's Tsunami Disaster* (2013).

HOLLY GAYLEY is affiliated with the University of Colorado at Boulder. Her publications include "Reimagining Buddhist Ethics on the Tibetan Plateau" (2013) and "The Ethics of Cultural Survival: A Buddhist Vision for Progress in Mkhan po 'Jigs phun's Heart Advice to Tibetans of the 21st Century" (2011).

DAVID N. GELLNER is affiliated with Oxford University. His publications include *Rebuilding Buddhism: Theravada Buddhism in Twentieth-Century Nepal* (2007) and *Borderland Lives in Northern South Asia* (2005).

TIM GRAF is affiliated with the University of Heidelberg. He has most recently completed a documentary film titled *Buddhism after the Tsunami: The Souls of Zen 3/11 Japan Special* (2013).

ELIZABETH GUTHRIE is affiliated with the University of Otago. She is author of "In Defence of the Nation: The Cult of Nang Thoranee in Northeast Thailand" (2007) and co-editor of *Cambodian Buddhism, History and New Religious Movements* (2004).

ELIZABETH HARRIS is affiliated with Liverpool Hope University. Her two most recent publications are "Sleeping Next to My Coffin: Representations of the Body in Theravada Buddhism" (2012) and "Memory, Experience and the Clash of Cosmologies: The Encounter between British Protestant Missionaries and Buddhism in Nineteenth Century Sri Lanka" (2012).

SANDYA HEWAMANNE is affiliated with the University of Essex. She is author of *Stitching Identities in a Free Trade Zone: Gender and Politics in Sri Lanka* (2010) and *Sri Lanka's Global Factory Workers: (Un)Disciplined Desires and Sexual Struggles in a Post-Colonial Society* (forthcoming, 2016).

HOLLY HIGH is affiliated with the University of Sydney. Her recent publications include *Fields of Desire: Poverty and Policy in Laos* (2014) and "Laos in 2012: In the Name of Democracy" (2013).

AMY HOLMES-TAGCHUNGDARPA is affiliated with Grinnell College. She is author of *The Social Life of Tibetan Biography: Textuality, Community and Authority in the Lineage of Togden Shakya Shri* (2014) and "Representations of Religion in 'The Tibet Mirror': The Newspaper as a Religious Object and Patterns of Continuity and Rupture in Tibetan Material Culture" (2014).

SARAH H. JACOBY is affiliated with Northwestern University. She is author of *Love and Liberation: The Autobiographical Writings of the Tibetan Buddhist Visionary Sera Khandro* (2014) and co-editor of *Buddhism: Introducing the Buddhist Experience* (2013).

MICHAEL JERRYSON is affiliated with Youngstown State University. His recent publications include *Buddhist Fury: Religion and Violence in Southern Thailand* (2011) and *Mongolian Buddhism: The Rise and Fall of the Sangha* (2008).

IRVING CHAN JOHNSON is affiliated with the National University of Singapore. He is author of *The Buddha on Mecca's Verandah: Encounters, Mobilities, and Histories along the Malaysian-Thai Border* (2012) and "Size Matters: History, Marginality, and the Politics of Building Big in a Small Community" (2011).

HIROKO KAWANAMI is affiliated with Lancaster University. She is author of *Renunciation and Empowerment of Buddhist Nuns in Myanmar-Burma: Building A Community of Female Faithful* and co-editor of *Buddhism International Relief Work and Civil Society*.

DANIEL W. KENT is affiliated with Whitman College. His recent publications include "Corporal Monk: Venerable Sudinna's Journey from the Sri Lankan Army to the Buddhist Sangha" (2014) and "Proof of Buddhism: Interpreting the Bodies of Sri Lankan Buddhist War Dead" (2007).

SUSANNE RYUYIN KEREKES is affiliated with the University of Pennsylvania. She is currently a Ph.D. candidate in the Department of Religious Studies, researching Buddhism, art, and material culture in Thailand.

HWANSOO ILMEE KIM is affiliated with Duke University. He is author of *Empire of the Dharma: Korean and Japanese Buddhism, 1877–1912* (2013) and " 'The Mystery of the Century': Lay Buddhist Monk Villages (*Chaegasŭngch'on*) Near Korea's Northernmost Border, 1600s–1960s" (2013).

TONGTHIDA KRAWENGIT is affiliated with the University of Otago. He is author of "The Form of Meditation Practiced and Taught by Khruba Srivichai and His Lineage" (2015).

JUDY LEDGERWOOD is affiliated with Northern Illinois University. She is author of "Buddhist Ritual and the Reordering of Social Relations in Cambodia" (2012) and co-editor of *At the Edge of the Forest: Essays on Cambodia, History and Narrative in Honor of David Chandler* (2008).

JY LEE is affiliated with Stanford University. He works in the fields of Asian and Asian American intellectual history and Korean business history.

JACQUES P. LEIDER is affiliated with L'Ecole française d'Extrême-Orient in Myanmar. His recent publications include "The Rise of Alaungmintaya, King of Myanmar (1752–60): Buddhist Constituents of a Political Metamorphosis" (2013) and "Kingship by Merit and Cosmic Investiture: An Investigation into King Alaungmintaya's Self-Representation" (2011).

CHIARA LETIZIA is affiliated with the University of Quebec. She is author of "Buddhist Activism, New Sanghas, and the Politics of Belonging among Some Tharu and Magar Communities of Southern Nepal" (2014) and "The Goddess Kumari at the Supreme Court: Divine Kinship and Secularism in Nepal, Divine Kinship and Politics" (2013).

SARAH LEVINE is affiliated with Harvard University. She is author of *The Saint of Kathmandu* (2008) and co-author of *Literacy and Mothering: How Women's Schooling Changes the Lives of the World's Children* (2012).

CHARLENE MAKLEY is affiliated with Reed College. Her most recent publications include "The Politics of Presence: Voice, Deity Possession, and Dilemmas of Development among Tibetans in the PRC" (2013) and *The Violence of Liberation: Gender and Tibetan Buddhist Revival in Post-Mao China* (2007).

JOHN MARSTON is affiliated with the Center for Asian and African Studies of El Colegio de México. He is editor of *Anthropology and Community in Cambodia* and *Ethnicity, Borders, and the Grassroots Interface with the State* (2014).

JUSTIN THOMAS MCDANIEL is affiliated with the University of Pennsylvania. His books include *The Lovelorn Ghost and the Magical Monk: Practicing Buddhism in Modern Thailand* (2011) and *Gathering Leaves and Lifting Words: Histories of Monastic Education in Laos and Thailand* (2008).

LEVI MCLAUGHLIN is affiliated with North Carolina State University. He is co-editor of *Kōmeitō: Politics and Religion in Japan* (2014) and author of "What Have Religious Groups Done after 3.11? Part 1: A Brief Survey of Religious Mobilization after the Great East Japan Earthquake Disasters" (2013).

DAVID L. MCMAHAN is affiliated with Franklin and Marshall College. He is editor of *Buddhism in the Modern World* (2011) and author of *The Making of Buddhist Modernism* (2008).

LEIGH MILLER is affiliated with Maitripa College. She is author of "The Afterlife of Images" (2012) and "The Work of Art in the Age of Self-Immolation" (2012).

JOHN NELSON is affiliated with the University of San Francisco. He is author of *Experimental Buddhism: Innovation and Activism in Contemporary Japan* (2013) and co-editor of *The Handbook of Contemporary Japanese Religions* (2012).

BRIAN J. NICHOLS is affiliated with Mount Royal University. His most recent publication is "Typologizing Religious Practice at Buddhist Monasteries in Contemporary China," in *Chinese Buddhism: Past, Present, and Future.* (2012).

CARINA PICHLER is affiliated with Civil Service International, Austria. She is author of "A Buddhist Way of Drug Rehabilitation in Thailand—Approaching Drug Addiction with Loving Kindness: An Interview with Phra Maha Narong Chaiyatha" (2013) and *Fahrrad fahren als Friedensarbeit—Über einen buddhistischen Mönch in Thailand* (2013).

VISISYA PINTHONGVIJAYAKUL is affiliated with Chandrakasem Rajabhat University. He recently completed his Ph.D. dissertation, "Performing the Isan Subject: Spirit Mediums and Ritual Embodiment in a Transitional Agrarian Society" at the College of Asia and the Pacific at the Australian National University in Canberra in 2015.

JUSTIN R. RITZINGER is affiliated with the University of Miami. His most recent publications include "Dependent Co-evolution: Kropotkin's Theory of Mutual Aid and Its Appropriation by Chinese Buddhists" (2013) and "If We Build It, He Will Come: Hope, Eschatology and the Modern Reinvention of Maitreya in China" (2013).

MARK MICHAEL ROWE is affiliated with McMaster University. His publications include *Bonds of the Dead: Temples, Burial, and the Transformation of Contemporary Japanese Buddhism* (2011) and "Death, Burial, and the Study of Contemporary Japanese Buddhism" (2009).

ROGER CASAS RUIZ is affiliated with the Australian National University. He is researching Buddhist monasticism among the Tai Lue of southern China.

JEFFREY SAMUELS is affiliated with Western Kentucky University. He is author of *Attracting the Heart: Social Relations and the Aesthetics of Emotion in Sri Lankan Monastic Culture* (2010) and "Intersecting Diasporas: Sri Lankan Buddhist Temples in Malaysia and Development across the Indian Ocean" (2013).

GREGORY A. SCOTT is affiliated with the University of Edinburgh. He is author of "Timothy Richard, World Religion, and Reading Christianity in Buddhist Garb" (2012) and "The Buddhist Nationalism of Dai Jitao" (2011).

ARTHID SHERAVANICHKUL is affiliated with Chulalongkorn University. He is author of "Phra Aphai Mani: A Classical Thai Epos on a Porcelain Bowl in the Ring

Collection" (2013) and "Thai Ideas about Hinayana-Mahayana: Correspondence between King Chulalongkorn and Prince Narisranuvattiwong" (2012).

NICOLAS SIHLÉ is affiliated with the Center for Himalayan Studies, France. He is author of *Rituels bouddhiques de pouvoir et de violence: La figure du tantriste tibétain* [Buddhist rituals of power and violence: The figure of the Tibetan tantrist] (2013) and "Written Texts at the Juncture of the Local and the Global: Some Anthropological Considerations on a Local Corpus of Tantric Ritual Manuals (Lower Mustang, Nepal)" (2009).

JESSICA STARLING is affiliated with Lewis and Clark College. She is author of "Neither Nun nor Laywoman: The Good Wives and Wise Mothers of Jōdo Shinshū Temples" (2013) and "Female Religious Affiliation in the Jōdo Shinshū: Wives, Mothers, and Nuns" (2013).

GITANJALI SURENDRAN is affiliated with Jindal Global Law School. Her Ph.D. dissertation (Harvard University) is titled "The Indian Discovery of Buddhism: Buddhist Revival in India, c. 1890–1956" (2013).

NICOLA TANNENBAUM is affiliated with Lehigh University. She is author of *Who Can Compete against the World? Power-Protection and Buddhism in Shan Worldview* (1995) and co-editor of *Founder's Cults in Southeast Asia: Ancestors, Agriculture, and Polity* (2003).

ANTONIO TERRONE is affiliated with National Chengchi University. He is author of "Messengers from Tibet's Past: The Role of Buddhist Charismatic Leaders in the Spread of Tibetan Buddhism in Contemporary China" and co-editor of *Buddhism beyond the Monastery: Tantric Practices and Their Performers in Tibet and the Himalayas* (2009).

ASHLEY THOMPSON is affiliated with University of Leeds. Her publications include *Calling the Souls: A Cambodian Ritual Text* (2004) and "Forgetting to Remember, Again: On Curatorial Practice and 'Cambodian' Art in the Wake of Genocide" (2013).

STEFANIA TRAVAGNIN is affiliated with the University of Groningen. Her recent publications include *Yinshun and His Expansion of Madhyamaka: New Studies of the Da Zhidu Lun in Twentieth-Century China and Taiwan* (2017) and "What Is behind Yinshun's Re-statement of *Mūlamadhyamakakārikā*? Debates on the Creation of a New Mahāyāna in Twentieth-Century China" (2012).

JONATHAN S. WALTERS is affiliated with Whitman College. He is author of "Apadana: Theri-Apadana: Wives of the Saints: Marriage and Kamma in the Path to Arahantship" (2014) and "Gods' Play and the Buddha's Way: Varieties of Ritual Levity in Contemporary Sinhala Practice" (2010).

Index